DRUIDS

DRUIDS:

Their Origins and History

Lewis Spence

BARNES
& NOBLE
BOOKS
NEW YORK

First published in 1949 as *The Origins and History of Druidism.*

Copyright © 1949 by Rider & Company
All rights reserved.

This edition published by Barnes & Noble, Inc.

1995 Barnes & Noble Books

ISBN 1-56619-894-1

Printed and bound in the United States of America

M 9 8 7 6 5 4 3 2

CONTENTS

Chapter I

INTRODUCTORY . . . . . *Page* 11

Chapter II

DRUIDISM IN CELTIC AREAS . . . 19

Chapter III

DRUIDISM IN CELTIC AREAS (*continued*) . . 35

Chapter VIII

PLACES OF WORSHIP . . . . *Page* 117

Chapter IX

DRUIDISM AND THE DIVINE KINGSHIP . 130

Chapter X

INFLUENCE OF OTHER CULTS ON DRUIDISM 139

PREFACE

A NEW investigation of the whole field of inquiry associated with Druidism, its origin and the historical and traditional material related to it requires no excuse. The erroneous views concerning the Druidic faith indulged in by a host of older writers and perpetuated by some modern antiquaries, have all but obliterated the realities of an important passage in the history of early European religion, and so many absurd theories and fantastic assumptions have been indulged in concerning its origins and general circumstances that the study of it has at last become the bane of the official historian and archæologist.

It has for some considerable time been apparent to students of Folklore and Comparative Religion that if the subject of Druidism be studied in relation to some of the later theories propounded by certain authorities on these sciences an entirely new construction can be placed upon its significance and beginnings. It is, I believe, through its associations with the newer theories respecting the history and origins of the Divine Kingship as presented in the works of Frazer, Cook and Hocart, and those connected with the history and archæology of early food-gathering and the worship of sacred food-bearing trees that it is possible to cast new light on the beginnings of the Druidic cultus.

In the first chapter of this book I have outlined my own thesis of the manner in which these theories reflect upon the theme of Druidic origins. In my belief the novel view of Druidism which I have presented practically substantiates the opinion of many previous linguistic experts that the Druids were indeed "Men of the Oak" and demolishes those statements which would otherwise explain the name of "Druid." Perhaps the strangest circumstance in connection with an obscure study is that those very philologists who regarded the Druids as "Men of the Oak" insisted so strongly on their association with the ancient stone monuments and circles of Western Europe.

The greater part of the present essay concerns the history of Druidism in the several areas in which it is known to have flourished, its priesthood and their functions, its theology and ritual, its places of worship, its magic and system of auspices. In the later chapters I have sought to co-ordinate this data with the theories of Frazer, Hocart and others concerning the Divine Kingship and the worship of sacred trees, and I have at last approached the much more difficult problem associated with the precise centre in which the Druidic faith had its inception and development.

Needless to say, such a task has been one of considerable complexity, and I cannot doubt that in some respects my suggestions will meet with adverse criticism. But I can only plead that I have honestly endeavoured to rehabilitate an important study which has undeservedly fallen into some disrepute, in the hope that it will once more commend itself to serious students of tradition.

L. S.

Chapter I

INTRODUCTORY

For more than a generation debate on the vexed question of the origin and significance of the cult of Druidism has been practically discontinued in this country, although it has proceeded in France and Germany in a manner sufficiently spirited. Controversy concerning it began to languish among us in the third part of last century and if certain empirical pens still pursued its discussion, the antiquary or archæologist of serious and sober proclivity regarded it as a dangerous if not discreditable bypath branching off the broad highway of history and frequented chiefly by cranks and charlatans. There was, indeed, one striking exception to this nervous dread of an interesting if questionable topic, the scholarly, sympathetic, and studiously fair essay entitled "The Druids," by Mr. T. D. Kendrick of the British Museum, which covered the entire ground available at the time of its publication in 1927.

And indeed it was not without reason that the prudent historian of the past eschewed a subject which had come to be associated with theories so fantastic that for sheer grotesquerie they rivalled the fabrications of Baron Munchausen or the vagaries of Sir John Mandeville. Aubrey and Toland had been among the first to resurrect the classical interest in Druidism which had expired at some time in the fourth century, and by the middle years of the Victorian era their successors in Britain and France had so garbled the whole testimony of Druidism by the exercise of ignorant surmise and absurd hypothesis, that the mere mention of Druids or Druidism appalled the official guardians of historical science. The Druids were Brahmans, they were the custodians of a mystic lore so potent in its magical effects as to make modern science seem a nursery pastime. Nothing in heaven or in earth was hidden from them. They were an offshoot of the Pythagoreans, of the Buddhists, of the Persian Magi. They "understood" the science of astronomy, they "understood" the deepest secrets of engineering, indeed there was nothing profound enough to baffle their understanding. So lofty were the ideals of their faith that it far surpassed all others in spirituality and divine wisdom.

Irritated by and contemptuous of this theatrical and even melodramatic treatment of a theme which appeared to them to have only a minor significance in European history, the modernists and freethinkers of the late nineteenth century poured upon its protagonists and their absurd notions the scorn of an outraged propriety. To them the Druids were merely the medicine-men of the Celtic peoples, *shamans, jossakeeds*, miserable jugglers and herbalists, the ministers of a superstition of the lower cultus. In their impatience they certainly assumed an attitude

towards the subject which now seems as undignified as the wild specu a-
tions of the fantasts whom they condemned.

A purely objective consideration of the Druidic faith in the light of
modern traditional knowledge reveals it as a system of belief not only
distinct from the speculations of its enthusiasts and its critics, but preg-
nant with interest for the student of folk-lore and comparative religion.
More especially is this the case when its circumstances come to be considered in association with some of the later theories which have within
our own generation made their appearance in the spheres of religious
science and archæology. That this is particularly so in respect of that
extensive body of evidence connected with the character of the Divine
Kingship has become fully apparent through the collection and exposition
of the proof relative to that subject by Frazer, Cooke, Hocart and other
outstanding students of tradition. Any fresh material associated with the
history of food-gathering among primitive peoples and with the worship
of trees as "food-givers" serves to widen the scope of our knowledge of
the elements which went to the making of the Druidic cultus. Indeed the
materials which would justify a new examination of the whole Druidic
question have been in the hands of students of folk-lore almost from the
beginning of this century, but through lack of emphasis and sympathetic
treatment this has not been readily manifest, nor has any endeavour
been made to place the study on a new basis in respect of the later evidence
of which I have spoken.

THE AUTHOR'S THESIS

The general thesis which the present writer seeks to maintain in this
book and which he hopes to justify, may now be stated briefly, although
the evidence which supports it must be retained for separate discussion
in a final chapter after the full record of Druidic history and religious rite
has been reviewed. Here only a bare outline, sufficient to furnish the
reader with the general argument, can be presented.

It is now known that in the food-gathering stage of society which
preceded the development of settled agricultural existence, certain trees
were regarded by mankind with reverence because of the provender they
yielded. In Europe these were chiefly the nut- and berry-bearing trees,
such as the oak, the hazel and the rowan, or mountain-ash. A great part
of Europe at that period was thickly covered with oak forests, the timber
of which was employed for building and firing, while the acorns they
yielded were ground into flour which was baked into small cakes for
human consumption. The acorn, indeed, appears to have been one of
the oldest and most important articles of food known to European man.
These circumstances led to the special adoration of the oak by the early
European races, and at a later stage of religious development it was
worshipped as a god, or as the abode of a god, whose attributes, as we

shall see, were associated with the weather, the firmament and the general idea of growth.

The Cultus of the Oak

That such a cultus of the oak underlay the ancient religions of Greece and Rome there is the fullest evidence, and that a similar cultus survived in some Slavonic countries until quite a late period is certain. The worship of the oak by European man at the food-gathering stage of his development and while oak forests continued to cover the greater part of our continent, appears to have been general all over Europe from the Caucasus to the Atlantic. The Celtic tribes evidently shared the belief with Slavs and Teutons. Among the Celts it came to be known by some term which has survived in English as "Druidism." But while, among the Greeks and Romans, the oak-cult, although it never entirely disappeared as a part of the national faith, assumed by degrees an ever-lessening importance, in the case of the Celts it appears to have remained as the chief element in their religion. That religion, like the Greek, Roman and Teutonic, developed in the course of time into a faith which could boast of a series of divine figures almost equally distinguished with those of Olympus. But, side by side with the worship of these, the cultus of the oak tree remained, almost until the end.

It is now fully apparent, to the present writer at least, that the Druidic cult was closely allied with that principle of belief which has come to be known to students of comparative religion as the doctrine of "the Divine King." Broadly speaking, this belief is associated with the idea that in the king, the son of heaven, is enshrined that magical vitality by virtue of which the forces of life in the region under his jurisdiction function regularly and satisfactorily—the growth of vegetation, of the crops, the production of animal life and even the fertility of human beings. Of this doctrine I hope to furnish a fuller account at a later stage. In what manner precisely it came to be associated with the Druidic cultus is not as yet clear, but that it was vitally bound up with that cultus can be proved beyond peradventure. It may be that the Sacred Kingship and the priesthood were originally one and the same and that the original cult contained both the germs of Druidism as we know of it and of the Divine Kingship. But this is also a question which can be more satisfactorily debated at a later stage.

Derivation of the Word "Druid"

As is notorious, and as might have been expected, the derivation of the word or name known in English as "Druid" has occasioned no little controversy. Here I will place before the reader as plainly as may be the several theories respecting the origin and significance of the term, and

when that has been done, will make an endeavour to arrive at a more
or less stable conclusion concerning its actual meaning.

In the year 1885, Professor Donald Mackinnon of the chair of Celtic
Languages in Edinburgh University furnished some notes respecting the
etymology of the term "Druid" to the Rev. Dr. J. A. Wylie for use in
that writer's *History of the Scottish Nation*, and as these notes are racy
of what has come to be recognized as one of the more important views
regarding its derivation, they appear to offer a suitable prelude to such
an examination as the present. Mackinnon gave it as his belief that
"Druid" is connected with and derived from the root that gives *drus* and
dendron in Greek as meaning "oak" and "tree" respectively; *drus*, "wood"
in Sanskrit; "tree" in English; *doire*, "a grove," and *darach*, "oak," in
Gaelic. After the fall of Druidism, thought Mackinnon, there was no
question that the word "Druid" took on the meaning of "a wise man"
simply and solely, and indeed there is plenty of evidence that it was so
used by early Christian scribes in Ireland. Nevertheless, Mackinnon gave
it as his belief that "Druid," in its original sense, was derived from the
word for an oak.[1]

Frazer examines the etymology of the word "Druid" with typical
care. "The very name of Druids," he says, "is believed by good authorities
to mean no more than 'oak men'." For this derivation he quotes Curtius,
Rhys, Kretschmer and Vanicek. "On this view," he remarks, "Pliny was
substantially right in connecting Druid with the Greek *drus*, 'oak,'
though the name was not derived from the Greek. However, this derivation of Druid has been doubted or rejected by some scholars," notably
D'Arbois and Schrader.[2] One instance which fortifies the view, however,
is the circumstance that at Mount Algidus in the Alban Hills, a height
covered with oaks, dwelt a Latin folk who were entitled to share the
flesh of the white bulls sacrificed to Jupiter on the Alban Mount and that
one of these tribes styled themselves *Querquetulani*, "the Men of the Oak."
(Pliny, *Natural History*, III, 269.)

Rhys, commenting on Pliny's derivation of "Druid" from the Greek
word *drus*, "an oak," says: "Had he possessed knowledge enough of the
Gaulish language, he would have seen that it supplied an explanation
which rendered it needless to have recourse to Greek, namely in the
native word *dru*, which we have in Drunemeton. . . . In fact, one has,
if I am not mistaken, been sceptic with regard to this etymology, not so
much on phonological grounds as from failing exactly to see how the oak
could have given its name to such a famous organization as the druidic
one must be admitted to have been. . . . According to the etymology here
alluded to, the druids would be the priests of the god associated or identified with the oak."[3] It may be said here, for completeness' sake, that
Maximus Tyrius asserts that the oak tree was the Celtic symbol of Zeus,
as it was also a Roman symbol of Jupiter.[4] Mr. Munro Chadwick approves
the "oak" etymology.[5] Concerning it, Macbain, perhaps the greatest

Scottish authority on Celtic linguistics in his day, flatly remarks: "it is yet the only one worth consideration of the many suggested."⁶ I may here be excused for interpolating the opinion that in my view no other derivation is consonant with the findings of modern folk-lore research. Indeed, as Macbain has it, "the sacredness of groves and of trees has not yet died out among the Celts." Camille Jullian thinks that the possibility of such a derivation as that of Druid from the oak should not be excluded. (*Hist. de la Gaule*, II, p. 85, note 7.)*

M. D'Arbois de Jubainville considered the word Druid to imply "very wise," or "master of knowledge." He thought that the Welsh term *derwydd* was an invention of some would-be *savant* of the Middle Ages, who derived it from the Welsh word for oak, and who perhaps had knowledge of the passage in Pliny.⁷ The late Professor Anwyl regarded D'Arbois' views on the subject as inconclusive.⁸ Mr. Kendrick is of the opinion that "the etymology of the word is still uncertain." The orthodox view, he says, quoting Thurneysen and D'Arbois, is that *"dru* is a

---

* At least one writer on Druidism has sought to connect the derivation of the word "Druid" with the widespread myth that mankind sprang from trees. Norse legend tells how the first man and woman, Ask and Embla, were created out of two trees found by Odin on the seashore. Indeed, the name "Ask" means "ash tree." (J. Grimm, *Teutonic Mythology*, p. 560; J. Rydberg, *Teutonic Mythology*, pp. 84–5.) The Central American "Popol Vuh" has it that the first men were fashioned from trees, and instances of stories which allude to a similar origin could be multiplied.

So it is not strange to find the French Celticist J. de Cambry, who published his *Monumens Celtiques* in 1805, preferring the not unreasonable hypotheses that the Druidic relationship with the oak may have been associated with such a myth, that it may have signified the former existence of an ætiological or explanatory myth that the first men were born of the oak tree. He thought that the Breton word *kenderv* implied "oak-kindred" (do we not still speak of "family trees"?). He points out that Homer, Vergil and Juvenal in certain verses allude to human birth as proceeding from the oak. He speaks of the *dryades*, who dwelt in oaks. The oak, he thought, was regarded as the parent of mankind, its house, its food-giver, its oracle. "And behold! This explains how the interpreters of the oracles of the oak, or of the god who resided within it, were named druids, druidesses, or the inhabitants of the oak." (pp. 324 ff.) My own ideas on the subject had been running in similar grooves long before I perused the work of Cambry, whom I recognize as the first begetter of this hypothesis, which I think has much to recommend it. Though one believes the Druids to have been priests of the oak-cult, it is surely not inappropriate to suggest that a myth like the Scandinavian once existed that early man, who owed so much to the oak for food and shelter, once actually believed himself to be descended from it, precisely as do those uncultured races in Africa, South America and Australia, who believe themselves to have kinship with certain plants or animals from which they derive sustenance. Strehlow has revealed that among the aborigines of Central Australia the belief obtains that the totemic ancestors were transformed into rocks and trees, "and especially into the mistletoe growing upon such trees," and that in these media live the *ratapa*, or spirits of the unborn children of the tribes, one only in each tree, rock, or sprig of mistletoe. (M. F. Ashley-Montagu, *Coming into Being Among the Australian Aborigines*, p. 78.) Respecting these beliefs I hope to add more in the final chapters of this book which will deal with the origins of Druidic belief.

strengthening prefix," and *uid* means "knowing," "so that a druid was
a very wise man."[9] But what renders this "the orthodox view"? If it is
so, it is certainly not that of the majority of etymologists. MacCulloch,
who claims that the word is "purely Celtic," follows D'Arbois in his
derivation, who, after all, merely adopted Thurneysen's view, but he
says that it is possible "that *dru* is connected with the root which gives
the word 'oak' in Celtic speech—Gaulish *deruo*, Irish *dair*, Welsh *derw*
—and that the oak, occupying a place in the cult, was thus brought into
relation with the name of the priesthood."[10]

Mr. C. E. Quiggin, in the *Encyclopædia Britannica*, asserts that no
ancient form of the word for Druid is known in Welsh, and that the
Welsh *derwydd* and *dryw*, Breton *drouiz* and *druz* are "all probably of
modern coinage." Professor J. E. Lloyd declares that no connection can
be established with *derva*, the Celtic original of *derw*, "oak," or its
congeners *deri*, *darik*, *daru*, of the same meaning.[11]

Mr. Whitley Stokes, a leading Celticist, connected "Druid" with the
Welsh word *dryw*, meaning "wren," a bird which the Druids, it is said,
kept in captivity for the purposes of divination through its twitterings.
He associated this Welsh term etymologically with the German *treu* and
the English "true." Thus, for him, "Druid" meant "truth-teller," that
is, a revealer of divine truth. But it would appear to be a weak assumption
that the priesthood was known by the name of a divinatory bird which
was regarded as singing or sheltering in the oak, rather than by the
title of the oak itself, the authentic object of worship—unless, indeed,
the wren was regarded as the spirit of the oak (as the god Picus, originally
a forest-god, was known to the Romans as a woodpecker, and a prophetic
or augural woodpecker at that), which seems not improbable in view of
that bird's connection with the lightning. To kill a wren in some parts of
France was regarded as a crime which might "bring down the lightning."
(C. Hardwick, *Traditions, Superstitions and Folklore*, p. 246.) But it
seems to me much more probable that the bird received its name *dryw*
from the Celtic name for the oak than that it gave its name to Druidism.

I must not even seem to press upon the reader the acceptance of that
etymology which maintains that the word which we know as "Druid"
implies a "man of the oak" or "minister of the oak," simply because it
chimes with the main part of my theory that the Druids were originally
and in particular the priests of an oak-tree cultus. Pliny's unfortunate
statement that the word was derived from the Greek *drus*, an oak, has
certainly awakened doubts of the genuineness of the belief that "Druid"
proceeds from an ancient Gallic or Celtic term associated with the oak
tree. It has indeed effected almost incredible mischief in arousing sus-
picions in the proverbially nervous and fretful mentality of the typical
philologist, who, goodness knows, is usually crochety enough without any
further temptation to be so! And we have the warning of Sir John Rhys
that one is apt to be sceptical concerning this derivation simply because

it is difficult to see how the oak tree could have given its name to so famous an organization as that of the Druids. Hard things have been said concerning the reasoning faculties of Sir John, especially by the hypercritical Rice Holmes, but in a very long experience of his writings I have never found him lacking in fundamental common sense when it came to the making of a serious and ultimate decision, and we must remember that in arriving at many he was acting as one of the pioneers of a renascence of Celtic criticism.

In all honesty, I profess my belief that some at least of the hypotheses which differ from what might be called the standard belief that "Druid" implies a priest of the oak-cult came into being not only because of a nervous dread that their protagonists must not countenance what seemed to be Pliny's "false etymology," but out of that queer intellectual pride which even the worthiest scholars display in the hope of achieving a reputation for superior insight. And as regards the late and secondary significance of "Druid" as a magician or "medicine-man," how many words have received an inferior implication through degeneration? Has not the word "villain," which originally denoted a farm-servant, come to imply a scoundrel, and "knave," a boy, or serving-lad, a rascally fellow? "It is pertinent to remark," says Mr. Allcroft, "that the thing which we call popular etymology is not peculiar to modern times, and that therefore it is in the highest degree likely that the confusion between 'wise man' and 'men of the oak tree' may go back to a very remote period indeed. It may be that philology is correct in asserting that Druid really means 'wise man,' but it may be equally true that as early as the days of Pliny the mass of even the Celts themselves had come to find another meaning in the name."[12] And have we not the caveat of Sir W. Ridgeway that "modern linguistic research has too often worked much mischief to historical inquiries"?[13]

So far as I am concerned, then, and for the purposes of this book, I must adhere to the finding that "Druid," in its original meaning, implies a priest of the oak-cult, and I think that the evidence which will be adduced in the latter chapters of this work will go to show that no other interpretation of the word is at all possible. It is, indeed, the very nature of this evidence which compels me to the adoption of such an etymology.

It seems necessary to say a word concerning the fame of the Druids throughout the Classical world, in view of the attitude of nescience concerning them on the part of some modern authorities. As the late Professor Edward Anwyl wrote: "One thing at any rate is clear, that the Druids and their doctrines, or supposed doctrines, had made a deep impression on the writers of the ancient world."[14] This makes it all the more amusing that some authorities on the Celtic past, and particularly that type of archæologist who confines himself almost exclusively to practical excavation, should assume an attitude of suspicion at the mere mention of Druidism. To be quite frank, a careful analysis of the remarks of some archæologists of note on the subject of Druidism makes it strikingly apparent that their knowledge of it is of the most superficial kind, about as profound, indeed, as that of the cranks and imaginative writers whom they deride. The plain truth is that the authentic material relative to the Druidic cultus is rather more generously documented in the literary sense than that which concerns many events of vital importance to European history—than, say, the invasion of Britain by the Anglo-Saxons, or the period of the Roman evacuation of this island. Indeed the evidence for its existence is greatly more convincing than that respecting the first introduction of Christianity into Britain, a subject which rests almost exclusively on a legendary basis, or on the merest conjecture. Compare, for instance, the material concerning the Druid Divitiacus and that respecting "Joseph of Arimathea." Roman poets sang of the Druids in terms of eulogy, even if they knew little of their principles, Druidism had been heard of in Egypt in the second century before Christ, and at least fourteen classical authors and Christian fathers, writing in three successive centuries, allude to it. Yet, in some quarters, we are invited to believe that it has no historical status whatsoever.

Chapter II

DRUIDISM IN CELTIC AREAS

DRUIDISM IN GAUL

ALL authentic accounts of the Druidic cult refer to it as practised and maintained among Celtic races only. This is not to say, however, that Druidism was a cult specifically Celtic in its forms or ideals or that it originated with the Celtic race. Faiths of a character closely resembling it existed among Teutonic and Slavonic peoples, in some instances until a comparatively recent period, and the probability is that it had its rise at a comparatively early phase in European history and that it came to be accepted by many of the racial groups which at one time or another made their way into our continent. In this chapter my intention is to provide a purely objective account of what we know of the history of Druidism in the several areas in which it functioned, irrespective of its religious practice.

But when European history commences, we find this particular type of cultus flourishing principally in certain areas in Gaul or France. The first notice we have of Druidism in Gaul is retrospective, and is contained in an early quotation to be found in the *Lives of the Philosophers* of Diogenes Lærtius, written in the first half of the third century A.D. He informs us that the Druids are alluded to in two lost works, one of them a supposititious treatise by Aristotle, which indeed is now known to be fabulous, and the other in a volume by a Greek writer, Sotion of Alexandria, written about a couple of centuries before the Christian era. Diogenes' words are: "the Celtæ and the Galatæ (that is the Galatians in Asia Minor) had seers called Druids and Semnotheoi, or so Aristotle says in the 'Magic,' and Sotion in the twenty-third book of his 'Succession of the Philosophers'."[1]

RACIAL DIVISIONS OF GAUL

At the date when Sotion wrote, about 200 B.C., says M. D'Arbois de Jubainville, the Druids had established themselves in Gaul.[2] At that period three specific racial groups shared that country among them. The Aquitani inhabited that part of it which lies betwixt the Pyrenees and the Garonne, the Celtæ occupied the area stretching from the south-eastern border through central France to the north-west, while the third part, stretching northward beyond the Seine and the Marne, was peopled by the Belgæ. It may be said at once that if the Aquitanian folk adhered to the Druidic faith, history supplies no details of its presence among them.[3] The theory that it functioned among the Belgæ has aroused considerable controversy. But there is ground for the assumption that the Belgæ did not practise the Druid faith. D'Arbois was of opinion that

the Belgic invaders of Britain coming from Gaul, found Druidism flourishing in the southern part of our island when they settled there in the
second century B.C. and that they carried it to Gaul.⁴ But other Celts
certainly preceded the Belgæ in Britain, and Rice Holmes thought that
"the date of the first mention of Druidism gives no clue as to the place
where it originated."⁵ According to Rice Holmes, it seems not improbable
that Druidism existed both in Aquitaine and among the Belgæ. But
Desjardins held that, according to the details of Cæsar's narrative, the
Romans came into contact with Druidism for the first time when they
passed the northern boundary of Roman territory in Gaul. He also
thought that Cæsar "intended his description to apply to the Belgæ."
But the absence of all evidence, historical or traditional, respecting the
presence of Druidism in either Aquitaine or the Belgic regions in Gaul
and Britain will, I think, serve to convince most people that it had no
abiding place in these areas.⁶

CÆSAR ON THE DRUIDS

The account of Julius Cæsar, as contained in the text of his Sixth
Book, the thirteenth and subsequent chapters, is by far the most complete
description of Druidism in Gaul which we possess, and merits a careful
summary. Two orders of men, he tells us, stood out saliently in the
scheme of Gallic life—the Nobles and the Druids. The latter dealt with
things sacred, they conducted the public and private sacrifices, and
interpreted all matters of religion. Young men in large numbers resorted
to them for the purposes of instruction and they were held in great
honour. They determined all controversies, public and private, and
adjudicated in cases of homicide and other crimes, also in suits respecting
inheritances and boundaries of property. Those who did not submit to
their decisions were interdicted from the sacrifices, and publicly shunned.
A chief Druid presided over them and he was succeeded at his death by
the most pre-eminent in dignity. If, however, there were several candidates for the office, an election was held, though on occasion they contended for the presidency in arms.

The Druids of Gaul, he continues, assembled at a fixed period of the
year at a consecrated place in the territories of the Carnutes (now identified
as Chartres) which was reckoned the central point of Gaul. All who were
engaged in disputes betook themselves there to submit to their decrees.
Druidism was *supposed* to have had its beginnings in Britain and to have
been brought thence to Gaul, and those who desired to gain a more
accurate knowledge of the system usually went to Britain to study it.

Military service was not exacted from the Druids, nor was tribute
levied upon them. These privileges induced many to "embrace this
profession." Such candidates must get by heart a great number of verses
and in some cases this necessitated a course of study extending to twenty
years. The lore in question was not reduced to writing, though in public

and private transactions they used Greek letters. Cæsar thought that the Druids left their beliefs unrecorded because they did not wish them to be divulged to the folk at large and because they thought it better to trust to memory. They believed that souls, after death, pass from one body to another, and that this doctrine incited valour and banished the fear of death. They imparted to youth many things respecting the stars and their motion, the extent of the world and of the earth, the nature of things generally and the power and majesty of the immortal gods.

The Gauls, he says, were greatly addicted to superstitious rites, and those who were afflicted by disease or threatened with danger in battle, made a vow that they would sacrifice men through the agency of the Druids. They made figures of vast size, the limbs of which were formed of osiers (wicker-work) which they filled with living men who were given to the flames. Such victims were usually criminals, but if malefactors were lacking, innocent folk took their places. The Druids handed down the tradition that the Gauls were descended from the god Dis, but they worshipped other deities, whom Cæsar identified with Mercury, Apollo, Mars, Jupiter and Minerva.[7]

Cæsar's statement, in my opinion, is not only of the greatest value as affording us a picture of the Druidic faith as it functioned in Gaul, but because it records traits in Druidism which can be compared with the religious ideas of peoples in a similar condition of culture, thus revealing the accuracy of his observations. Not only so, but it exhibits so many precise analogies with what we know of Irish Druidism as to justify the exactitude of the accounts which have come down to us concerning that system. Nearly every one of the particular points Cæsar records concerning Druidism in Gaul—the instruction of youth by the priests, the mnemonic character of that instruction, the doctrine of the transmigration of souls, the study of nature-lore and the addiction to human sacrifice, might have been recorded of religions of the lower cultus in many parts of the world, and more particularly in ancient Ireland.

Not only so, but Cæsar's account is to some extent ratified in its general correctness by those of other Classical writers upon Druidic affairs in Gaul. It is not improbable that these may merely have played "the sedulous ape" to Cæsar, but the theory that all of them did so is absurd. Diodorus Siculus wrote some fifty years after the great Roman, but his account of the Gallic Druids is almost entirely devoted to augural and other religious matters of which Cæsar says nothing and which will be dealt with in their appropriate place. Strabo (54 B.C.–A.D. 24), is somewhat reflective of Diodorus, but he also describes circumstances which his predecessor omitted, referring chiefly to ritual usage. Ammianus Marcellinus, who flourished in the fourth century A.D., adds but little to Cæsar's account. Pomponius Mela, who wrote in the Claudian period, the middle of the first century A.D., copies the great Julius closely, while Lucan is merely rhapsodic. On the whole, however, the circumstances which most of these writers detail, apart from those already mentioned in the Cæsarian account, serve to amplify it and fill in the picture. In any case, their descriptions of Druidism, saving those parts of them which merely reflect Cæsar's, will be dealt with in later chapters, and are practically confined to brief details concerning the Druidic attitude to religion, rite and law.

That the Gaulish Druids controlled the civil administration of Celtic Gaul is borne out by Cæsar's account, and it would seem that clan or intertribal dissensions were brought before their court at Chartres. But, as M. Camille Jullian remarks, the administrative part of their power was probably due to the circumstance that, although each tribe in Gaul had its own Druids, all the Druids were associated in a permanent federation, like priests of the same cult, in what he calls a "church," which necessitated the existence of a hierarchy, and of periodical assemblies.⁸

But the Druidic organization could not hope to oppose the Roman power when that attained the complete conquest of Gaul. Comprising as it did the most powerful and intelligent section in the community, it became for the Gauls the symbol of patriotic resistance to the Romans and to the invaders a nucleus of native strength and individuality which must at all costs be broken down. Not long after Cæsar's entry into Gaul the Gallic chief Vercingetorix rebelled against Roman authority, and during an entire year Cæsar was engaged in a life-and-death struggle with this able young leader. With his fall, it may be said, Druidism in Gaul virtually collapsed, and prominent Druids began to take sides, some with the Romans, some with native leaders.

Vercingetorix, the son of Celtillus, who had been the most powerful chief in Gaul, recalling that his father had endeavoured to restore the monarchy, became a kind of Gallic Robert the Bruce, who in all likelihood desired at once to expel the Romans from his native soil and to regenerate the royal power. His organizing abilities were considerable and soon he had a large force at his command. He was indeed hailed by his supporters as "king." And here, I believe, we approach the crux of the reason for the Druidic downfall in Gaul, that its associations were so intimately connected with the idea of what has come to be known as the "Divine Kingship" that it was almost impossible to disentangle them from it without doing fatal violence to the faith and its tenets. True, the monarchy had come to be detested in Gaul and a powerful Republican party jealously contested its claims and had even punished Celtillus, the father of Vercingetorix, with death for seeking to restore it in his own person. Even so, the tradition surrounding it appears to have been one of great potency and, if my theory is correct, as it certainly is in respect of Irish Druidism, the Gallic Druids seem to have supported its tradition in the person of Vercingetorix, and to have sought to restore it for religious reasons. Be this as it may, its final collapse after the defeat of Vercingetorix appears to have precipitated the downfall of official Druidism in Gaul.[9]

Sir John Rhys, indeed, appears to have surmised that some such condition brought about the final catastrophe of Druidism in Gaul, when he wrote: "In Ireland . . . druidism and the kingship went hand in hand, nor is it improbable that it was the same in Gaul, so that when the one fell, the other suffered to some extent likewise. It would thus seem probable that druidism had here and there begun to lose a good deal of its power and influence during the revolutions which had resulted in the abolition of the ancient kingship in most of the more important Gaulish communities mentioned by Cæsar."[10] It seems to me that much credit is due to the great Welsh Celticist that he succeeded in unveiling the cause of the downfall of Gallic Druidism at a time when the theory of "the Divine Kingship" had as yet not been advanced.

SUPPRESSION OF GALLIC DRUIDISM

Roman measures for the suppression of Druidism in Gaul appear to have been gradual. In the reign of Augustus, Roman citizens were prohibited from taking part in the religion of the Druids.[11] Their rites, or some of them, particularly human sacrifice, were repugnant to Roman usage. In the reign of Tiberius (A.D. 14-37) the Roman senate issued a decree directed chiefly against the ritual abominations of the order.[12] According to Pomponius Mela, human sacrifice was modified from outright slaughter to a mere drawing of blood from the victims led to the altar.[13] But the most drastic measure was that effected under the Emperor Claudius (A.D. 41-54). Severe as it was, however, it did not succeed, but was followed by the more practical policy of Augustus, who established a new magistracy in Gaul which superseded the Druids as judges, Romanized the Gallic religion and substituted for it the *Gutuatri* or *flamens*, whose office will be the subject of description in a later chapter.[14]

The Druids, now reduced to the condition of a despised and probably peripatetic minority, seem speedily to have degenerated into a species of medicine-men or magicians, lurking in forests and wild places. Indeed Lucan tells us that as early as the period subsequent to Cæsar's conquest, they had retired to their sacred groves.[15] But in the year 71 of our era certain Druids issued a prediction that the Capitol of Rome would be reduced to ashes. It had been threatened, said they, four and a half centuries before by the famous invasion of Rome by the Gauls, and when it was finally destroyed, dominion would pass to the Gallic peoples north of the Alps.[16] These prophetic Gauls were perhaps the same persons who revolted against Rome after the death of Nero.

Certain persons in Gaul are alluded to by the poet Ausonius as surviving descendants of the Druids at the end of the fourth century. He says of the rhetorician Attius Pateras:

> "Thou, born at Bayeux, with Druids for thy ancestors,
> Derivest thy sacred race from the temple of Belenus."

while of another, Phœbicius, he sings that he was "a hymner of Belenus" "descended from a family of Druids," and held a professor's chair at Bordeaux.[17] St. Eloi, or Eligius, Bishop of Noyon (640–685), has been suspected of Druidical leanings, although he preached against paganism, and St. Beuno, in his dying hour, exclaimed: "I see the Trinity and Peter and Paul and the Druids and the saints."[18]

Religious councils launched anathemas against the performance of pagan rites in Gaul. The 23rd canon of the Council of Arles, held in the year 442, formally proscribed the worship of trees, stones and fountains, as did that held at Tours in 567. The Council of Leptines, near Binche, held in 743, lashed the Belgians for their pagan superstitions and issued a prohibition against their continuance.

DRUIDISM IN SOUTHERN BRITAIN

For generations antiquarian opinion in this island, founding its beliefs upon the allusions of Julius Cæsar to British Druidism, maintained that the Druidic cult not only flourished in what is now England and Wales, but that it actually had its inception there. To-day, it would seem that authoritative sentiment is unfriendly to the theory that Druidism originated in Britain. Nor does it stop there, for the more conservative among those writers who have discussed the subject appear to entertain the belief that the Druidic cult never prevailed in Southern Britain at any time.

Here I shall place the somewhat tenuous evidence for the former existence of Druidism in what is now England before the reader, later discussing the statements of those authorities who deny its former presence in that area. In his *Gallic War*, Cæsar tells us that "this institution (Druidism) is *supposed* to have been devised in Britain, and to have been brought over from it into Gaul; and now those who desire to gain a more accurate knowledge of that system generally proceed thither for the purpose of studying it."[19] Let me indicate that one important circumstance concerning this statement has not been sufficiently commented upon. It was written in Gaul, where Cæsar was intimately associated with the Æduan chief Diviciacus, who was probably a Druid, and from whom he must have obtained his information concerning the cult. So much, indeed, is admitted on all sides. If Diviciacus provided him with this particular piece of intelligence, it must surely be regarded as accurate. Communication between Gaul and Britain was frequent and continual, and the Æduan Druid could scarcely have been mistaken in his estimate of the presence and importance of his cultus in Britain. At the same time, it must be pointed out, Cæsar qualifies his assertion by saying that Druidism is "*supposed* to have been devised in Britain," and does not more precisely affirm it as a fact.

But this by the way. It must be admitted, however, that definite historical information concerning the existence of Druidism in Southern

Britain is disappointingly scanty, and that those writers who claim that it never actually flourished there have thus sound reasons for their convictions.

No further allusion to Druidism in Britain was made by classical writers until a century after Cæsar had written his *Commentaries*. Tacitus, recording affairs in Britain as they presented themselves in the year A.D. 60-1, tells us that Suetonius Paulinus, the military Governor of the British Colony, uneasy because the island of Anglesey afforded a refuge to fugitives from Roman power who were fomenting rebellion among the neighbouring tribes, attacked their stronghold in force. The defence was a fanatical one. The defenders were inspired by furious women clad in sable garments, who brandished burning torches, and uttered frantic cries of encouragement to the warriors. These were reinforced by Druid priests, who raised their hands to heaven in tragic supplication, pouring maledictions upon the Roman invaders. At first the legionaries quailed and stood motionless at this horrid spectacle of Celtic wrath. But, encouraged by their general, they advanced to the attack, bore down the resistance of the frantic Britons, slew numbers of them, and cut down the groves of their worship.[20]

Pliny the Elder, writing in the sixth decade of the first century, remarks that Britain still celebrates the magic art "with such ceremonies that it might seem possible that she taught magic to the Persians." He adds that, thanks to the Romans, an end was put to "this monstrous cult," and as he is writing of Druidism, we can only assume that his references to "magic" and "cultus" apply to the circumstances of the Druid faith. In a few brief sentences he gives the impression that, while the cult of Druidism in Britain had been suppressed, its magical traditions still lingered on, and this may perhaps be regarded as inferential that it formerly had a definite existence in the southern parts of our island.[21]

In short, the three allusions to which I have referred—those of Cæsar, Tacitus and Pliny—are the only three authentic passages respecting Druidism in Britain which we encounter in classical literature. Even these have been assailed as being of much too slender and unsatisfactory a character to permit of their acceptance as the foundations of a belief in the former existence of a Druidic cultus in Southern Britain.

Those writers who seek to clarify the Druidic "position" in Britain, as apart from Gaul or elsewhere, scarcely inspire us with much confidence so far as the manner of their demonstration is concerned. In some instances they preface their arguments with a definite denial of the presence of the Druidic cultus in South Britain, while only a few pages farther on, when faced with some circumstance unfriendly to their thesis which they find it difficult or impossible to ignore, they falter and appear to give a partial admission to the argument they seek to dispose of. Few indeed arrive at such conclusions of definite value as the importance of the subject demands, and on the whole it may be said that their findings are quite as unsatisfactory as those of their opponents who devoutly believe in the presence of Druidism in the English-Welsh area on grounds either insufficient or fantastically conceived. Miss Eleanor Hull, a proficient in Celtic lore, left the question suspended in an atmosphere of uncertainty.[11] James Fergusson, in his now classical *Rude Stone Monuments*, which ranks as a modern work, though published in 1872, remarks that "Neither Cæsar, however, nor any one else, ever pretended to have seen a Druid in England. Suetonius met *'Druidæ'* in the Island of Anglesea (Mona), but none were ever heard of in Wiltshire, or Derbyshire, or Cumberland, where the principal monuments are situated."[12] Here Fergusson associates Druidism with stone monuments, as though the presence of the one proved that of the other.

Mr. T. D. Kendrick, of the Department of British and Mediæval Antiquities of the British Museum, is among those who have dealt with the subject of Druidism in Britain with conspicuous and deliberate fairness. He indicates that "so far as England is concerned, there is no reference to druids at all, and it seems obvious that in this country they were of negligible importance as an organized body after the Claudian conquest." Elsewhere in his book he summarizes his findings concerning the probability of the existence of Druidism in South Britain. The Druids of Gaul were known to a Greek writer as early as 200 B.C. If, therefore, Druidism in Britain pre-dated the Gaulish form of the cultus, it might have come down from an antiquity preceding the Celtic period in England, the La Tène period of the early Iron Age, which commenced in this island about 500 B.C. It may thus have been of aboriginal origin and have been grafted upon Celtic faith. But is there any good reason why the invading La Tène Celts should not have introduced it into England? Indeed Mr. Kendrick elsewhere remarks upon the unlikelihood that the guardians or professors of the Celtic religion should have adopted the cultus from "defeated natives," and definitely states that the Druidic priesthood of Gaul "must have been of Keltic origin."

Mr. Kendrick's supposition is racy of that theory which upholds the notion that Druidism was not a faith typical of the Indo-German or "Aryan" peoples, a doctrine which I shall review when I come to deal with the origins of Druidism as a whole. Here it is only necessary to say that I believe the Druidic cult to be considerably more ancient than the Early Iron Age in Western Europe, at least it was so on the Continent, and that I am aware of reasons which so clearly substantiate this belief as to render further comment scarcely necessary in this section. Nor can I see why Druidism should not have been the common possession of Aryan and non-Aryan peoples in Europe.

Mr. Kendrick concludes that no evidence exists of a Celtic priesthood in Britain of such power and status as that which existed in Gaul. He thinks that Celtic folk from the Marne area who had mingled with the native Marne population settled in Britain and incorporated its faith with their own. This admixture gave to British "Druidism" a character more antiquated and thus seemingly of greater authority and longer establishment than that of Gaul. The legend of this more authoritative tradition grew with the passage of the centuries until at last we find it reflected in the statement of Cæsar. The "Druidism" of Britain was a Druidism sustained by kings and chieftains. In this island it probably had no other priesthood, although certain "British elders" may have undertaken the care and upkeep of its sodality. Mr. Kendrick, however, applies to this conclusion the description of an hypothesis only.[14] His observations generally relate so intimately to the question of the origin of Druidism that I must deal with them in the chapter reserved for the discussion of that problem.

Professor Sir John Rhys gave it as his first opinion that Druidism reached Gaul "undoubtedly through the Belgæ who had settled in Britain."[15] Later, he held that the Belgæ were preceded in Britain by other Brythons, and in any case he denied that any Brythonic-Celtic people ever had Druids. Druidism was a religion of the non-Celtic natives, and it "possessed certain characteristics which enabled it to make terms with the Celtic conquerors both in Gaul and in the British Islands."[16] Still later, he found that Druidism had been "evolved by the Continental Goidels, or rather accepted by them from the Aborigines,"[17] thereby referring its invention to another Celtic stock. In his *Celtic Britain* (fourth edition, 1908, pp. 72–3) he says: "It is hard, however, to accept the belief, recorded by Cæsar, that druidism originated here, and was only imported into Gaul: the probability rather is that the Celts found it both there and here the common religion of some of the aboriginal inhabitants of the West of Europe." But the proof that Druidism had a specific racial origin is totally lacking. That at one time it was a cult of the folk of the European forest-regions we shall see.

The case for the existence of British Druidism was supported by D'Arbois de Jubainville, who inferred its presence in the island from Cæsar's statement that Druidism originated in Britain, and thought that it was of Goidelic origin. He believed that it had been imposed upon Brythonic conquerors from Gaul by the native Goidels of Britain. (It is, of course, hardly necessary to indicate that people of Goidelic stock are not thought to have settled in the south of England, although traces of them may appear in the south-west.) Subsequently to this acceptance, he thought, the Goidels imported Druidism into Gaul from Britain.[18] D'Arbois points to an allusion in the "Cophur in dà muccado," one of the prefaces of the *Táin Bó Cualnge*, to the *Druid do Bretnuib*, that is "the Druid of the Britons," in justification of his belief in the existence of Druidism in what is now England in the first century B.C. The Druid in question, however, may have belonged to one of the British tribes in what is now Southern Scotland, although we have no authority for believing that these tribes ever cultivated the Druidic faith.

Mr. Kendrick is inclined to believe that in those British districts where Roman rule was established, Druidism rapidly diminished until it became "completely ineffective and moribund." He considers it "significant that Tacitus does not even mention Druidism in the 'Agricola,' a biography that is principally concerned with the events of a seven years' administration of the island."[29] We certainly hear nothing of Druids or Druidism among the Iceni of Norfolk and Suffolk in the accounts of the rebellion of Boadicea. This appears all the more strange, because I believe, as I stated in a work descriptive of that rising, that the aristocracy of the Iceni, if not that people as a whole, had a Gallic origin.[30] Indeed we find Boadicea herself officiating as a divineress, though not as a priestess, as has erroneously been stated by Kendrick and others. The Greek writer Cassius Dio describes her treatment of the Romans in the sack of Londinium in gruesome detail. She celebrated her victory, he tells us, by hanging up the Roman or Belgic women of London in the grove of the goddess Andraste, after barbarously impaling them.[31] We know that impalement was a Druidic method of sacrifice. Andate, or Andraste, it may be said in passing, was a deity of the Vocontii of the south-east of Gaul, who appear to have known her as Andarta[32] and it is difficult to believe that her cult existed in Britain. The evidence of Dio is, in my opinion, dubious, and if a part of it seems to substantiate the presence of Druidic rite, his reference to Andraste arouses suspicion.

BRITISH TRADITIONS OF DRUIDISM

If we turn now to tradition pure and simple, we discover little which may reasonably be attributed to a memory of actual Druidic practice in Britain. Naturally it is essential that memorative traces of this description should be subjected to the closest scrutiny. In the first place, it is not a little remarkable that the folk of ancient Ireland nourished the belief that Druidic magic originated in Britain. Their heroes and seers are again and again spoken of as acquiring the highest proficiency in the magic art only by sojourning in Alba.[33]

I am of opinion, too, that the fact that Druidism in some form flourished in Scotland and Ireland for some centuries after the Romans evacuated Britain fortifies the belief that it formerly functioned also in the "English" Celtic areas. That the Druidism of Scotland and Ireland in the immediate post-Christian centuries was by no means merely a species of fetishistic magic but definitely a faith having an ethical background of its own and a tradition of pseudo-scientific character, will, I hope, be proven in these pages beyond peradventure.

In many parts of England and Scotland small herds of white cattle were long preserved, some of them to the present time, and it appears to me as highly probable that these may have been the fragmentary remains of what had once been Druidic herds set apart for the purpose of sacrifice. I will deal with the subject at some length in a later chapter, but here I may remark upon the pious and even jealous care with which these herds have been maintained throughout the ages, and until the present era in some cases. This zealous tradition is revealed in more than one ancient manuscript which records the maintenance of these herds. It is certainly remarkable that only white cattle, those of a colour especially associated with Druidic sacrifice and of a primitive type, should have been preserved and segregated, while those of other colours of the ancient breed were comparatively neglected. In some instances, too, legends concerning the fate of the families who owned these herds have come down to us, and certain of these tales appear to hold a more or less religious significance.

Possible Druidic Place-names

So far as places or sites in England associated with the name of Druid are concerned, it seems to me that the importance of these has been stressed too much in supporting the argument for the existence of British Druidism. A stone found near Port St. Mary in the parish of Rushen, Isle of Man, bears an inscription in Ogham characters, and this has been read "Dovaidona Maqi Droata," that is "(the stone) of Dovaidona, son of the Druid." The relic appears to date from the fifth century of this era.[14] If Celtic authorities be correct in their rendering of this inscription, says Mr. Kendrick, "we can at least say that there were druids (in the Irish sense) in Man as late as the fifth or sixth century." As we shall see, quite a number of Druidic traditions are associated with the island.

A few places in England appear to bear names of Druidic significance. In Gloucestershire we find Stoke Druid, near which standing stones of a kind associated in the popular imagination with the Druids are situated. It seems, however, impossible to trace the designation to remoter times. Stanton Drew, in Somersetshire, at which stone circles are situated, has also been linked with Druidic tradition, but the land so called was certainly the property of a family named Drew.[15] This family held and gave its name to other manors where there are no putative Druidical remains. Apart altogether from the assertions of romantically-minded antiquaries, popular folk-lore has associated the Druids with standing stones of one description or another at Stonehenge, Avebury, the circle at Saddleback near Keswick, the Carn Leskys, or "Cairn of Lights" at Land's End, the "Grey Wethers" on Dartmoor, the "Giant's Chair" in the Scilly Isles, said to have been the throne of an arch-druid, the "Druid's Stone" at Fountain Dale in Nottingham, Arbor Lowe, near Buxton, and numerous other places. But tradition and tradition alone asserts their association with the Druidic cultus, and the very circumstance that it is linked with rude stone monuments is perhaps the best evidence of their non-Druidic character.

DRUIDISM AND ROMANTICISM

Mr. Kendrick, in the first chapter of his excellent treatise *The Druids*, has been at some pains to prove that the Saxon invasion blotted out the memory of the Druids in England, and that "a knowledge of the former existence of the priesthood was regained slowly and laboriously in the sixteenth century as a result of the return to a study of the ancient historians. . . . The theory, now so popular, that the druids built the megalithic monuments was an invention of the late seventeenth century, successfully promulgated, in the succeeding century, by Romanticism."

The real begetters of this notion were Aubrey, Toland, Stukeley, and Camden. But the Romantic Movement in the late eighteenth and early nineteenth centuries carried the process farther, and poets found in the Druid and the mysterious influences which surrounded him the material for which they craved. It is becoming more and ever more definitely recognized that folk-lore and popular belief are powerfully influenced by literature, both ancient and contemporary. Thus some of the West Highland folk-tales collected by J. F. Campbell reveal the traces of acceptances from *The Arabian Nights* and other literary sources, while scores of localities in our island owe their "legends" to the comparatively recent fabrications of poets and novelists. The rootless or fictional legend is indeed one of the most serious pitfalls in the path of the inexperienced collector of tradition. A notorious instance in point is the manner in which Arthurian legend has in some cases attached itself to localities in Germany where it can be shown to have had an introduction in late mediæval times only, through the agency of minnesingers and weavers of romance.

One is bound to admit in face of the sheer lack of evidence that the case for the existence of Druidism in what is now England is indeed one of the most threadbare in the annals of archæology. If we except the statement of Cæsar, not a single authentic historical reference to Druidism in England is forthcoming. So far as tradition is concerned, the record is almost equally bare. A passage in Nennius' *Historia Britonum*, compiled according to some authorities in the year A.D. 680, and referred by others to the year 800, has been assumed by some to refer to the Druids. Nennius says that the British prince Vortigern, abhorred by all for his nameless crimes, sought counsel of his magicians, or wise men.

The Irish version of his work, written at some time in the twelfth century, translated the word *magos* as "Druids," and from this it has been assumed either that the personages so described were actually Druidic priests, or that they were sorcerers, such as the later Irish Druids are believed to have been by many authorities. The date of this occurrence is given as the year A.D. 452. It is certainly by no means impossible that a caste of elders devoted to mystical or occult practices actually did exist in Southern Britain at this period. But we have no explicit and parallel evidence which might justify such a belief, and the entire circumstances of the passage, associated as it is with the ensuing combat between the frankly allegorical dragons representative of the Saxon and British races and the first appearance of the prophet Merlin, appear to me as basically mythical.[30]

The only safe conclusion which it seems possible to arrive at in the circumstances is that, if Druidism ever did function in the area now known as England—a contingency supported by Cæsar's statement alone —it was so speedily extirpated after the invasion of Claudius in A.D. 43 as to leave little or no traces of its former existence behind. I have already stated my belief that its disappearance in Gaul was perhaps due to the downfall of the native monarchies with which it must have been so closely identified, the "Divine King" being regarded as the central figure in its cultus, as I hope to prove. That it flourished so long in Scotland and Ireland was probably due to the continued maintenance of the sacred kingship in these countries as an institution.

DRUIDISM IN WALES

If, now, we turn to the evidence for the existence of Druidism in Wales, what do we find? We have already seen that a Druidic cult assuredly functioned in the island of Anglesey, a part of the Welsh area. "Druidism," wrote Sir John Rhys, "is far harder to discover in the oldest literature of the Welsh" (than in records relating to Ireland or Scotland) but "it is possible there to recognize the Welsh counterpart of the Goidelic god of Druidism, namely in Math Vab Mathonwy."[31] "Among the oldest instances in Welsh poetry of the use of the word *derwyddon*, 'druids,' " he says elsewhere, "is one where it is applied to the Magi, or Wise Men, who came with presents to the infant Jesus."[32] The poem referred to will be found in the *Book of Taliesin*.

In short, practically all the Druids referred to in Welsh literature are those who appear in the poetry associated with that later Welsh bardism which seems to have assumed the title, and to some extent the functions of Druidism. "In Wales there had been Druids as there were Bards," says Canon MacCulloch.[33] But I can trace no mention of any except at a late period. The bard Gwalchmai (1150-1190) says in his elegy on the death of Madog, Prince of Powys: "Would to God the day of doom were arrived, since druids are come bringing the news of woe." Cynddelw, his contemporary, in his panegyric on Owen Gwynedd, exclaims: "Bards are constituted the judges of excellence, even Druids of the circle, of four dialects, coming from the four regions." Elsewhere, in a poem recited at a bardic contest, he alludes to: "Druids of the splendid race, wearers of the golden chains," as though they were still existing. In still another poem addressed to Owen Cyveilcawg, Prince of Powys, he makes repeated mention of the Druids. Llywarch ab Llewelyn (1160-1220) also speaks of the prophecies of the Druids as though they were his contemporaries. Philip Brydydd (1200-1250), President of the Welsh bards, mentions the chair he holds, adding that none in the presence of the grave Druids of

Britain could aspire to it who were undistinguished in their art.

These allusions make it perfectly clear that in later centuries, when Christianity had long been established in Wales, the Druidic cultus, as then understood, must have assumed the form of a bardic sodality, the doctrines of which were associated with a species of poetic mysticism.

I have neither space nor inclination to discuss at any length in this book the present position of ancient Welsh literature as it is understood and treated by the foremost critics in Wales. Indeed I have already reviewed the subject in a recently published volume, *The Magic Arts in Celtic Britain* (pp. 133–6). Here I will only say that the leading critic of Welsh literature, Professor W. J. Gruffydd, remarks of old Welsh poetry as found in the famous Triads and elsewhere, that "such translations of it as have appeared (including Rhys's, the best) are mere guesswork, and no theory of any kind may be built upon them."[40] It is not, however, necessary, I feel, to assume that simply because these poems have been badly translated their contents are other than authentic, in part at least.

Here, of course, I am concerned with them only so far as they refer to Druidism or its personnel. Apart from those allusions to it which I have already mentioned, a considerable number are to be found in ancient Welsh literature which appear to have some association with the cult of the oak tree. In a poem entitled "The Wand of Moses" we find allusions to the "wood-circle of feathered oak trees," which would seem to imply a grove. In "The Battle of the Trees," a poem by Taliesin, a Welsh bard who may have flourished in the sixth century, Algernon Herbert, whose scholarship seems so strange an admixture of critical care and wayward fantasy, found a quatrain which appears to throw some light upon the Welsh use of the word "Druid":

> "The rapid oak tree,
> Before him heaven and earth quake;
> In every land his name is mine."

"That is to say," continues Herbert, "I style myself a derwydd from the name of the tree derw. . . . Moreover, the poets of the same age not only used the style of derwydd, but that of mael-derw, which title (seemingly confined to one person, the arch-druid) signifies the efficient man, the proficient or adept, of the oak tree." Here Herbert is undoubtedly correct in his recognition of the meaning of the term. He says elsewhere: "Derwydd is the plainest of all British nouns, being formed of derw, an oak, and ydd, 'a termination of masculine nouns'." If Herbert's derivation of the Welsh word for "Druid" be as correct as his remarks upon its meaning as applied to the cultus, we have here a very definite example of the use of the term "Druid" in a Welsh poem the manuscript of which is believed to date from the last quarter of the thirteenth century, but the content of which is probably much older. I can do no more than bring the passage to notice, as its linguistic implications must rest upon the judgment of the guardians of Celtic philology.[41]

"The Red Book of Hergest" makes allusion to "The scions of oak from the grove," and in the poem known as "The Wand of Moses" (lines 76–7) we find the following:

> "Each exalted woman's praise hath been sung
> By some of the Druids."[42]

But these quotations represent only a few random gleanings from ancient Welsh poetry on the subject of Druidism and many others might be instanced. It is evident, I think, that most of them, particularly the last, are the compositions of a body of men who were proficient in the bardic art, but who appear by some means which it now seems impossible to fathom, to have retained, or revived the tradition of much of the ancient cultus of the oak and its more mystical and allegorical significance. As Mr. Kendrick expresses it: "The basic assumption that the mediæval Welsh bards were a continuation of the Druidic hierarchy . . . is not by any means an extravagant or ridiculous belief."

When the sacerdotal powers of the Druids vanished, he suggests, they may have been "merged in the bardic class." "The survival of the calling of the professional bard is only a token of Keltic custom, and not a proof of connection with Druidism. The most that can reasonably be claimed is that some bards of special distinction may (in earlier times) have been possessed of the Druidic doctrines," but he refrains from the belief that by the mediæval period the ancient Druidic lore had descended to any of them.[43] My own opinion is that these poems reveal a good deal more of the Druidic spirit and "philosophy" than most authorities would care to admit, but I freely grant that the means by which it descended to the Welsh bards remains among the obscurities. One thing, however, is manifest. The bardic class appears to have survived as a caste in Wales in unbroken continuance from the early British centuries, and if that be granted—and I fail to see on what grounds it can be refuted—we have good reason to believe that it must have retained and preserved much of the lore of the Druidic cultus with which it had once been contemporary and closely allied. It would seem, too, that that cultus actually did flourish in Wales in the early Roman period, as we are almost compelled to believe from the evidence concerning the existence of Druidism in Anglesey. Elton maintains that the Welsh bards "retained a stock of tropes and allusions which derived their origin from the ancient British paganism," but that their works "contain nothing which can be treated as a real doctrine of tradition."[44]

The statement is typical of the species of treatment to which these poems have been subjected by English critics. A careful comparison with Irish myth, indeed, reveals many of the Welsh bardic allusions as belonging to the common stock of Celtic belief. M. D'Arbois, however, points to the circumstance that the name of the Druids does not appear in the most ancient Welsh laws nor in those attributed to Howell-Dda, nor in any of the Latin texts composed to the order of that prince in the tenth century.

DRUIDIC PLACE-NAMES IN WALES

Certain place-names in Wales might appear to enshrine Druidic memories. Cerrig-y-Drudion, in Denbighshire, is now translated as "Stones of the Heroes," and not of "the Druids," as the misleading spelling "Druidion" formerly led some investigators to believe. Rowland examined certain place-names of alleged Druidic association in Anglesey —Caer-Edris, "the City of the Astronomers," and Cerrig-Brudyn, "the Astronomer's Circle." He thought them traditional rather than natively original.⁴⁵ Toland also cited such place-names in the island as Tre'r Driu, "the Town of the Druid," and Tre'r Beirdh, "the Town of the Bards." He also mentions Caer Dreuin, "the City of the Druids" in Merioneth-shire.⁴⁶ Probably none of his translations would find favour with philologists to-day.

DRUIDIC RELICS IN THE ISLE OF MAN

Traditional material respecting the Druids is associated with the Isle of Man. Archbishop John Spottiswood of St. Andrews, who wrote in the seventeenth century, tells us in his *History of the Church of Scotland* that Man, for long an appanage of the Scottish Crown, was the centre of Caledonian Druidism, the affairs of which were governed by a "president" who dwelt in the island. But Cratylinth, a mythical king of Alba, or Scotland, expelled the Druids and extirpated their superstitions. The legend, for it seems to be little more, is repeated by Sacheverell in his *Survey of the Isle of Man*. He alleges that Man rather than Anglesey was the principal seat of the Druids and seeks to prove as much from the circumstance that it was anciently known as *Sedes Druidarum* and *Insula Druidarum*. A tradition also exists that Dothan, the eleventh King of Scotland, left his three sons in the Isle of Man to be educated by the Druids. Corbed, alluded to as the first (mythical) King of Scotland, is said to have been reared by the Druids of the island.⁴⁷ All this may, or may not, indicate the presence of an ancient tradition that the Isle of Man was formerly a centre of Druidic activity, and the fact that the island was at one time closely associated with the legend and possibly the worship of the Celtic god Manannan may have lent colour to such a supposition.

A tradition exists in Man that when St. Maughold landed on its shores, its Druids were in the act of making a human sacrifice upon one of the stones of the circle called the Lonan, or Cloven Stones, situated in the uorth-western part of the island in the little village of Baldrine. The saint sprinkled holy water upon the sacrificial stone, thus extinguishing the fire which burned there and splitting the stone itself asunder, by which means the human victim was released. The Druids, dismayed at what appeared to be a miracle, fled incontinently.⁴⁸

As I have already indicated, a stone containing a Druidical inscription has been discovered in the Isle of Man.

Chapter III

DRUIDISM IN CELTIC AREAS (*continued*)

SCOTLAND

IF we seek for data concerning the presence of Druidism in Scotland during the early Christian centuries, we shall certainly meet with a more ample measure of encouragement. One of the first allusions to the cultus in that region states that certain Irish-Pictish Druids were driven into Scotland from Hibernia. "From them are every spell and every charm and every *sreod* (sneeze) and voices of birds and every omen"—in short, all magic in Scotland proceeded from them.[1]

St. Columba, on his arrival in Scotland in the latter part of the sixth century, found himself opposed by a powerful Druidic sodality precisely as did St. Patrick in Ireland. Columba is said to have come from Ireland for the especial purpose of converting the Picts from paganism to Christianity. He came into contact with Druidic priests at the Court of King Brude, which was situated somewhere to the north-east of Loch Ness, and there and elsewhere, we are told, he entered into what can scarcely be otherwise described than as magical contests with them. Columba seems to have made evident his hostility to Druidism in no uncertain terms. Like most devoted protagonists, he had a one-track mentality. He says:

> "It is not with the *sreod* (sneeze) our destiny is,
> Nor with the bird on the top of the twig,
> Nor with the trunk of a knotty tree,
> Nor with a *sordan* hand in hand.

> "I adore not the voice of birds,
> Nor the *sreod*, nor a destiny on the earthly world,
> Nor a son, nor chance, nor woman ;
> My Druid is Christ, the Son of God."[2]

At the hall of King Brude he encountered the Druid Broichan, who had been tutor to the King. Almost at once he commenced to poach upon the Druidic preserves. He converted an entire family and baptized them. A few days later, one of its members, a young man, fell seriously ill. The local Druids upbraided the parents with their infidelity to the tribal faith. The young man died, but Columba raised him from the dead, thus justifying the faith of the youth's parents.[3] The Christian magic was more powerful than the Druidic.

Broichan the Druid had an Irish bondmaid whom Columba asked him to liberate. When the obstinate pagan refused to do so, the saint assured him that did he not obey his injunction, he would surely die. Columba later informed his followers that Broichan had been smitten by an angel with severe illness. At that moment messengers arrived to plead that Columba would come to Broichan's assistance. Columba agreed to do so if the Druid would set the girl free. This Broichan did, whereupon Columba placed a white pebble in a cup of water. The stone miraculously floated on the surface of the liquid, and when Broichan had drunk of the same he was cured. (Adamnan, *Life of St. Columba*, W. Huyshe's translation, pp. 146–7.)

We obtain a glimpse of the species of worship of the Picts under Druidism when we learn that they adored a certain fountain. So holy was it that if any drank of its waters, or bathed within it, they were afflicted with leprosy or partial loss of sight. But after Columba had blessed it, the "demons" who haunted it were exorcised.* Broichan the Druid, however, was not minded that his opponent should proceed on his conquering path unhindered, for he warned him that should he embark upon the waters of Loch Ness, he would cause the winds to blow unfavourably and a great darkness to envelop his vessel. Undaunted, the saint duly entered his boat, whereupon a violent and contrary wind commenced to blow and it became exceeding dark. But Columba called upon Christ, so that his barque was borne along safely in the teeth of the gale.*

We are informed that Columba travelled through Northern Pictavia, establishing monasteries and small Christian communities, yet Adamnan, his biographer, records but two specific instances of his conversion of individuals to the Christian faith. The saint appears to have assumed a position of importance at the Court of King Brude and the Druids seem to have withdrawn themselves from his sphere of influence. But it is idle to assume from this that Druidism in Pictavia was otherwise than a definite system of belief, a mere fetishism of the lower cultus, as Hill Burton and other historians who were unacquainted with the tenour and general nature of its principles have averred.* Hill Burton actually denied the presence in Scotland and Ireland of the Druidic cult, but as Skene remarks: "Here he must find himself face to face with a body of evidence which it is impossible, with any truth or candour, to ignore."*

It is not contended that the tenets of Druidism composed a cultus of superior intellectual and philosophic character, or that its principles were those of an exalted spirituality. But it is certainly not to be classed as mere magic or "witchcraft" alone. The very fact that the Druids took such strong exception to the baptism and conversion of a "peasant" family by Columba makes it plain that they did so on "religious" grounds. For the passage makes it clear that they extolled *their own gods* as more powerful than the God of the Christians; nor could the Pictish Druids have objected to their people's recognition of that God on the score that it in any way controverted the ideas of a system founded on magic alone and which had not the sanction of a belief in divine beings.

Columba succeeded in his mission and in the time-honoured manner of the ecclesiastic managed so to arrange the affairs of the kingship in the small Scottish colony of Dalriada, in Argyll, that he was at length enabled to dictate even the royal succession. There is a tradition that on his arrival in the island of Iona he encountered two Druids disguised as bishops, who pretended to have planted the Christian faith there. He commanded them to depart, an order which they politely obeyed. But, as Skene indicates, this story is due to O'Donnel, who introduced it into his *Life of St. Columba*. The "Druids" appear to have been the remains of "a church of seven bishops, which here, as elsewhere, preceded the monastic church." According to tradition, it appears that Druids must have been familiar in what is now Scotland long before Columba's day, for we learn that King Cormac of Tara sent in the third century for Druids to Alba to practise magic on his behalf against the King of Munster.[8]

POSSIBLE DRUIDIC SURVIVALS IN SCOTLAND

It is not improbable that certain practices recognized in Scotland at a much later period as of popular if magical acceptance, may have been of Druidic origin. The subject of Druidic bull-sacrifice is discussed on a later page, but here it may be remarked that in the year 1656 the Church Presbytery of Applecross in Ross-shire, took action against certain persons for sacrificing bulls on the 25th of August, "which day is dedicate, as they conceive, to St. Mourie, as they call him." In 1678 the Presbytery of Dingwall took similar disciplinary action against four Mackenzies for sacrificing a bull in an island in Loch Maree.[9] This island of Inis Maree, or Mourie, has an enclosure, or stone dyke, in which are the remains of a chapel.

Near it stands an oak tree, into whose trunk nails and coins are still driven as "offerings." Pennant states that St. Mourie, or Maree, was in his day the patron of the district and "that the oath of the country is by his name."[10] The ruined chapel was circled by the devotees in dance or procession. That "St. Mourie" was an earlier divinity there can be little doubt. Mr. A. B. Cook is of opinion that Mourie was the successor of a "divine king" connected with the oak and sacred well at Inis Maree, the god or spirit of which was incarnate in him. The sacrificed bull may have incarnated the spirit of the god.[11] The island appears at an earlier time to have been known as *Eilean mo righ*, "the island of my king," or perhaps as *Eilean a Mhor Righ*, "the island of the great king," where a local king may have been worshipped as identified with a god. Indeed some sixty or seventy years ago the people of the place still alluded to Mourie as "the god Mourie," as Mitchell assures us from his personal inquiry. Other sacrifices of bulls were very frequent in Scotland and throughout Britain.

In the Highland rite of *taghairm* a seer was wrapped in the hide of a newly-slain bull and stretched himself beside a waterfall or at the foot of some wild precipice believed to be haunted by spirits, who communicated to him what he desired to know respecting the future. The rite persisted until the middle of the eighteenth century and is in consonance with what we know concerning Druidic auspices in Ireland.[12] That it may also have been practised in Wales may perhaps be inferred from a passage in the *Mabinogion* tale "The Vision of Rhonabwy," in which a warrior of that name beheld a vision whilst sleeping on the skin of a yellow heifer.

DRUIDIC PLACE-NAMES IN SCOTLAND

Other reminiscences of the Druidic faith in Scotland will be recorded in future pages in connection with the several departments of cult-practice and belief, and will be noted in the index. So far as Scottish place-names which appear to indicate Druidical associations are concerned, certain small huts in Skye, capable of holding only one person, are known as *Teg-nin-druinich*, or "Druid's House," which would suggest that they may have been the dwellings of hermit Druids.[13] The island of Iona is still known to some Highlanders by its ancient name *Inis Druineach*, or *Nan Druihean*, "Druid's Isle," and the Irish called it *Eilean Drunish*.[14] Are these denominations to be classed with the "silly tales of the Druids" "vended in Iona," alluded to by Dr. Reeves in his *Vita Columbæ?* (p. 436). Surely they cannot be imputed to the fantasies of Stukeley, Toland and those other Druidic enthusiasts who discovered "the never-failing Druids" everywhere, and who seduced a credulous peasantry into believing the "fiction" of Druid establishment in the island, as they considerably antedate in their use and origin the period when the antiquaries in question set to work on the "Druid legend." As M. D'Arbois has said, it is a historical fact, incontestably established, that Druidism existed in Great Britain among the Picts north of the Wall of Antonine until the close of the sixth century. Indeed this region had never at any time been subject to Roman domination and there is no reason why Druidism should not have flourished there unhindered. (*Les Druides*, p. 88.)

DRUIDISM IN IRELAND

For some time it has been fashionable to believe that Druidism in Ireland was, if not merely a distorted reflection of the Gaulish system, something even more negligible and approaching the lower type of fetishism. Indeed most modern writers on the subject appear to have arrived at a consensus of opinion concerning its lowly condition. That view, I feel, is no longer entitled to acceptance or even tolerance, and I hope that I will be enabled to make it perfectly clear in the course of this book that Irish Druidism was not only the equal of the sister system in Gaul, but in some respects superior to it. That it was moreover a religious cultus and not merely a body composed of magicians or "medicine men," is, as we shall see later, proven by its close connection with the institution of the Divine Kingship. As the late Miss Eleanor Hull, a trusted authority, expressed it: "the (Irish) Druids occupied a position and carried on functions in every way corresponding to those existing in Gaul. We find them as a well-organized body of men holding a position of authority, the counsellors of kings, the promulgators of legal decisions, the inspirers and controllers of armies. We hardly open a page of early Irish writings without coming into contact with them either as soothsayers and magicians or prophets; or as priests, carrying out the rites and sacrifices."[15] Keating, the seventeenth-century historian of Ireland, even suggested that when Cæsar spoke of the original home of Druidism he may have referred to Ireland rather than to Britain, an idea which might commend itself did not the Continental evidence make it plain that the origins of Druidism were certainly not insular.[16]

Nor was tradition affectionate to such a notion, for it averred that Druidism was introduced into Ireland at some time about the year 270 B.C., a statement which chimes to some extent with what we know of Hibernian relationships with the Continent at that epoch.[17] Keating avers that the Druids came to Ireland along with the mythical Tuatha Dé Danann.[18] Druids are frequently referred to in the Irish *Book of Invasions* as belonging to the several immigrant tribes which settled in the island at various times. The ancient myth of Partholan avers that he brought Druids to Ireland in his train. The Nemedians, who competed with the Fomorians for the soil of Ireland, had Druids of their own, as also had the Fomorians, though in some of these instances, I believe, the word "Druid" has been employed to convey the meaning of "magician" or "wise man."

The traditional association of the Irish Druids with the *Lia Fail*, or Stone of Fàl (the so-called "Stone of Destiny"), which figured so largely in the coronation ceremonies of the High Kings of Ireland, reveals that not only were these monarchs inseparably connected with the cultus of the Divine King in Ireland, but that their relationship with that cultus was a religious as well as a mystical one. The tradition further links them as intimately with the Tuatha Dé Danann, a race who appear as pre-eminently divine or godlike in the mythology of Ireland. This particular link between the Druidic body and a pantheon of godlike beings has indeed been neglected as supplying a reasonable degree of proof of the religious status of Druidism. The Tuatha Dé may be said to have been the deific nucleus of the Druidic institution in Ireland, and O'Curry alludes to the Dagda, the chief deity of this pantheon, as "a druidical chief or demi-god."[19] But the Firbolgs, who defended the soil of Ireland from Danann intervention, could also boast of "Druids," as did the later Milesians who supplanted the Tuatha Dé.[20]

O'Beirne Crowe, in his *Religious Beliefs of the Pagan Irish*, gave it as his opinion that Irish Druidism was a reflection of that of Gaul, a belief in which Professor Sir John Rhys appears to have concurred.[21] But he did so merely on the grounds that in both countries the Druids were pre-eminently "magicians," a theory which obviously calls for revision when the weight of modern evidence unfriendly to it comes to be considered. Mr. Kendrick lays some stress upon the fact that important assemblies were held in Ireland at fixed intervals and concludes that "we cannot fairly assume that Irish Druidism lacked that co-ordination of its members such as obtained in Gaul." "It is significant," he adds, "that the Druids of Ireland were servants of the primitive festival-system in its Central-European form."[22]

In the triune *Life of St. Patrick* we are told that "the gentiles were about celebrating an idolatrous solemnity accompanied with many incantations and some magical inventions and other idolatrous superstitions, their kings being collected, also their satraps with their chief leaders, and the principal among the people and Magi and enchanters and soothsayers and doctors, inventors of all arts and gifts, as being summoned before Laogaire in Temar." This work also describes how Patrick was challenged by the "Magus," or Druid of King Lœgaire to a magical contest, an account of which the reader will find in the chapter which deals with Druidic sorcery. He was also opposed by the "Magi," the sons of Amolugid.

MISTAKEN CRITICISM OF IRISH DRUIDISM

Of the early history of Druidism in Ireland, says MacBain, "We have no direct information. It is only when Christianity has been long established and Druidism a thing of the remote past that we have writers who speak of the Druids; and in their eyes the Druids were but magicians that attended the Courts of the pagan kings. . . . In all the numerous references to them in Irish chronicles and tales there is no hint given of Druidism being either a system of philosophy or religion; the Druids of Irish story are mere magicians and diviners, sometimes only conjurers." To the priests and annalists of Christendom, of course, the Druids were merely "conjurers," but so were the priests of Christendom to the Druids. They challenged the Christian missionaries to magical contests, and as the priests and missionaries almost invariably triumphed over them, an unbiassed reader, a Hindu or Mahometan, who knew nothing of the authentic spirit of Christianity, might well be pardoned if he assumed therefrom that the early Christian missionaries in Ireland were greater proficients in the occult arts than were the Druids. Judging from this, he might easily conclude that Christianity possessed "no system of philosophy and religion." Macbain's argument is flagrantly unsound in its premises.

Macbain proceeds to say that the Irish Druids could not have been a priestly class, an assumption I shall contest when we come to consider the Druid priesthood more particularly. He adds, "it is quite true that we have, at least, an echo now and then of the time when Druidism in Ireland or Scotland was something different, and when even human sacrifices were offered"; and to illustrate his statement he proceeds to describe the well-known incident of St. Columba's immolation of St. Oran, by burying him beneath the foundations of the first church at Iona, thereby possibly strengthening the impression in the mind of his hypothetical "unbiassed reader" that Christian magical practice was every whit as discreditable in its recognition of barbarous magical practice as was Druidism itself![23]

In a passage which speaks well for his fairness of view and his insight into underlying verity, Mr. Kendrick gives it as his opinion that "it is conceivable that a pre-Keltic priesthood of the requisite authority existed in Ireland." "Legend, winnowed by disapproving Christianity, may have left us with a very imperfect residue of fact." "The evidence hints the other way." The certainty that the Druids of Ireland were servants of the Celtic festival-system "goes to the very heart of the problem."[14] It has been averred that the Irish Druids did not recognize the oak as a sacred tree, giving that position to the mountain ash. But as I shall indicate in a later passage, Irish literature is by no means lacking in references to the sacred character of the oak. At the same time, Mr. Kendrick believes that Druidism in Ireland was "a very faint reflection of the Gallic system, and one that speedily became isolated and degenerate." As the general opinion stands, this is a most liberal view of the Druidic situation in Ireland. Even so, it is not sufficiently broad to satisfy my own impressions regarding its status.

THE PRIESTHOOD AND THE BARDS

The Irish Druids were composed of two classes : the priesthood and the *Filid*, who were both bards, prophets and diviners. The latter caste, as may have been the case in Wales, long survived the former, retaining much of the lore of the associated and more strictly religious body. As we shall see, books and curricula concerning the training and methods of the *Filid* survived to a late era, and the instruction of the youth of Ireland was in the hands of the Druidic caste. Many of the ancient tales referring to the Druids allude to them as lighting and attending to the sacred fires associated with the Celtic festivals, thereby revealing their priestly status. As we shall see, too, evidence is not wanting that they adored certain idolatrous images. Yet O'Curry, who collected many such references, drew the conclusion that "there is no ground whatever for believing the Druids to have been the priests of any special positive worship."[15]

DRUIDISM AND THE KINGSHIP

But the actual and important position of the Druidic caste in Ireland is revealed by its association with the kingship there, and it is manifest that the rites and ceremonies connected with the choice and inauguration of a monarch in Ireland who was responsible for the welfare of the country, the growth and fructification of the crops, the multiplication of cattle and even of human beings, were in the hands of the Druidic caste. When most of the modern opinions unfriendly to the belief in an actual Druidic priesthood in Ireland were penned, this important theory of the Divine King and his functions was either imperfectly understood, or, in some cases, had not as yet been advanced. When we approach it in its proper place it will readily be recognized that it provides an entirely different view of the question of the status and functions of the Druidic priesthood from that which had been previously entertained concerning it, and indeed more than one perspicuous writer on the subject has already realized the necessity for revising his views upon Druidic priestly function and position in relation to it. Here it is necessary only to refer to the point in a general review of Druidism in Ireland, in which a narration of the detailed proof would be out of place, more particularly as it is bound up with analogies drawn from Druidic practice elsewhere and from the religious history of other lands.

Certain statements unfriendly to the Druidic caste, and put into the mouths of contemporary pagans occur here and there in Irish Celtic literature. Thus we find a lady from the Land of the Gods declaring that: "the faith of the Druids has come to little honour among the upright, mighty, numberless people of this land. When the righteous law shall be restored it will seal up the lips of the false black demon; and the Druids shall not longer have power to work their guileful spells."[26] It is almost beyond doubt that such hostile sentiments are the interpretations of priestly redactors.

We read also that King Cormac, "the Magnificent," whose era is said to have been A.D. 177, did his utmost to suppress Druidism. In revenge, a Druid named Maelgen so wrought upon a demon that the fiend placed a salmon bone crosswise in the king's throat as he sat at meat, and choked him.[27] King Loegaire, we are told, was one of the earliest converts to the Christian faith, but his son, the more traditionally minded Lughaid, obstinately refused to deny the faith of his ancestors and because of his adherence to it was struck by lightning and so perished.

Evans Wentz was informed by the caretaker of the "Purgatory" at Lough Derg that the old people in the neighbourhood nourished a legend that the vicinity of the lough, and the island it contains, were the last stronghold of the Druids in Ireland.[28] Beneath the soil of this island there were said to exist labyrinthine caverns where strange rites were celebrated and extraordinary visions were beheld, and it may possibly be that these structures and beliefs were the surviving relics of a centre formerly employed for the purposes of Druidic initiation.[29] The spot enjoyed a European celebrity throughout the middle ages.

King Diarmuid Mac Ceurbhail, who occupied the throne of Ireland in the year A.D. 528, and who is described as "half a Druid and half a Christian," made war upon a chieftain because he had destroyed a sacred cow.[30] Numerous colleges of Druidesses are alluded to in Irish lore and certain oak-groves in Ireland have been associated with Druidic tradition, although it has been strenuously affirmed by more than one authority that the oak was not adored by the Irish Druids. Yet in ancient Irish law seven "noble" or distinguished trees were noted, among them the oak, which was said to belong to "the high sacred grove," and severe penalties followed upon its destruction. Even St. Columba besought the Almighty to spare the sacred oak-grove at Derry, and declared afterward that much as he feared death and hell, he dreaded still more the sound of an axe in the grove of Derry.[11] Many place-names in Ireland are associated with the oak in its religious capacity.[12]

What I have said respecting Druidism in Ireland in this place will be added to materially in the chapters which deal with the several phases of Druidic belief and polity, and indeed it is not until these have been considered that the entire evidence regarding its importance can be realized. Even so, I think I have made it plain that statements derogatory to that importance must at least be reviewed, if not rejected in part.

To sum up the position and attributes of the Irish Druids from the evidence already supplied and from that still to be adduced in these pages, it is possible to say that they composed a definite priesthood practising specific religious rites and ceremonies, that they were closely identified with the cultus of the Divine King, that magic and augury were employed by them, that they instructed the youth of royalty and nobility and possessed a well-defined curriculum of study. There is good evidence that they recognized the oak as among the trees of the sacred grove and that the Celtic seasonal festivals were celebrated by them. That they acted as counsellors to the Irish kings is proven by the very numerous allusions to their tenure of this office in ancient Irish literature. But what has so far been written concerning them here must be accepted as merely prefatory and preparatory to the consideration of their position in the Druidic structure as a whole.

THE GALATIANS

It is not improbable that still another area of Druidic worship and practice may have existed in Asia Minor. In the third century before our era a horde of Celtic conquerors settled in a part of that peninsula which came to be known as Galatia. The religious meeting-place of this folk bore the purely Celtic name of Drynemetum, "the sacred grove of the oak." Here twelve "tetrarchs" met annually along with three hundred minor officials as composing a great national Council.[13] Arrian tells us that they paid sacrifice to Artemis, under which name a Celtic divinity may be disguised.[14] But that they adored the oak tree and had brought its worship from their ancient home in Europe is scarcely to be questioned, as the Celtic etymology of the name of their place of convention makes plain. Were these "tetrarchs" Druids and priests as well as law-givers and administrators? I see no good reason to doubt that they were, although the evidence is much too scanty to permit of positive conclusion.

There appears to have been a Gallic equivalent to the Galatian Drynemetum, for Fortunatus, a French bishop and Latin poet of the sixth century, in one of his songs, alludes to a certain Uernemetis:

> "Nomine Uernemetis uoluit uocitare uetustas,
> Quod quasi fanum ingens gallica lingua refert."

While Gregory of Tours mentions place-names composed of similar verbal elements.

Chapter IV

THE DRUIDIC PRIESTHOOD

T HE title of this chapter will at once reveal the writer's attitude to the officiants of the Druidic cultus, making it plain that no question remains in his mind of their status as a priesthood. Those who deny that the Druids composed a priesthood must have done so without reflecting that the servants of practically all the faiths of the lower cultus combined the character of magician or sorcerer with that of priest, even those of the early Egyptian and Brahmanic religions acting in this double capacity, though in some cases there was specialization. If the priesthoods of Egypt, Babylonia, India, Greece and Rome performed acts magical and are yet described as "priests," for what reason, it may be asked, should the Druids be classed merely as "shamans" or "witch-doctors"? It may be retorted that Egypt and Greece developed faiths of a much loftier and more spiritual type. But they had expanded from equally humble beginnings, while Druidism appears to have been suppressed at a juncture of affairs when, as all the evidence reveals, it was about to develop into a system of belief which might at a later era have equalled in spirituality the cults of Egypt and Hellas. Its "philosophy" at least appears to have aroused the enthusiasm of classical writers and poets, and even the early Christian fathers seem to have regarded its tenets as praiseworthy.

If the Druids were not priests, neither were the officiants of the rites of the early dynasties in Egypt, nor those of the Babylonian deities. Clement of Alexandria classes the Druids along with the priesthoods of the Egyptians, the Chaldeans and the Assyrians. And, as we shall see, the servants of the Druidic cult, like those of other cults, were divided in their several capacities into ritual officiants, poets, law-makers, judges, and so forth. It may be remarked that this division appears to have been recognized in all the Druidic areas, with the possible exception of Scotland, respecting which we have no evidence on this particular point.

In dealing with this question, however, we must regard the Druidic priesthood as not differing in any manner in the several areas in which it functioned so far as its basic beliefs were concerned. Slight local distinctions there may have been, but all the evidence points to the fact of its having maintained a common tradition of practice and discipline in all the areas in which it existed.

That the Druids were recruited from the higher ranks of the nobility in Gaul, or at least from the aristocracy, is clear enough from Cæsar's account of them. He describes them as one of the two classes of "persons of definite account and dignity in Gaul,"[1] while Pomponius Mela alludes to their disciples as *nobilissimi Gentis*.[2] "Over all these druids," says Cæsar, "one presides, who possesses supreme authority among them."

He says nothing of the title borne by this personage. When this functionary died, the most pre-eminent candidate succeeded him; or another might be elected; or a duel might ensure the acceptance of the most warlike.⁸ There appear to have been "Arch-Druids," or at least chief Druids, at some of the early Irish Courts. We read of Dubhtach Mac Ui' Lugair, Arch-Druid of King Mac Niall, that he became a Christian convert, and an Arch-Druid is said to have been established in the Isle of Man by King Finnan in 134 B.C. The Arch-Druid of Ireland, says Bonwick, was known as *Kion-Druaight* or *Ard-Druaight*.⁴ According to the *Life of St. Patrick*, too, there was a chief Druid, or *primus magus*. These latter statements, however, may well be due to the systematizing propensities of late annalists, or merely to the imagination of modern writers.

THE SEVERAL CLASSES OF DRUIDS

The statements of Greek and Roman authorities reveal that the Druidic caste was divided into several classes, which undertook the functions of priests, diviners, magicians, poets, teachers, leeches and legal administrators. In all probability these offices overlapped, certain individuals acting in more than one capacity. Cæsar alludes to the Druids as though they were primarily a religious body who also acted as judges and moderators in private disputes. He makes no mention of a bardic class. Diodorus, however, specifically refers to "composers of yerses, whom they call bards," as well as to "philosophers and theologians who are held in much honour and are called Druids," and to soothsayers.⁵

Strabo enumerates the classes of men who are held in great honour in Gaul as Bards, *Vates* and Druids, thus seeming to separate the first two from the Druidic caste, as does Diodorus. The Druids, he tells us, decide public disputes and study natural and moral philosophy.⁶ The term *Ouateis* (*vates*) he employs, is merely the Greek equivalent for "diviners," although the Latin form, *vates*, also means "a poet." Ammianus Marcellinus, quoting from the last work of Timagenes, classes them as Bards, *Euhages* and Druids, thus also separating the Druids from the other Gallic officials. Dottin thought that the *ouateis*, or *vates* of Strabo were identical with the "diviners" alluded to by Diodorus. The *vates*, he believed, presided over sacrifices and drew omens from them. D'Arbois was of opinion that they were functionaries of similar office to the augurs of Rome. The *Euhages*, Ammianus tells us, "strove to explain the high mysteries of nature."⁷ The very explicit manner in which these three prime authorities set the Druids apart from the other learned bodies appears to me to fortify the belief that they formed a class exclusively priestly. Dottin considers the *Euhages* of Ammianus Marcellinus as identical with the *vates* of Strabo or the *manteis*, or diviners of Diodorus. Lucan, in his *Pharsalia* mentions only Druids and Bards.⁸ Pliny speaks of "Druids and the whole tribe of diviners and physicians."⁹

In Ireland, the members of the Druidic caste appear to have acted as priests, magicians, and teachers. They were classed as Druids, *Filids* or "learned poets," who were superior to the lesser poets, or Bards, and who also appear to have functioned as prophets or diviners. These two latter classes, the *Filids* and Bards, survived the suppression of the Druids proper in Ireland. All three of these offices in Erin, Druids, *Filids* and Bards, correspond to those known in Gaul, the Druids, *Vates* and Bards.[10] This correspondence, however, it is only proper to say, has been denied by Irish and other authorities of eminence, as has the priestly function of the Irish Druids.[11] It cannot, however, have escaped the more solicitous students of Druidism that the mention of all ritualistic functions has been deliberately suppressed in the Irish texts by Christian annalists and editors, and this, to a great extent, I believe, accounts for the somewhat absurd and quite unscientific notion that the Druids of Ireland were exclusively "magicians" who wielded no priestly function.

THE BARDIC CLASS

I have already furnished some account of the Bardic class in treating of its position in Wales, but must here add certain important particulars concerning its more general history. The Gallic Bards, says Ammianus, "celebrated the brave deeds of their famous men in epic verse to the strains of the lyre."[12] Diodorus employs practically the same terms in describing them.[13] Occasionally the Irish Bards seem to have acted as diviners, and in an ecstatic state to have poured forth a flood of poetry which concluded with a prophetic declaration. In Ireland, too, their satirical qualities were famous, and sometimes the reverse.[14] The *Filids* of Ireland, the higher poetic caste, employed spells, and a feature of Bardic training in Ireland was the study of traditional incantations which were believed to produce magical results.[15] A good deal of traditional matter concerning the Irish Bards may be gleaned from the texts. It is said that they studied for twelve years to gain the barred cap and title of *Ollamh*, or teacher. The metres employed by them were exceedingly varied. "The Dialogue of the Two Sages" supplies the qualifications of a true *Ollamh*. Some peripatetic minstrels claiming descent from the ancient Bards survived into the eighteenth century. A good deal of information of this kind concerning them will be found in the interesting, if not very precise, little work of Bonwick.[16]

More authoritative material regarding the ancient status of the Bards may be summarized as follows: They appear to have undergone a severe course of instruction in the magical arts, in the recitation of tales, the study of grammar, the deciphering of the Ogham script, as well as in "philosophy" and law, and in poetical composition. That they possessed a "secret" dialect is known (was it the Shelta Thari as current among modern Irish tinkers, as has been averred ?), and they seem to have been versed in the significance of obsolete and abstruse terms. The Druids proper in Ireland appear to have passed through such a Bardic curriculum as a part of their general training. The recital of genealogies was also included in Bardic education.[17] In *The Book of Ballymote* we read of the courses of instruction in incantations which the Irish Bards studied during the ninth year of their initiate. These are set down without much reference to their classification, and range from the spells which instruct one in the manner in which a horse might be prevented from stumbling to charms which should be used upon entering a new house. In this book, too, we find much express information concerning the course pursued by the *Ollamhs*.[18] One ancient Irish MS. deals in the form of question and answer with the degrees conferred upon a *Filid*. It tells us that in order to graduate, he must submit his compositions to an *Ollamh*, a master of the poetic art. Before doing so, he must be in possession of "the qualifications of the seven orders of poets." If successful, the King then conferred the degree upon him, it being understood that he was an innocent and upright man, pure in learning and in speech, and that he was not a homicide, a robber nor an adulterer. (E. O'Curry, *MS. Materials of Ancient Irish History*, p. 462.)

We find at least one Irish Bard stopping the growth of the corn by the use of magic, while another caused his enemy's life to be shortened by his incantations.[19] O'Beirne Crowe alludes to the Irish Bards "practising incantations like the Magi of the Continent and in religious matters holding extensive sway," as well they may have done in times when the offices of Druid and Bard were well-nigh one and the same. A Bard might be refused nothing. Racy of the extraordinary influence wielded by the Bards and of their sacrosanct character, is the tale which recounts how Aithirne, a celebrated Ulster poet of the time of Conor MacNessa, travelled through Ireland making the most outrageous demands of every king with whom he sojourned. Eachy MacLuchta was at the time King of Southern Connaught and possessed but one eye. The malicious Bard, when quitting his dominions, demanded his remaining eye, which the unhappy king at once plucked out and gave him. Eachy was led to the neighbouring lake to wash the blood from his face, and ever afterwards, says tradition, this sheet of water has been known as Loch Derghderc, that is "the Lake of the Red Eye." (P. W. Joyce, *The Origin and History of Irish Names of Places*, p. 171.)

In the writings of classical authors we encounter references to certain classes of Druidic officiants whose titles are more than a little obscure. Diogenes Lærtius alludes to the *Semnotheoi*, in association with the Druids.[20] He appears to be quoting from Sotion of Alexandria. This is the only reference to the name, the etymology of which is obscure. M. Camille Jullian seems to be of opinion that it may refer to the priests of the Celtic Galatians of Asia Minor, who adored the oak in the grove of Drynemetum. Lærtius states that "the Celts *and the Galatæ* had seers called Druids and *Semnothei*." Does the term "Druids" refer to the priests of the European Celts, while *Semnotheoi* refers to those of the Galatians?[21] J. Cambry states that it is the same as the Breton *hénan*, that is, "very old," or "venerable," the superlative of *hen*, "old." He compares it with the tribal names *Senones*, the title of a Gaulish people of Cisalpine and Transalpine Gaul, and that of the Sennotes, a tribe of Aquitanian Gaul, both of which, he says, have the meaning of "ancient"; and with the territorial name of the "Druidesses" of the Isle of Sena. (*Monumens Celtiques*, pp. 321-2.) The name *Saronides* has by some writers been fancifully applied to the Druids, but it is merely an early Greek appellation for the oak, or those who affected its worship.

THE GUTUATRI

But when we consider the title *Gutuatri* associated by others with the Druidic caste, we at once encounter a difficulty. This title appears in several inscriptions of Gallo-Roman origin, two at Autun, one at Mâcon and another at Le Puy, and it seems probable that these refer to persons who, although they functioned as officials of the Romanized Gallic faith after the suppression of Druidism, were still very surely the servants of that Latinized cultus who had taken the place of the Druids after their expulsion, and whose loyalty was confined to Rome. In any case, they seem to have been mere officiants at the minor shrines of local gods. M. Camille Jullian thinks that they "were transformed into *Sacerdotes*," according to the Roman custom, "when dealing with cults other than Roman."[22]

Less probable appears the decision of Canon MacCulloch, that the *Gutuatri* "were a Druidic class, ministers of local sanctuaries, and related to the Druids as the Levites were to the priests of Israel."[23] The word may be derived from *gutu*, "voice," and may thus imply "a speaker."[24] It would seem, too, that the inscriptions which apply to the *Gutuatri* post-date the suppression of Druidism in Gaul. Rice Holmes, again, remarks: "I doubt whether it is possible to prove that in pre-Roman times the gutuater was not a Druid."[25] But where is there any mention of *Gutuatri* "in pre-Roman times"? He repeats this phrase in his *Cæsar's Conquest of Gaul.*[26] The "Gutuater," alluded to by Hirtius, the continuator of Cæsar's *Commentaries*, was almost certainly one Cotuatus, and Hirtius has confused his name with the title.[27]

The *Gutuaters*, according to Dottin, were the priests of local cults at the epoch of Gallo-Roman influence. D'Arbois has much to say concerning the *Gutuatri*. He thought the name to be derived from the Q-Celtic word *guth*, meaning "voice," that is, they were the "speakers," or orators, those who invoked the gods. They acted as priests of the temples or of sacred groves. There were, he says, *Gutuatri* in Gaul in the time of its independence, as Cæsar condemned to death a *Gutuater* of the country of Chartres. This man, alluded to by Cæsar, was the same as the person mentioned by Hirtius. The circumstances, then, seem to make it plain that the *Gutuatri* were merely the local priests of the Druidic cultus in later Roman Gaul, the officiants of the Gallo-Roman form of worship. That the *Gutuatri* were a *secular* clergy, as D'Arbois suggests, appears improbable. (*Les Druides*, pp. 1–7.)

PRIESTLY CHARACTER OF THE DRUIDIC CASTE

At the commencement of this chapter I touched upon the question as to whether the Druids actually functioned as priests, but here I must deal with it more expressly. Appealing to the classical evidence, we find that Cæsar tells us that the Druids were "*concerned with divine worship, the due performance of sacrifices public and private and the interpretation of ritual questions.*" Speaking of the Germans, he says: "They have no Druids to regulate divine worship," which surely makes it plain that he means to say that Gallic Druids *did* "regulate divine worship." Diodorus Siculus refers to the Druids as "philosophers and *theologians*," and states that no one in Gaul performed a sacrifice without their assistance, because they were "*learned in the divine nature.*" Strabo practically repeats his statement. Ammianus Marcellinus avers that "they professed the immortality of the soul." Pomponius Mela states that they claimed to know, among other things, "the will of the gods," and that they believed in immortality. Lucan alludes to their "holy rites"; Pliny refers to them as "priests," although he also speaks of them as "magicians." Tacitus mentions their "altars." If we are to judge of their status from the tenor of these references alone I cannot see how it is to be maintained that they did not compose an authentic priesthood, a sacerdotal body of officiants whose duty was the maintenance of a religion somewhat above the lower cultus and the performance of its ritual offices.

Origen, the Christian father, declares that the Druids were worshippers of one god.[18] If we turn to modern authorities of standing, we find that the more perspicacious among them endorse the view that the Druids were priestly officiants. They were certainly priests, says Kendrick, but "they were a good deal more than mere priests." "We must be prepared to believe," he adds, "that druidism professed, or was in sympathy with, all the known tenets of ancient Keltic religion, and the gods of the druids were the familiar and multifarious deities of the Keltic pantheon." Elsewhere, he indicates that "the druids of Ireland were servants of the primitive Keltic festival-system in its Central European form."[19]

Dr. Julius Pokorny believes them to have been the priests of an oak-cultus.[20] Professor Camille Jullian, the foremost French authority on the subject of the Druids, gives it as his opinion that "the analogy between druidism and the ancient priesthoods is complete." "Two points remain, however, in which the druids do not resemble the priests of classical antiquity, but rather recall those of the East. First, though each tribe in Gaul had its own druid or druids, all the druids were associated in a permanent federation, like priests of the same cult. Although they were not formally a clergy, they did form a church, like the bishops of the Catholic church, and this church necessitated both a hierarchy and periodic assemblies." For, argues M. Jullian elsewhere, "the doctrine and the clergy of a religion have an origin most different: behold Christianity."[81]

"In Gaul, and to some extent in Ireland," says the erudite Canon MacCulloch, an authority whose keen observation probes to the heart of every subject he examines, "the Druids formed a priestly corporation." They were not, he thinks, a monkish type of clergy, as Bertrand has mistakenly suggested, and do not appear to have led a communal existence. "They practised a series of common cults." "It is impossible to doubt that the Druids in Ireland fulfilled functions of a public priesthood." "One fact shows that they were priests of the Celtic religion in Ireland. The euhemerized Tuatha Dé Danann are masters of Druidic lore. Thus both the gods and the priests who served them were confused by later writers." Indeed these gods were so closely identified with Druidism that this fact alone makes it impossible to doubt that the Druids were their servants. "The opposition of Christian missionaries to the Druids," Canon MacCulloch adds, "shows that they were priests; if they were not, it remains to be discovered what body of men did exercise priestly functions in pagan Ireland."[82]

"The evidence that they were sacrificing priests is conclusive," remarks Miss Eleanor Hull, an authority of large experience. "Tara, in St. Patrick's Day, is called 'the chief seat of the idolatry and druidism of Erin'."[83] "The function of the druid," says Keating, "was to regulate the concerns of religion and the worship of the gods, to offer sacrifices, to divine and foretell, for the use and advantage of the King and country."[84] How closely to the heart of the Druidic problem did this antique writer come. The latter part of his statement probes almost to the core of the Druidic enigma.

M. Hubert is of the opinion, briefly stated, that the Druids of Gaul resembled the Arval Brotherhood of Rome, a body who performed the worship of Dea Dia, who was perhaps a cereal deity, Acca Larentia.[85] A fact which lends colour to this assumption is the close association of this sodality with the Roman kingship and the expiatory sacrifices offered up by it in its grove if any damage were done to the same, such as the breaking of a bough from one of its trees, or their destruction by a stroke of lightning. The custom seems to link with the procedure at the Arician grove as described by Frazer, a matter to which I will return at a later juncture.

As was almost bound to be the case, the argument that the Druids were otherwise than a definite priesthood practising certain rites and functioning as the servants of a faith, is represented with but little cogency. Macbain, who seems to have considered it "modern" and "scientific" to cavil at their priestly status, remarks that "the Druids were rather the philosophers and divines of the Gauls (can he have meant "diviners"?), and as what we know of their opinions and practices is somewhat remarkable, it is better not to confuse their system with the ordinary Aryan religion of the Gauls." No "customs or religious survivals" can "be referred to Druidic belief or usage." "In Ireland there is no hint given of

Druidism being either a system of philosophy or religion." "There is no reference to these Druids being a priestly class."[36]

O'Curry, at the conclusion of his lectures on the Druids, pronounced the general verdict that "there is no ground whatever for believing the Druids to have been the priests of any special positive worship."[37] It is obvious that the collection he had brought together of Druidic magical occurrence and rite had proved too much for him and had blinded him to the numerous examples of actual religious procedure which ancient Irish literature reveals as associated with Druidism in Erin. Nor could he have known of the implications of its connection with the Divine Kingship. And, of course, he was writing of Druidism in Ireland alone and made no comparisons with its Continental phase. Nor did he make allowances for the inspired dislike for everything pagan revealed by the Christian annalists of his country.

As regards the specifically priestly nature of Druidism, Rhys is brief in statement. "The Celts had their druids to attend to religious matters . . . The Celts delivered religious matters over to their druids, that is, to their magicians and medicine-men acting as priests."[38] This is trite enough, but not uneloquent, even if it place Druidic belief and practice on a decidedly low level.

I am unable to perceive any good reason why the title of priests may not be granted to the members of the Druidic brotherhood. That they fulfilled other functions as well as the priestly is beside the question, for when in the course of human history did a priesthood fail to avail itself of mundane power when the opportunity was granted it? And, as the science of modern Comparative Religion asserts, the function of priest and king was originally one and the same, reasons were not lacking why a developed priesthood should naturally cling to the shadow of that royal authority which it had formerly enjoyed. I repeat that the sole objection to the view that the Druids formed a priesthood, but were merely "medicine-men" or "shamans" practising a low form of magic, proceeds from the practical archæologist, who as a general rule can scarcely be regarded as a specialist in religious science.

As regards the organization of the Druidic priesthood, Mr. Kendrick is of opinion that it was conceived on a national basis in Gaul. He indicates that the Druids held national assemblies, as at Chartres, and that they acknowledged the sway of an Arch-Druid. No "intertribal jealousy or dispute," he thinks, disturbed their relations. They wielded an "enormous influence" over educated public opinion as instructors of the young, and their decrees had a "formidable religious sanction." Their conditions of service were not of such a character as might be associated with the popular idea of them as "mysterious ancients holding aloof from the common world." So much, indeed, may be ascertained from the terms of a passage in Cicero's *De Divinatione*, in which he describes Cæsar's friend the Æduan Druid Diviciacus as having a "knowledge of nature which the

Greeks call 'physiologia' " and as habitually making predictions, "sometimes by augury, and sometimes by means of conjecture." He was, in short, a great political priest, and no mere fetishist or tribal "medicine man."[39]

Important Druidic assemblies held on fixed dates were also celebrated in Ireland, and attended by delegates coming from distant places, and this alone makes it clear that a considerable degree of organization attended the affairs of Irish Druidism.[40] The fact that the Druids were exempt from military service in Gaul seems to point to their apartness as a special class of religious and political officials. Their division into classes, indeed, makes it clear that these had been developed in the course of generations as special offices from one original class in which all had functioned as priest, seer and poet. But it is frankly impossible altogether to disentangle the functions of the Druids one from another and to set them apart, and the probability is that there was a great deal of overlapping between the various degrees, both in Gaul and Ireland. Especially was this bound to be the case with those Druids who were isolated in the more remote regions, or who served the lesser shrines scattered across the land. We cannot believe that each holy place, well, or tree, or each hamlet or village possessed its definitely assigned Druid, diviner and bard. The officiant in such localities must surely have fulfilled all three offices, or at least those of priest and magus.

Cæsar declares that the Druids had the right of interdiction or "excommunication" in such cases as those in which unruly people refused to submit to their verdict in legal affairs. "If any one, either in a private or public capacity, has not submitted to their decision, they interdict him from the sacrifices." This appears to connect the offices of priest and judge. As judges, they decided, but if the guilty, or he who was worsted in a lawsuit, failed to agree with their decision, they banned him from public worship.[41]

THE DRUIDS NOT A CELIBATE CASTE

The Druids, both in Gaul and Ireland, were not a celibate priesthood. As Ammianus remarks, they were "an intimate fellowship" (*sodaliciis adstricti consortiis*) yet this did not prohibit them from taking wives, as was the case with some ancient priesthoods. They were certainly not a species of monks, dwelling in community, as M. A. Bertrand would have us believe.[42] M. Dottin has something to say concerning Ammianus' description of their status as a sodality when criticizing the theory of Bertrand. The term *sodaliciis*, he remarks, is not doubtful, but it is difficult to determine Ammianus' precise meaning in his use of the term *consortiis*. He concludes, however, that it has merely a corporative significance and not a cenobitic one, as M. Bertrand imagined (*Antiquities Celtique*, pp. 288–9). As regards the Irish Druids, the ancient texts seem to make it probable that the Druidic priesthood was in some cases a hereditary one, as was the early Christian priesthood in Scotland and

Ireland down to the eleventh century, the sons succeeding their fathers in office. Mention of the children of Irish Druids is made in several places.[44]

DRUIDIC REGALIA AND COSTUME

This seems to be the place to give some details concerning the regalia and costume of the Druids. They were, says Strabo, attired in variegated garments embroidered with gold.[44] Were these "variegated garments" an early form of tartan? They also wore golden torques, or neck-pieces. Some "authorities" on ancient British costume assert that the Druidic priests were garbed in white, while the bards wore green, but for this statement there is no positive evidence. Mog Ruith, the famous Druid of Munster, when he went to do battle with the Druid of another tribe, donned a "dark-grey, hornless bull-hide and white-speckled bird head-piece," the latter to assist him in his magical flight through the air. A Druid in attendance upon an Irish king is described as wearing a speckled white cloak, and ear-clasps of gold in his ears. This was Tulchinne, the Druid of the King of Tara, who juggled with the nine swords which he carried.[45] From Pliny's account of the cutting of the mistletoe, we learn that on the occasion of this rite the garb of the Druids was white, and that their feet were bare.[46] Nine Druids destroyed by the gentle St. Patrick, who brought down fire from heaven upon them, were clothed in white vestments. The luckless pagans had "feigned themselves saints," says the monkish chronicler, and had no right to the spotless garb they wore.[47]

In the *Táin Bó Cualnge*, the Druids are described as wearing sandals.[48] Traditional Irish lore says that the Arch-Druid's head was surrounded by an oaken garland on special occasions, and that this was surmounted by a golden tiara set with adder-stones. At the altar, however, the Arch-Druid wore a white surplice fastened at the shoulder with a golden brooch. These two latter statements are, of course, really fanciful, and I feel that those of Strabo are nearest to the truth, having regard to the very slight knowledge we actually possess concerning the nature of early Celtic costume.

THE DRUIDIC TONSURE

There seem to be reasonable grounds for assuming that the Druids wore a special tonsure, shaving a part of the head. Rhys thought that the tonsure in Britain "was merely a druidic survival."[49] Gildas halts his anathemas against his British countrymen long enough to tell us what this tonsure was actually like. "The Romans say that the tonsure of the Britons is reported to have originated with Simon Magus, whose tonsure embraced merely the whole front part of the head from ear to ear, in order to exclude the genuine tonsure of the Magi, whereby the front part alone was wont to be covered." He goes on to say that this Roman belief is mistaken, and that the pagan tonsure originated in Ireland.[50] Rhys was convinced that the passage, though it had not, perhaps, been included in the original text, was written before the Druidic tonsure had disappeared.[51] Simon Magus was, of course, that Samarian sorcerer mentioned in Acts viii, who later went to Rome to spread his heresies there. Among other magical acts, he flew through the air, on beholding which, St. Peter charitably prayed that he might fall, whereupon he crashed to earth at Nero's feet. In Irish legend he is said to have assisted the Druid Mog Ruith, to whose feats of magical flight I have alluded, in the manufacture of his celebrated wheel, the Roth Fail, which had the property of flight. In Ireland Simon came to be regarded as a Druid, probably because the word *magus*, or magician, was employed as a Latin equivalent for "Druid."[52]

In the letter which, in the year A.D. 710, Abbot Ceolfrid despatched to Nectan, King of the Picts, on the subject of the Catholic Easter and the use of the tonsure, he remarks on the tonsure of Simon Magus. "Upon the top of the forehead, it does seem indeed to resemble a crown (that is the crown of thorns) but when you come to the neck, you will find it cut short."[53]

The Druidical tonsure was effected by shaving all the hair in front of a line drawn over the crown from ear to ear. The coronal tonsure, as affected by the Church of Rome, was not adopted by the Irish Church until the year A.D. 896, as the Mac Firbis MS. makes clear. The frontal tonsure thus appears to have been in use among the early Scots and Irish Christian clergy. Rhys thinks that it was "probably a druidic tonsure continued."[54] Says Herbert: "The story goes that it was brought into fashion in Ireland by the swineherd of King Leogaire, and at his suggestion almost universally adopted. But Leogaire was the very king under whose reign Patricius (St. Patrick) pretended to have been an apostle, and whom he is said to have converted. And the office of a royal swineherd is the same, in which all legends agree that Patricius himself was employed."[55]

THE QUESTION OF INITIATION

I will conclude this chapter with a brief examination of such tolerable evidence as is to be found concerning the possible existence of a ceremony of initiation to which the Druidic aspirant may have been subjected prior to his acceptance as a member of the cultus. As regards the actual existence of such a rite there is no consensus of opinion among authorities of standing, perhaps for the reason that they have not sufficiently examined the question. And the more imaginative writers who have sought to prove that such a rite existed have in most cases allowed their enthusiasm to get the better of their judgment. The sober sense of Canon MacCulloch finds that Cæsar's statement that the Druids would not permit their sacred hymns to be written down but taught them in secret, implies that "they communicated secrets to the initiated, as is done in barbaric mysteries everywhere. . . . These are kept secret not because they are abstract doctrines, but because they would lose their value and because the gods would be angry if they were made too common." He adds that: "If the Druids taught religious and moral matters secretly, these were probably no more than an extension of the threefold maxim inculcated by them according to Diogenes Lærtius: 'To worship the gods, to do no evil, and to exercise courage.' To this would be added cosmogonic myths and speculations, and magic and religious formulæ."¹⁰ I feel, however, that the subject holds further implications.

The fact is that certain passages in the old Welsh poems and writings allude to circumstances which reveal almost direct analogies concerning rites with those which we know from classical authorities to have been celebrated in connection with the Greek mysteries. In the mysteries of Eleusis, at one point, a herald summoned the neophytes to embark upon the sea. On the fifteenth day of the month Boedromion the mystics went "to the sea," or rather to the salt lakes at Rheitoi, between Athens and Eleusis, and bathed therein. This day came to be known as *Alade Mystæ*, that is "the mystics to the sea." In a Welsh poem in the *Myvyrian Archaiology*, attributed to one Gwydno, the British novice is said to have embarked on the sea in a coracle, being assured by the hierophant, or master of the ceremonies of the goddess Ceridwen, that only the unworthy risked the fate of drowning. "The conduct of the water will declare thy merit." The rites are said to have been associated with the cult of the goddess in question, the keeper of the cauldron of inspiration. This ceremony took place on the evening of the 29th of April. Here there is no mention of Druidism, but it is not impossible that the rite in question may have been derived from its practice. Gildas alludes to the existence of pagan ceremonies in Britain and fulminates against the pagan conditions still in vogue in the several British principalities in the sixth century.

In the mysterious poem known as "The Spoils of Annwn," ascribed to the bard Taliesin and roughly translated by Skene in his *Four Ancient Books of Wales*, we read of Gwair, or Gwydion, who underwent a strange experience in "the prison of Caer Sidi," and who afterwards remained for the rest of his life a bard or prophetic poet. Does this imply that he underwent some process of initiation? In another ancient Welsh poem "The Chair of Taliesin," the writer speaks of the god Dovydd, "on behalf of the assembly of the associates qualified to treat of mysteries," and alludes to the cauldron of inspiration and its mystical ingredients. The poem also alludes to a bath for the immersion of the neophyte.

Again, in a poem quoted in *The Myvyrian Archaiology* we find circumstances which seem reminiscent of initiatory practice. Arthur and Kai, his henchman, enter into a mystic conversation with the guardian of a sanctuary. The place seems to have been a sacred grove. Slight as these references may appear, and confused by reason of imperfect translation, I feel that when taken along with many other hints and allusions to the subject of secret initiation in ancient Welsh poetry, they may possibly indicate the former presence of some system of arcane belief in Celtic Britain, or perhaps the influence of a late and imported Hellenic secret doctrine in this island. But we have no means of identifying them directly with Druidic belief, except that they deal with mythical personages and events in that Celtic system of religion of which the Druids were certainly the officiants.

Chapter V

THE DRUIDIC PRIESTHOOD *(continued)*

THE DRUIDIC CURRICULUM

THAT young men desirous of entrance into the Druidic sodality underwent a special course of training of a mnemonic kind is expressly stated
by Cæsar. "Many," he says, "embrace this profession of their own accord
and many are sent to it by their parents and relations. They are said there
to learn by heart a great number of verses; accordingly some remain in
this course of training twenty years."[1] The passage gives the impression
that none might become a Druid until he had committed to memory a mass
of rhymed material. Pomponius Mela, writing on this subject, states that:
"They teach many things to the nobles of Gaul in a course of instruction
lasting as long as twenty years, meeting in secret either in a cave, or in
secluded dales."[2] The passage, of course, is merely borrowed from Cæsar.

As regards the nature of the instruction given, we know from Irish
lore that the tenets of Druidism were taught both to numbers of youths,
and separately, and that young women of distinguished birth were also
instructed by Druids. The neophytes of the Druidic caste in Ireland had
to pass through a course of specialized study which occupied many years,
at the end of which they proceeded to a more definite examination of the
principles of magic. The courses of study included the recital of tales, the
rules of grammar and the writing of the ogham script, the subjects of law
and philosophy and a very thorough grounding in the composition of
poetry. Still later, the Irish Druid appears to have applied himself to the
task of acquiring the secret language of the bards.[3] According to the
Tripartite Life of St. Patrick we learn that two Druids of King Loegaire,
the brethren Mael and Coplait, had been set apart by that monarch for
the instruction of his daughters Eithne the Fair and Fedelim the Rosy.

Indeed it was a Druid who first gave St. Patrick his early instruction.[4]
Cuchullin is said to have been taught at a seminary of which the Druid
Cathbad was the principal.[5] When Cuchullin was interrogated in after-
life as to the benefits he had obtained from Cathbad's instruction, he
replied that it had introduced him to a knowledge of the arts of the god of
Druidism and had given him skill in interpreting visions, or dreams.
Judging from this, then, Druidic teaching may have been, or may have
been thought of, as a system of instruction partly religious, partly magical.
Joyce says that the Irish Druids were the exclusive possessors of whatever
learning may have been known in pagan times and that no one was capable
of public employment who had not received instruction at their hands.
Enough evidence exists to make it perfectly plain that both in Gaul and
Ireland the Druidic caste wielded exclusive power in the matter of the

education of the ruling class. So far as Gaul is concerned, M. Camille Jullian seeks to modify this opinion. He writes: "If it were said absolutely that they directed the schools, the expression would be unsuitable. But they gathered round them the young men of the Gallic families and taught them all that they knew or believed concerning the world, the human soul and the gods. A few of these scholars stayed with their masters until they had reached the age of twenty years; but it is clear that those who were to become priests received the lion's share of attention."[6]

DRUIDIC COLLEGES

A good deal has been written concerning the existence of colleges among the Druids, but it must be admitted that an atmosphere of uncertainty surrounds this part of the subject. Some writers have made free play with the rather scanty evidence. Allcroft speaks of "systematic schools, with all the needful concomitants. Druidism must have had its equivalents for professors, lectures, class-rooms, courses, examinations and degrees. The students must have required lodgings also, and if their numbers were really so large, this means that each educational centre was a community in itself, a 'college.' The druidical educational system must have been something very closely resembling monasticism."[7] Pomponius Mela states, following Cæsar, that the Druids met to instruct the youth of the nobles "in secret either in a cave or secluded dales."[8]

That the Druidic schools had anything "monastic" about them, is, as Canon MacCulloch has said, "purely imaginative." The early Irish Druids are said to have formed arcane groups. *The Book of the Four Masters* refers to the existence of a settlement known as Mur Ollavan, "the City of the Learned," as early as the year 927 B.C., a quite hypothetical date for the existence of such a community.[9] The shrine of St. Brigit at Kildare is said to have been the later Christian site of a much older community of Druidesses who preserved the holy fire there.[10] Toland asserts that a Druidical college at Londonderry was converted into a monastery by St. Columba. The Rev. W. L. Alexander thought that a Druidic college existed in "the Isle of the Druids," that is Iona, until A.D. 563-4, when Columba arrived in that island. Equally imaginative writers claim that at the Wiltshire Ambresbury there is a Mount Ambrosius at the foot of which, according to local tradition, there stood a college of Druidesses. "It is probable that, as at Chislehurst, the mound is honeycombed with caves cut in the chalk, where these druidesses lived."[11] But who, or what, inspired this "local tradition," and when?

In the same way the tradition concerning the Pheryllt of Snowdon is in no sense accountable to authority, although fugitive allusions concerning them are occasional in the ancient Welsh poems. They were said to be a mystical brotherhood who dwelt in the secret city of Emrys, situated on Snowdon, a site identified by Gibson, the commentator of Camden, as occupying the summit of "the Panting cliff," and with certain ruins of a

fortification there known as Broich y Dinas, on the top of the height of
Penmaen. In the *Book of Taliesin* "the Books of the Pheryllt" are
alluded to in connection with the myth of the goddess Ceridwen. And an
ancient Welsh manuscript quoted by Dr. Thomas Williams asserts that
this brotherhood maintained a college at Oxford prior to the foundation of
that University! The term for ancient metallurgical art in Welsh is
Celvyddydan Pheryllt, "the arts of the Pheryllt." But there is nothing to
associate this tradition with Druidism in any way, and it appears as
representative of that phase of legend in which a modicum of obstinate
and reiterated statement gives rise to a sentiment that an ancient group of
facts has been overlaid by a patina of fanciful elaboration.

Although Cæsar states that the Druids did not commit their secret
knowledge to writing, he remarks elsewhere that they knew how to use the
Greek alphabet. In the Irish tale of Mider and Etain we hear of a Druid
named Dalan who was able to read ogham characters. "The Yellow Book
of Lecain" declares that St. Patrick at one time burned one hundred
and eighty books of the Druids, and this act, it seems, so inspired Christian
fanaticism against Druidic literature that the converted set to work in
all parts of Ireland, and did not rest from their barbarous task of destruction "until all the remains of the Druidic superstition were utterly
destroyed." Toland, quoting Dr. Kennedy, says that Patrick burnt 300
volumes, and rightly terms the act "a dishonour upon human understanding." We decry the Moslems for burning the great library at
Alexandria, while we excuse the early Christian fanatics for destroying
the monuments of Celtic antiquity, in the self-same spirit as their Spanish
successors consumed the hieroglyphic books of the Aztecs and Maya in
Mexico and Central America! When Cuchullin, who had been instructed
by Druids, left an ogham script on a pillar-stone as a message, those for
whom it was intended resigned the task of its decipherment to the
Druids.[11] In St. Patrick's magical contest with the Druids at Tara, the
king suggested that both the Christian and Druidic antagonists should
cast their books into the water so that he in whose volume the letters
remained decipherable might be declared the minister of truth.

THE DRUIDS AS JUDGES

Cæsar, in his account of the Druids, tells us that they occupied the
position of judges. "They determine respecting all controversies, public
and private; and if any crime has been perpetrated, if murder has been
committed, if there be any dispute about an inheritance, if any about
boundaries, these same persons decide it; they decree rewards and punish-
ments; if anyone, either in a private or public capacity, has not submitted
to their decision, they interdict him from the sacrifices. This among them
is the most heavy punishment . . . nor is justice administered to them when
seeking it."[18] The chief seat at which causes and trials were held and
adjudicated seems to have been Chartres, the ancient capital of the

Carnutes, which was regarded as the centre of Gaul and of Gallic life.
M. Camille Jullian is of opinion that this assize "came into competition
with the jurisdiction of the ordinary magistrates of the cities," and that
"it remains to be discovered to what extent this tribunal was attended,
its sentences executed and its jurisdiction respected. It may be that in
the last century of independence these druidic assizes were but the
survival of very ancient institutions, then falling more and more into
desuetude."[14] But the likelihood is that one cause and one alone could
have brought them to such a pass—the gradual decline and destruction
of the institution of the Divine Kingship.

M. Georges Dottin ventured to define the more precise nature of the
pecuniary fines inflicted by the Druidic judges, and the premiums awarded
by them to those injured. "*Poenis,*" he believed, describes the sum which
the defender paid, or, were he bankrupt, which his family was mulcted in;
proemia, on the other hand, designates the award made to a family for the
death of one of its members, or to one who had been wounded or injured.[15]
M. D'Arbois de Jubainville thought that Cæsar, in speaking of the
Druidic laws, referred to a juridical code or system which did not exist
in his time, but which was of more ancient provenance.[16] He believed
that the principal cases adjudicated by the Druids were criminal, and
above all, homicidal, those, in fact, in which fines and damages were
fixed by "la loi de talion," that is the *lex talionis*, the law of retaliation.

Homicides were put to death by burning, which was considered a sacrifice pleasing to the gods.[17] These sacrificial fires, says Strabo, were thought
to assist the growth of the crops, a statement which reveals the association
of Druidic law and practice with the institutions of the cultus of the Divine
King as clearly as anything is capable of doing.[18] "The Druids," adds the
Greek chronicler, "are considered the most just of men." There seems to
be some reason to infer that the Druids elected the chief magistrates among
the Gauls, for Cæsar expressly states that in 52 B.C. the Æduan *Vergobret*,
or chief magistrate, was elected "by the priests, according to the usage of
the state."[19] The question of the actual degree of authority wielded by
the Druids has aroused much controversy. But the sapient, if somewhat
magisterial Rice Holmes, in summarizing the debate, finds no grounds for
believing that the Gallic Druids exercised undue and tyrannical influence,
as the nobles had common interest with them and would agree with them
in most matters, although he admits the possibility that they may have
employed their spiritual powers against ambitious aristocratic individuals
on occasion.[20]

Diodorus Siculus mentions that the Druids were in the habit of
pacifying their people and restraining them from what seem to have been
inter-tribal quarrels. "Often when the combatants are ranged face to
face, and swords are drawn and spears bristling, these men come between
the armies and stay the battle, just as wild beasts are sometimes held
spellbound."[21] Strabo says that "in former times they even arbitrated

in cases of war and made the opponents stop when they were about to line up for battle."[33] This does not seem to apply to their Irish brethren, who, on occasion, proved themselves "bonny fighters." In a battle which was joined between the Tuatha Dé Danann and the Milesians, many Druids are said to have been slain on both sides, and, as we have seen, certain Irish Druids were believed to have fought each other in the air. At least one Irish Druid acted as a herald, King Dathi of Connaught sending him to Feredach, King of Scotland, calling upon that ruler for submission and tribute, which were refused, although time was courteously granted to enable the Scot to muster his forces for battle.[33]

Druidic leechcraft seems to have been chiefly concerned with the use of herbs, which were employed in a semi-magical manner. The mistletoe, as we shall see, was used as an antidote to poison, or for the cure of wounds. The selago (probably lycopodium) was thought to preserve one from accidents and its smoke, when burned, healed diseases of the eye. It was gathered with the right hand through the left sleeve of the tunic. Vervain, or verbena, was believed to dispel fevers and other maladies.and was regarded as an antidote against snake-bite.[34] Pliny says that the Druids also used a certain marsh-plant called *samolus* (a herbaceous plant of the primrose family) as a charm against the diseases of cattle. It must be gathered with the left hand while one is fasting. (*Nat. Hist.*, XXIV, 104.)

In several cantons in northern France the groundsel was plucked with certain ceremonies on the day of St. Roch and blessed by a priest. It was employed as a panacea for the complaints of cattle and was believed to be the *samolus* of the Druids. (Reynier, *Economie publique et rurale des Celtes*, p. 196.) But, according to Grimm, *samolus* may have been the *anemone pulsaltilla* (*Teutonic Mythology*, p. 1207). In Ireland Druids appear to have acted as leeches. When Cuchullin lay on his sickbed, his wife Emer remarked that had his friend Fergus been ill "Cuchullin would never have rested until he had found a Druid able to discover the cause of that illness."[35] When warriors from Britain attacked the hold of an Irish chieftain at Enniscorthy, they employed poisoned arrows which caused lethal wounds. But a Druid ordered great baths of the milk of white kine to be prepared in which the wounded were bathed, when they speedily recovered.[36]

Keating tells us that it was the duty of the Irish Druids to act as genealogists and annalists "to preserve their generations of descent and their transactions in every expedition that befel them in coming to Ireland."[37] Although the statement has absolutely no authority behind it, the guess is probably correct enough, as the bards or priests of primitive races are almost inevitably the conservators of its royal and noble pedigrees.

DRUIDESSES

So frequent are the allusions to "Druidesses," or women associated with the Druidic cult, in both classical and ancient Irish literature, that the existence of these can scarcely be denied. Roman inscriptions reveal the presence in Gaul of a priestess or *antistita* of the goddess Thucolis at Antibes, while at Arles two inscriptions were discovered commemorating similar female functionaries.[28] These may or may not have been associated with the Druidic cultus, but to judge from another inscription found near Metz, which refers to "*Arete Druis Antistita, somno monita*," it would appear probable that such was the case. It seems not unlikely that women continued the functions of the Druidic *Vates* or prophets when the order began to fall into desuetude and ill-repute, as has certainly been the case in other primitive religious sodalities. Women in sable robes were found attending the Druids in Anglesea, and Tacitus tells us that they encouraged the Britons to withstand the Romans. But there is no evidence that so long as Druidism was in a flourishing condition women actively functioned as priestesses, or that they were even admitted to the order.

The Continental *Dryades* of the third century alluded to by some classical authors appear to have been divineresses or "spaewives" rather than priestesses proper, and the name by which they were called at a time when the Druidic cult had long been abandoned appears to have been a traditional ascription due to folk-memory. Ireland had its *ban-filid* or *ban-fathi*, prophetesses or divineresses, but we also encounter the term *ban-drui*, or druidess, in ancient Irish literature. In *The Book of Leinster*, for instance, we read of "three Druids and three Druidesses" (Fol. 75b).

Tradition avers that the shrine of St. Brigit and her nuns at Kildare, where a sacred fire was piously maintained, was formerly a community of Druidesses, virgins who were called from their office *Ingheaw Andagha*, that is "Daughters of Fire." At Cluan-Feart, says legend, there existed a retreat for Druidical women, who could raise storms, cause diseases and fatally smite their enemies.[29] Even in the Irish mythical period we read of Druidesses. Three Druidesses of the Tuatha Dé Danann, Badbh, Macha and Mor Kegan, are said to have brought down darkness and showers of blood and fire upon the Firbolgs at Tara for three days, according to the *Book of Invasions*. The names of other Druidesses, real or mythical, have been preserved in Irish literature. We hear of a Druidess named Geal Chossach, "the white-legged" of Inisoven, in Donegal, and of another named Milucrah, "Hag of the Waters," who transformed Finn into an old man by means of water from Lake Shabh Gullin. One known as Ban Draoi ("Druid Woman") may represent only the general type of the Druidic enchantress. The Druidess Bodmall reared the hero Finn "in the wilderness."[30]

Several tales of the manner in which Druidesses prophesied their future greatness to Roman emperors are recorded. When in the year A.D. 235 Alexander Severus was starting on an expedition the purpose of which was to deliver Gaul from the Germanic tribes, a Gaulish Druidess cried out to him in her native tongue: "Go forward, but hope not for victory, nor put trust in your soldiers."[31] When Diocletian was still a common soldier, he tarried at an inn in the land of the Tongri in Gaul and when he came to reckon with his hostess, the woman upbraided him with his meanness. In jocular vein he retorted that he would be more liberal when he became an Emperor. "To which the Druidess replied: 'Laugh not, Diocletian, for when you have slain the Boar, you will indeed be Emperor.'" Diocletian rose in rank and slew many boars in hunting expeditions, but at last he killed the prefect Arrius, surnamed "the Boar," and the prophecy of the Druidess came to pass.[31] Vopiscus, who relates this story, tells another concerning the Emperor Aurelian. He once consulted a number of Gaulish Druidesses concerning the possibility that his descendants would retain the imperial crown. But they replied that the line of Claudius would become the more illustrious in the Roman annals.[32]

Here I should indicate that the French Celticist M. Toutain, in his essay, "Les Pretendues Druidesses Gauloises," (in *Mélanges Boissier*, pages 439-42) is inclined to question the authenticity of these prophetic women both on philological and racial grounds. He states that the term *dryas*, as used by Vopiscus and Lampridius when writing of these women, means a "nymph," whereas older authors never employ this word when speaking of the Druidic caste, the Greeks using *druides* or *drudæ*, and the Latins *druidæ*. These forms would not yield a feminine *dryas*. Again, the incidents recorded in connection with them took place in that part of Gaul close to the boundaries of Germany. Thus Severus lost his life near Mayence, while the incident related of Diocletian took place near the Mause. He adds that it is remarkable to read of Druidesses in the third century A.D., since no author of the first century even alludes to them. Nor does he believe that the wild women of Anglesey were Druidesses, but merely female fanatics. D'Arbois de Jubainville believed such women to be mere soothsayers. (*Revue Celtique*, Vol. XXVI, p. 350.)

That such women were divineresses and not officiants or practising priestesses—mere spaewives in fact—seems probable. All that we know of the strictly conservative nature of Druidism in its palmy days in Gaul pleads against the supposition that rites of any description would be delegated to women, although in certain instances they may have functioned as "acolytes" or assistants, more particularly in Ireland, where they seem to have acted chiefly in a magical capacity.

INSULAR COMMUNITIES OF WOMEN

Women associated with some religious caste and whom several authorities have identified as "Druidesses" seem to have dwelt in certain islands off the coast of Gaul. In the Isle of Sena, or Sein, off Pont du Raz, on the western coast of Brittany, dwelt nine virgins known as Gallicenæ, who were described by Pomponius Mela as possessing magical power over the weather. They were consulted by mariners as to its control by occult means, and could transform themselves into animal shapes. Near the mouth of the Loire, says Strabo, lay another island on which no man dared set foot. It was inhabited by women called Namnites, who appear to have worshipped a deity resembling Bacchus. This god had a roofed temple in the island, but it was the custom of the resident priestesses to unroof it once a year, replacing the thatch before sunset. Each woman brought a bundle of building material to the work, but should any of them permit her burden to fall to the ground, she was instantly torn in pieces by her companions. It is noteworthy that later Norse lays retain memories of such cults in the Channel Islands, allusions being made in the Helgi lays to the existence of sibyls or hags such as Mela mentions, in Guernsey and other adjoining insular localities.

In his *Histoire de France*, M. Martin stated his belief that these insular women were the servants of the Celtic goddess Ceridwen, and that they were Druidesses. Mr. Kendrick believes them to have been the priestesses of an indigenous faith, non-Druidic in character. Other writers, MM. G. Dottin and S. Reinach among them, are of opinion that the tales concerning these female insular castes were borrowed by early voyagers, such as Pytheas and Posidonius, from the Homeric poems, particularly the Odyssey, and the passages relating to Circe and her insular enchantments. But though certain parallels are apparent, there does not appear to be any basic resemblance between the factors of the Hellenic and those of the Celtic accounts, and it should here be added that all of these narrations are probably to be referred to the lost work of Hecatæus of Abdera, which described the voyage of Pytheas to the north-western portions of Europe.[34]

"That there were female Druids is certain," remarks Frazer in a footnote; but he does not afford any other proof than a reference to the stories of Vopiscus and Lampridius.[35] J. F. Campbell inferred that the name of the Scottish Highland *gruagach*, a description of female brownie, may have some connection with the *groac'h* or *grac'h*, a name given to the sacred women who dwelt in the Isle of Sein.[36] Elsewhere he likens the *gruagach* to the Druids, but he (or she, according to locality) is the depressed domestic representative of a solar deity to whom offerings of milk were made.

We find a parallel to the priestesses of Sein, perhaps, in the legend of the nine sorceresses or fairies of Gloucester, who guarded the thermal waters of that ancient city.[37] One of them, indeed, appears again in the legend of Peredur, who, it was prophesied, should overcome her and her dread sisters.[38]

INDIVIDUAL DRUIDS

Not a little information regarding individual Druids is to be gleaned from various sources, and as this carries with it a certain enlightenment respecting Celtic ideas concerning the caste, I propose to devote the following pages to such of this material as is available. I have already alluded in passing to the Æduan Druid Diviciacus, the friend of Cæsar, who aided him materially by urging his Gallic countrymen to accept the Roman yoke. Cicero, in a letter to his brother Quintus Cicero, who had served in Gaul with Cæsar, mentions that Diviciacus spent some time in Rome with this Quintus, that he had a knowledge of nature "which the Greeks call 'physiologia,'" and that he was in the habit of making predictions "sometimes by means of augury and sometimes by means of conjecture."[39] Diviciacus, says Mr. Kendrick, was thus no mysterious and secluded ancient, but a man of affairs, a ruler of the Ædui and a politician and diplomatist of established repute throughout the whole of Gaul, who actually travelled to Rome on a diplomatic mission. Cicero's account of him, he adds, compels us to enlarge our ideas of the Druidic functions. M. Saloman Reinach, on the other hand, is of opinion that Diviciacus was an Æduan noble who had received a Druidic education, and not a member of the priesthood proper, a statement of which the evidence of Cicero practically disposes for the Roman author alludes to him as a Druid.[40]

We find some evidence respecting another person who was possibly a Gaulish Druid, Chyndonax by name, in the writings of the French antiquary Guenebauld, who died in 1630. In 1621 he published his *Le Reveil de Chyndonax, Prince de Vacies, Druide Celtique.* In the year 1598, in Guenebauld's own vineyard, at a place called Poussat, near Dijon, in the vicinity of an old Roman road, the turning of a great stone revealed a curiously shaped coffer in which was enclosed a glass cinerary urn. On the coffer was an inscription in Greek, which stated that "in this tomb in the sacred wood of the god Mithra is contained the body of the High Priest Chyndonax. May the gods guard my ashes from all harm." The burial seems to have been a comparatively late one, and indeed two centuries after this find a Roman cemetery was discovered on the site. But the inscription does not mention that Chyndonax was a Druid, although it is known that later Druidism was strongly affected by Mithraism, and the probable date of the interment seems to militate against his Druidic status.[41]

In ancient Irish literature we find almost innumerable references to individual Druids. At an evening banquet King Dathi asked his Druid, Finnchaemh, who it was that built the noble and royal court in which they sat. The Druid answered that it had been built by King Eachaidh Aireamh (who is said to have flourished about a century before the Christian era) and then recounted to him the tragic circumstances which followed its erection. It seems to have been this Druid whom Dathi sent on an embassy to Scotland, in circumstances already described.[42]

Cathbad, the Druid, to whose fame as an instructor of youth I have already alluded, appears to have flourished about the beginning of the first century A.D. and held the office of chief or royal Druid to King Conchobar at Emania. According to some accounts, he was the father of

Conchobar, by the famous virago Nessa. As I have already remarked, he was the instructor of Cuchullin in Druidic arts.[43]

Three Irish Druids of consequence—Moel, Blocc and Bluicne—are traditionally believed to have been interred at the royal residence at Tara. The three stones which are said to mark their graves are now known by the respective names of these priests. Professor Macalister ventures the suggestion that these Druids were buried alive "and the stones set over them at some rite of initiation, foundation or inauguration," and that "the personalities of the Druids passed into the stones that were set on them."[44] The stones known as Blocc and Bluicne were considered as of special importance in connection with the ordeals which the Kings of Tara had to undergo before their election, for the person who aspired to sovereignty must drive his chariot between them. If they accepted him, they would open before him to let his chariot pass through.[45] The three Druids in question, as we shall find, are also associated with the legend of the Lia Fail.

It is recorded that the Druid Caicher foretold to the Milesians that Ireland was their ultimate destination while they were yet upon their way from Egypt to Spain.[46] Fer Fi, the son of Eogabal of the *Sidh*, or hill-dwelling of that name, brother to the goddess Ainé and foster-son of the sea-god Manannan Mac Lir, was a Druid of the Tuatha Dé Danann. Fer Fi was a notorious adept in shape-shifting, and occasionally took the form of a dwarf at Lough Gur, near the ruins of Desmond Castle in County Limerick. A gentleman who once spoke disrespectfully of this dwarf was warned by a frightened peasant: "Whisht, he'll hear ye." Fer Fi also assumed the shape of the *bean-nighe*, the fairy-housekeeper, or brownie of Castle Desmond, and at Tara once took the form of a woman to assist his enchantments.[47]

Another outstanding Irish Druid was Mog Ruith, who is said to have aided Simon Magus, the opponent of St. Paul, in the manufacture of a portentous wheel which had the property of bearing one through the heavenly spaces. Mog Ruith, we are informed, was Arch-Druid of Erin, and after drinking of the wells of Druidic knowledge open to him in Ireland and Scotland, he travelled with his daughter Tlachtga to Italy, where they made contact with Simon Magus and assisted him in his contention with the Christian apostles. The trio were responsible for the magical wheel in question, the *Roth Fáil*, or *Roth Rámhach* ("Rowing-wheel") by means of which Simon sailed through the air, thus demonstrating that his magical powers were superior to those of his Christian opponents. When their invention crashed in Rome, in view of the Emperor Nero, and Simon was seriously injured, Tlachtga bore its shattered fragments back to Ireland. These consisted of two masses of rock, one of which she set up near Rath Coole, in the county of Dublin, and the other in Tipperary. He who looked at these stones was smitten with blindness, and whosoever touched either of them perished instantly. The

wheel appears to have been symbolic of the sun, and the myth of Mog
Ruith bears a certain resemblance to that of the Greek Icarus. Mog Ruith,
on one occasion, by his spells and magic fires, drove King Cormac and
his Druids from the kingdom of Munster. He did battle in the sky with
the opposing Druid Ciothruadh, worsting him in an aerial combat.[48]
By shooting an arrow into the air and marking the place of its descent, he
discovered a spring of water which relieved the thirst of the men of
Munster, whose sources of supply had been sealed up by the sorceries of
King Cormac's Druids. For this service he received a grant of land in
Fermoy, where, says tradition, some of his descendants still survive
under the names of O'Duggan and O'Cronin.[49]

John Toland in his *History of the Druids* (pp. 90–92) provides a list of
celebrated Irish Druids: "The Druid Trosdan, who found an antidote
against the poysoned arrows of certain British invaders. Cabadius,
grandfather to the most celebrated champion Cuculand; Tages, the father
of Morna, mother to the no less famous Fin Mac Cuil; Dader, who was
killed by Eogan, son to Olill Olom, King of Munster; which Eogan was
married to Moinic, the daughter of the Druid Dill . . . Dubcomar, the
chief Druid of King Fiacha; and Lugadius Mac-Con, the abdicated King
of Ireland, was treacherously run thro' the body with a lance by the
Druid Firchisus. Ida and Ono, Lords of Corcachlann, near Roscommon,
were Druids; whereof Ono presented his fortress of Imleach-Ono to Patric,
who converted it into the religious house of Elphin, since an episcopal
see. From the very name of Lamderg, or Bloody-hand, we learn what
sort of man the Druid was, who by the vulgar is thought to live inchanted
in the mountain between Bunncranach and Fathen in the county of
Dunegall. Nor must we forget, though out of order of time, King Niall
of the Nine Hostage's Arch-Druid, by name Lagicinus Barchedius, who
procured a most cruel war against Eocha, King of Munster, for committing
manslaughter on his son."

In the later chapters of this book mention will be made of other Druidic
personages in many associations. The intention here is to supply some
general information concerning the most outstanding figures in Druidic
history and tradition and to reveal how familiar that tradition was,
both on the Continent and in Ireland. It will be noticed that the name of
Merlin, the celebrated enchanter of Britain and the counsellor of King
Arthur, is not numbered among the above. But nowhere in any authentic
document prior to the publication of Geoffrey of Monmouth's *Historia*
is his name to be traced, and tradition alone has accorded him the name
and title of Druid.[50]

Chapter VI

DRUIDIC THEOLOGY AND RITUAL

WHATEVER the general theological system of the Druids, it must, if my conclusions are correct, have originated in the worship of the oak tree as a source of provender in early times. In Chapter XVII of his *Commentaries* (Book VI) Cæsar wrote that "they" worshipped gods, including Mercury, Apollo, Mars, Jupiter and Minerva. In the chapter (XVI) which precedes this, he had been dealing with the subject of Gaulish rite and religious belief in connection with which he mentions the Druids as the ministers of Gaulish sacrifices. The personal pronoun "they" alludes therefore to the Gauls, and, by implication, to the Druids also. The deities in question, although Cæsar confers upon them the names of Latin divinities, were certainly the equivalents of gods included in the Celtic pantheon, so that we are left with the inference that the Druids were their priests.

In chapter XVIII of the same book (VI) Cæsar tells us that the Gauls assert that they are descended from the god Dis, and says that this tradition has been handed down by the Druids; so that we can only conclude that the Druids were the source of their religious traditions. "In short," as Mr. Kendrick observes, "we must be prepared to believe that druidism professed, or was in sympathy with, all the known tenets of ancient Keltic religion, and the gods of the druids were the familiar and multifarious deities of the Keltic pantheon."[1] Dis, in Roman myth, is the god of the Underworld and of the dead, the Roman equivalent of the Greek Pluto. For this reason, continues Cæsar, the Gauls (in his honour) reckoned time not by days but by nights, so that the night preceded the day. We find much the same conditions in Irish myth, where the gods of the Fomorians, the powers of darkness, are in point of time anterior to the Tuatha Dé Danann, the gods of day and of life. Indeed M. D'Arbois equated the Dis of Cæsar with the Irish god Bilé, the root of whose name is associated with the idea of death.[2] The Druids, says Pomponius Mela, "professed to know the will of the gods," which appears to make it plain that they were expressly the servants of the gods.[3] Here Mela almost certainly refers to their augural capacity and office.

The matter contained in the great number of verses which the Druidic neophytes were compelled to learn by heart was probably, as Professor Macalister observes, contained "in sacred hymns composed before the introduction of writing, and, like the Vedas in ancient India, preserved by oral tradition, because they would have been profaned were they to be committed to the custody of this novel art." This body of traditional verse, if it were so great as to engage the study of a man for twenty years, as Cæsar tells us it occasionally did, "must," Macalister thinks, "have been at least as extensive as the material at our disposal for the study of classical Latin.''⁴ We have seen that it probably contained a myth respecting the god "Dis," but the likelihood is that it embraced an entire mythology, as complicated and as complete in its way as those of Greece and Rome. If Irish myth, as we know it, was the production of Druidism as it survived in the writings of Christian scribes, then its extensive character is apparent and it is not straining the probabilities too far to believe that Gaulish Druidism possessed at least an equally comprehensive mythology.

Strabo tells us the Druids asserted that the souls of men were "indestructible."⁵ Lucan, in one of his rhapsodies, apostrophizes them as follows: "It is you who say that the shades of the dead seek not the silent land of Erebus and the pale halls of Pluto; rather, you tell us that the same spirit has a body again elsewhere, and that death, if what you sing is true, is but the mid-point of long life."⁶ "With grand contempt for the mortal lot," says Ammianus Marcellinus, "they professed the immortality of the soul."⁷ This, however, is a subject which will receive the more serious discussion it deserves in a later chapter.

THE GODS OF DRUIDISM

The question has been posed more than once as to whether the Druidic cultus centred its adoration in any one particular deity. As we shall see, the Druids invoked a god during the mistletoe rite, while Maximus of Tyre speaks of the Celtic image of Zeus as having been symbolized in a lofty oak.⁸ The Irish hero Cuchullin is made to say that the Druid Cathbad instructed him concerning the arts of "the god of druidism" (dé druidechta). This, says Rhys, "doubtless meant the divinity with whom the druids as magicians had to do and with whose aid they practised their magical arts. We are," he adds, "unfortunately not told the name of this god, but it is natural to suppose that it was the chief of the Goidelic pantheon," whose miracles were mostly of an atmospheric nature associated with the phenomena of the weather. He goes on to say that it is possible to recognize the Welsh counterpart of this Goidelic, or Irish, god of Druidism (who was probably Nuada) in the figure of Math Vab Mathonwy, who appears in a well-known Welsh mabinogi, or tale.

Math was probably superseded as the god of Druidism in Wales by Gwydion, as the former deity is said to have handed on to him the whole apparatus of illusion and fantasy.⁹ But it must be admitted that these ascriptions occur in Irish and Welsh accounts which are at least a thousand years in date after Druidism had disappeared as an influence in Gaul, and that therefore it is difficult to believe that they can refer to deities in any way associated with Druidism in that region. The likelihood is that they are racy of a period when Druidism was regarded by Christian scribes as mainly a corpus of magical art and little more, and when a folk-lore interpretation was placed upon its memorabilia. But this is not to say that the details concerning the association of especial gods with Druidism are lacking in a certain degree of authenticity. The great mass of material concerning Druidism which is to be found in Irish Christian writings cannot altogether be regarded as inventive in character, and must in the ultimate have been obtained either from still earlier manuscripts or from tradition, whether official or popular.

It is only proper to state that Professor Macalister is of opinion that Nuada "is actually the sky-god . . . In fact the equivalence of certain of the legends of Nuada with some of those of Zeus has been pointed out by Rhys, D'Arbois and Cook." He also indicates that in Irish myth we read of a certain girl called Mess, whose name may be translated as "Acorns." "The king of birds obtains access to her and a son called Conaire is born to her." We hear of another female personage in Irish mythology known as Odba (i.e., "Timber-knots") of whom was born three sons, one of them the god Lug, the sun-god. These incidents, thinks Macalister, are fragments of one story. Now "the oak tree is the tree of the thunder-god, and when a deity is born of wood-knots or acorns as the result of the attentions of a bird, we naturally look for the woodpecker. In modern Irish folk-lore, the king of the birds is the wren; he may be a deputy for the woodpecker, which was once a native of Ireland, but is so no longer. . . . This throws some light on the mysterious line in the doggerel rhyme of the wren-boys: 'Although he is little his family's great'." (*Tara*, pp. 119–21.)

Professor Macalister's reference is, of course, to the rhyme chanted by boys in Ireland and England at the ceremony known as "the hunting of the wren," on December 26th. As we have seen, the name of this bird has been said by some authorities to be associated with the root from which Druidism took its name. It was evidently thought necessary to hunt and kill the wren and to carry it round the district, and then to eat it sacramentally to obtain its divine influence. Macalister suggests that the wren may have been a surrogate of the woodpecker in Ireland. The assumption is that the woodpecker, the bird of the oak, fertilizes that tree, and of this union the sun-spirit is born. The wren was certainly associated with lightning. The Roman god Picus took the shape of a woodpecker, and was also connected with the oak. (Rendel Harris, *The Ascent of Olympus*, pp. 4–5.) So that, were the wren the counterpart of the woodpecker in Ireland, it does not seem to be straining probability too far to see in it the spirit of the oak, and therefore a Druidic deity in bird form. In brief, the Roman myth of the oak and its bird-god appears to have been duplicated in Ireland.

Presently, we may agree that the *original* god of Druidism was a spiritual conception of the oak tree, like the Greek Zeus and the Roman Jupiter, as Maximus of Tyre asserts, and that this conception, at a much later date, achieved a more elaborate "personality." At the same time, it appears to me as not improbable that the ancient spirit of the oak tree may, at a later stage of Druidic development, have been represented by the Gaulish god known as Cernunnos. A monument at Rheims reveals a

sculpture of this deity, horned, and in a squatting posture, holding a bag
from which issues a profusion of acorns or beech-mast, the "fruit" of the
oak tree. The acorns drop between a stag and an ox, which was certainly
a "Druidical beast" or symbol. The god, like the animals he feeds, is
horned. Rhys was of opinion that he resembled the god Dis, adored by
the Druids, according to Cæsar. It has been stated by me elsewhere that
the spirit known as "Herne the Hunter," who, horned and threatening,
haunted an oak in the royal forest of Windsor, is a British form of this
deity, and this legend, it seems to me, supports the view that such a god
resembling Cernunnos was known also in Britain.[10]

It has been repeatedly asserted that the gods Taranis, Teutates and
Belenos were associated with the Druidic cult in Gaul and even in Britain,
and a brief examination of the claims of these deities to a Druidic connection seems to be called for. Taranis, who has been identified with
Jupiter, was certainly a god of thunder and lightning, so that his status
as a Druidic deity seems by no means improbable. To him also is credited
the fertility of the soil. Sacrifices were, appropriately enough, made to
him by fire. Taranis, I think, may have symbolized the lightning spirit
which inhabited the oak in the first and original sense, and in that aspect
he may gradually have developed into a god. M. Camille Jullian, a prime
authority, definitely identifies all three deities mentioned above as "The
sovereign deities" of the Druids. (J. A. MacCulloch, *Religion of the Ancient
Celts*, p. 30 f. ; Diodorus Siculus, xxxi, 13 ; C. Jullian, *Cambridge Mediæval
History*, p. 462 ff.)

Teutates, identified by the Romans with Mercury, and sometimes with
Mars, was the Gallic war-god. He, too, appears to have been associated
with the thunder, and bore the hammer symbolic of the thunderbolt in
many mythologies. The name, according to Rhys, has a royal significance.
It seems to me that he may also have been connected with the oak cultus.
(C. Jullian, *op. cit.*, p. 463 ; J. Rhys, *Hibbert Lectures*, p. 46.)

Bel, Bilé or Belenos, the last his Gallic appellation, who is associated
so frequently with the Druidic faith by writers serious and the reverse,
was certainly the god of the *Beallteinn* fire-festival, with which he is
definitely connected, as we know, by Cormac's "Glossary." It is now
merely absurd to attempt to dissociate his Irish and British forms which
last are distinctly the same (see W. J. Gruffydd, *Math Vab Mathonwy*,
p. 172 ff.) from that by which he was known in Gaul, or to pretend that
he had no connection with the *Beallteinn* festival. Beli gave these festivals
his name in Britain and in Ireland the Druids are known to have officiated
at them, as we have seen. So I cannot see why the Irish form of the god,
Bilé, may not be regarded as a Druidic deity. It would seem to follow that
in Gaul his worship was also Druidic. (C. Jullian, *op. cit.*, p. 462; Rhys,
op. cit., p. 46.)

That the Tuatha Dé Danann of Ireland were gods associated with the
Druidic cultus may be inferred from the statement in an ancient

manuscript that "all who are adepts in Druidical and magical arts are the descendants of the Tuatha Dé Danann."[11] The discussion of this part of the subject may perhaps be fittingly concluded by quoting the statement of Diodorus that the Druids alone "knew the gods and divinities of heaven."[12]

It appears to have been regarded as essential that at least one Druid should be present at every sacrifice. According to Diodorus Siculus, it was "a custom of the Gauls that no one performs a sacrifice without the assistance of a philosopher, for they say that offerings to the gods ought only to be made through the mediation of these men, who are learned in the divine nature, and, so to speak, familiar with it."[13] Professor Anwyl construed this as meaning that the "philosopher" in question was "apparently a Druid in addition to the sacrificing seer, the theory being that those who were authorities on the divine nature were to the gods intelligible mediators for the offering of gifts and the presentation of petitions."[14] But Cæsar distinctly avers that the Druids were the *performers* of such sacrifices. (Book VI, Chap. xvi.)

The Worship of the Oak

It now becomes necessary to examine with close fidelity the whole circumstances of the ancient cultus of the sacred oak in Europe, but before approaching that subject more particularly, it appears essential to say a few preliminary words on the worship of trees in general, so that the reader who has no knowledge of the topic will be enabled to pick up the threads of the general argument. Perhaps no writer has so clearly demonstrated the successive steps in the history of tree-worship as the late Sir James Frazer, and here I propose to summarize his account of it, briefly noting his chief arguments apart from the very numerous examples by which he illustrates his thesis.

The savage, he says, believes the world in general to be animate (that is, with him the law of animism prevails) and trees and plants are no exception to the rule. Trees were regarded by primitive man as ensouled or inhabited by spirits. Sometimes only particular species of trees are so tenanted. In some instances, again, the souls of the dead are thought to animate them. Among some tribes such trees are conceived as the ancestors transformed, and they must not be injured or defaced. In the majority of instances the spirit is viewed as incorporate in the tree. If the tree dies the spirit dies along with it. But according to what seems to be a later form of the belief, the tree is not the body but merely the dwelling of the tree-spirit, which can leave it and return at pleasure. In some cases entire groves are regarded as sacred and inviolable because they are thought to be inhabited or animated by sylvan deities. In this phase, "an advance has been made in religious thought. Animism is passing into polytheism." The tree-spirit has become a forest-god. "He begins to change his shape and assume the body of a man in virtue of a general tendency of early thought to clothe all abstract spiritual beings in concrete human form . . . The powers which he exercised as a tree-soul incorporate in a tree, he still continues to wield as a god of trees." Trees considered as animate beings are credited with the power of making the rain to fall, the sun to shine, and flocks and herds, and even human beings to increase, and at a later juncture the fully developed tree-god is found to possess the self-same powers. In some parts of the world, too, the belief prevails that tree-spirits have the power to quicken the growth of the crops, thus revealing that they are regarded as gods of growth in general.[15]

There is also good evidence that trees are worshipped not only because they enshrine spirits, but for a more practical reason, one which bears more precisely upon the question at issue—because they are "food-givers," that is because they or the spirit which animates them furnish primitive man with nuts, or fruit, by way of provender. The idea is entirely similar to that which is associated with the worship of food plants and cereal grain-plants, only it is plain that the adoration of food-bearing trees must have preceded that of grain-bearing plants, a condition which in most instances could scarcely have come into vogue until the period at which agriculture was adopted. Among the people of certain Fijian islands, a man would never eat a coconut without first asking its leave, and addressing it as "chief," while to cut down a coconut palm among the Waniki of East Africa was considered a serious crime.

To acquire palm-wine in Togoland necessitates a felling of the palm-tree, and this is accompanied by an expiatory ceremony.[16] Among the Celts the rowan and hazel were regarded as the bearers of celestial fruits, and their divine exemplars were supposed to be planted in the Celtic paradise. Hazelnuts and rowan-berries were regarded as divine fruit, which yielded, in the first instance, poetic inspiration, and in the second a wine conducive to longevity, and many legends are told of their virtues.[17] The rowan was, indeed, as Rhys remarks, "the Celtic counterpart to the soma-plant of Hindu mythology," with all its associations of mystery and magic. The hazel was indeed a god. It was worshipped as such by one of the eponymous kings of Ireland, MacCuill, "Son of the hazel."[18] In the *Rennes Dindsenchas*, an ancient Irish document, we read that a place known as Mag Mugna, "the greatest of oaks," bore acorns, apples and nuts, a combination of the three sacred fruits of the Celts. As we shall see, the oak was regarded in the same manner in many parts of Europe, as a sacred food-yielding tree.

Trees, then, are regarded by uncultured peoples as "the ancestors transformed." Now we know from the records of tribes in the lower phases of human progress, the Australian aborigines, for example, that trees, rocks and other natural objects are regarded as the dwelling-places of human spirits after death, those spirits indeed which await reincarnation in a new human body and which lie in wait in such receptacles until a possible human mother passes their lair, to enter her body and to be reborn therefrom. (See J. G. Frazer, *The Belief in Immortality*, Vol. I, p. 93 ff.; M. F. Ashley-Montagu, *Coming into Being Among the Australian Aborigines, passim.*) Among some Australian tribes the mistletoe which clings to such trees is believed to contain the souls of spirit children waiting to be reborn. (Ashley-Montagu, *op. cit.*, pp. 78, 79, 91, 94.) This, as Mr. Ashley-Montagu indicates, is not necessarily connected with the process of reincarnation, but of ordinary incarnation, and it seems to me not impossible that such an idea may explain the Druidic reverence for the mistletoe.*

In this chapter the worship of the oak will be dealt with in a strictly objective manner, in relation to the Druidic and other European cults, all theoretical observations on the subject being omitted until the final and conclusive chapters. In primeval ages the continent of Europe was covered by dense forests, and particularly with those in which the oak tree featured. Indeed, it was not until the late mediæval period that most of these disappeared, and their presence must have had a profound influence upon the life and habits of European man. Enormous oak-trunks in a petrified state have been excavated from bogs and dried-up lake-dwellings in Europe, and from peat-deposits in Scotland and Ireland, and mosses in Yorkshire.[19] Oak timber was employed in the construction of primitive lake-dwellings and artificial islands, canoes were hollowed from oak-trunks and oak timber was employed for firewood. It is also evident from stores or heaps of acorns which have been discovered in the dwellings in these lake-villages that their inhabitants subsisted upon the acorn as an article of food even at a period when they had adopted the agricultural state of life to some extent and grew wheat, barley and millet. In the valley of the Po great quantities of stored acorns have been found and these were eaten as food by the folk as well as by their swine.[20]

That acorns were an article of diet for human consumption in primitive times can be proved from many a passage in classical literature. Speaking of the manner in which the righteous will be rewarded, Hesiod, in his

* As will be seen, I have in a later passage explained the Druidic adoration of that plant as arising out of a belief that it symbolized the male essence of the god or spirit of the oak. This notion of mine, however, might appear to be vitiated by the circumstance that some of the Australian aboriginal tribes do not regard paternity as a factor in the birth of children and that among them the belief prevails that the human mother is impregnated solely by the type of ancestral spirit alluded to above. May not the Druidic idea have been a distortion or adaptation of the older notion, as found among the Australian tribes and other primitive folk, adopted at a later period when human paternity came to be recognized as a fact? That European man believed that men were born from trees seems established. The god of the oak was certainly a male spirit. This, I think, fortifies my argument that the fact of paternity was known to the people who worshipped the oak, even in early times. In Greece, Rome and among the Celts the oak-spirit was a male. We seem, indeed, to encounter here a later phase of the idea which inspired Australian notions of birth. Nor, I may add, do all Australian tribes believe that paternity plays no part in the begetting of children.

Works and Days, composed in the seventh century B.C., says that for them the earth yields her riches and that the oak in the mountains puts forth acorns. According to Pausanias and Galen, the Arcadians were eaters of acorns. Pliny, in his *Natural History*, says that in his day, in times of dearth, acorns were still ground and baked into bread. Strabo tells us that the mountain folk of Hispania in his time, the century before Christ, lived upon acorn bread for the greater part of the year. In Greece and Spain the peasantry still eat acorns, and even in England and France they have been regarded as food by the poor in time of famine. Homer, in his "Hymn to Aphrodite," alludes to the "man-feeding" oak. Juvenal, in his first satire, speaks of mankind as born of the opening oak which, mother-like, fed man with her own acorns, while Ovid says that the first human food was supplied by "acorns dropping from the tree of Jove." In the Irish *Book of Leinster* we read that during a revolt of the plebs every ear of corn bore but one grain and every oak only one acorn, which seems to reveal that the acorn was regarded as an article of food, classed as it is with grain.

It is scarcely surprising, then, that the oak tree loomed so largely in the religious ideas of early European man. Its mast fed him, its twigs and branches served him for firing, its timber provided him with building material, his swine were fattened upon its acorns. He worshipped the tree itself for its benefactions and doubtless for its favours to come, and, when he came to believe that it was animated by a powerful spirit, he conceived it as the abode of a god.

The worship of the god of the oak was common to most of the peoples of Europe. In ancient Greece the god Zeus was revered in oak-form at the famous shrine at Dodona, in Epirus, which he shared with his spouse Dione, who at this spot was regarded as his wife instead of Hera. The oldest relic in the sanctuary was an oak tree, from the rustling of whose leaves the attendant priests ascertained the will of the gods. Near at hand stood an iron basin or gong, the clanging of which is thought to have mimicked the thunder.[11]

The people of Platæa, in Bœotia, held a movable festival at which they laid before a grove of oaks an offering of meat. Should a raven bear off a portion of this, and settle upon a particular oak, that tree was felled and its wood shaped into an image. This was dressed as a bride, and at the jubilee of the *Great Daedala*, a nature festival, which was celebrated once in every sixty years, all the images collected within that period had animals sacrificed to them by fire, the idols themselves being included in the conflagration. The myth associated with this ceremony recounted that Hera had forsaken Zeus after a quarrel, and that to ensure her return, Zeus circulated the story that he was about to espouse the nymph Platæa, the tutelary genius of the region. He ordered an oak to be cut down and this was dressed as the prospective bride. In jealous wrath Hera tore off the bridal veil which concealed the wooden statue, and thus becoming aware of her husband's stratagem, was reconciled to him.[22] In all likelihood the ceremony represented the marriage of the oak-god with the oak-goddess, while the above story was invented at a later time, to "save the face" of the goddess Hera. As we shall see, both Greek and Roman kings claimed to be descended from Zeus and Jupiter, and to share their powers of fertility.

Zeus, as the oak-god, wielded the powers of rain, thunder and lightning. Frazer was of opinion that this view of oak-gods generally as rain-bringers and lightning-wielders arose from the notion that as fire on earth was generated by the rubbing together of oaken sticks, so in heaven it was produced in a like manner. Zeus' power as a rain-god was merely consequent upon his aspect as a god of the thunder-and-lightning.[23]

In Italy the oak was sacred to Jupiter and on the Capitolian Hill at Rome he was worshipped as the god of the oak and of the rain and the thunder.[24] The probability is that the sacred tree of Nemi, rendered famous by Frazer in *The Golden Bough*, was an oak, the centre of a similar tree-cult.[25] The Germans certainly worshipped the oak, which was dedicated to the god Donar or Thunar, the Lord of the Thunder, the great fertilizing power.[26] Among the Slavonic peoples the oak was the sacred tree of the thunder-god Perun, whose image at Novgorod represented a man holding a thunder-stone. His priests dare not let the sacred fire of oak wood which burned in the vicinity go out except at the risk of their lives. It is noteworthy that oxen were sacrificed to him.[27]

Among the Lithuanians the god Perkunas, the deity of thunder and lightning, was associated with the oak, and when Christian missionaries cut down his groves, the folk lamented. He also had perpetual fires burned to him. The Dominican friar Simon Grunau, who for long sojourned in Prussian Poland in the early part of the sixteenth century, mentions these doings as within his knowledge, and although the veracity of his account of them has been questioned, it has been confirmed by Mæletius and Rostowski, and agrees too precisely with what we know of the circumstances of other oak-cults to be in any sense an invention.

Moreover, Peter of Dusburg, whose account dates from 1326, speaks of a High Priest of the Prussians, revered as a Pope, who maintained a perpetual fire at Romow.[28] The Lithuanians sacrificed to oak trees for plentiful crops, says Rostowski. The Esthonians, who are not Slavs, worshipped the oak in the person of the god Taara, and smeared the oaks with the blood of beasts once a year. They also sacrificed oxen to it, praying for rain and good crops.[29] Tylor alludes to a grove in a Siberian forest where gaily decked idols, "each set up beneath its great tree swathed with cloth or tin-plate, endless reindeer hides and peltry hanging to the trees around, kettles and spoons and snuff-horns and household valuables strewn as offerings before the gods" composed a strange picture of a holy grove at a later stage. (*Primitive Culture*, Vol. II, p. 224.) The close resemblance of all this Slavonic and other evidence to what

Pliny has to say concerning the rite of the mistletoe, shortly to be described, led Professor Rhys to remark: "Seeing the importance of sacred trees in the ancient cult of the chief god of the Aryans of Europe, and the preference evinced for the oak as the tree fittest to be his emblem, or even the residence of his divinity, I am inclined to regard the old etymology of the word druid as being, roughly speaking, the correct one," that is, "men of the oaks."[30] The evidence is, I believe, irrefragable that in ancient times the worship of the oak obtained over a wide area in Europe and that among the Slavonic peoples it survived until the fourteenth century at least.

The oak was by no means the only tree adored by the Celtic peoples, and they appear to have adopted local tree-cults from some of their neighbours, as Canon MacCulloch indicates. He thinks that they accepted the cult of the beech and the god of some coniferous tree from the Ligurians, while "forests were also personified or ruled by a single goddess, like Dea Arduenna of the Ardennes, and Dea Abnoba of the Black Forest."[31]

The perpetual fire maintained by the nuns of St. Brigit at Kildare, a place whose name means "church," or "shrine of the oak," is reminiscent of those which certain Slavonic peoples burned to the genius of that tree, and the saint's maidens may innocently have preserved, down to the reign of Henry VIII, a fire which glowed to the glory of Brigit, the ancient pagan goddess, the patroness of bards, physicians and smiths. No man might set foot within the fence which surrounded her sanctuary.[32] The oak was certainly a sacred tree in pagan Ireland, but in later times it appears to have been supplanted as a Druidic tree by the yew. Indeed, Dr. Pokorny assures us in italics that "the Irish Druids are never mentioned in connection with the oak." Their holy tree, he says, was the yew. They bore wands made of its wood and the Druidic fire was kindled by yew faggots.[33] This appears to be the case, indeed it is confirmed by O'Curry, but I think Pokorny exaggerates when he remarks that "the Druids must have been once the priests of a people who did not know the worship of the oak." To cut down an oak was an offence in pagan Ireland, and even Columba deplored the destruction of an oak-grove at Derry and forbade the felling of oaks.[34] So I prefer to believe that the oak was originally the Druidical tree in Ireland and that for some reason unknown the yew superseded it, as the wren superseded the woodpecker as its genius in bird-form.

At least one relic of yew-worship appears to have been known in England. Tupper, in his *Farley Heath* (p. 69), mentions that "on Merroe Downs, in Surrey, are two distinct concentric groves of venerable yews a thousand years old with remnants of little avenues, possibly Druidic." The age of these may readily be discounted. There are far too many Irish place-names connected with the oak to permit of the belief that it was not regarded as a sacred tree in pagan times, and the notion that the Irish Druids had *never* adored it at any time when all other Druids did so, is one that scarcely commends itself. To fortify such a theory it would also be necessary to explain why so many early Christian churches in Ireland were erected on the site of oak-groves, for it was proverbially customary with the early Christian missionaries to build their churches on the sites of pagan shrines.

FOLK-LORE OF THE OAK-CULT

In many parts of Europe superstitions concerning the oak strengthen the theory that its worship must formerly have been widespread. As an example of this type of surviving reminiscence, the Copt Oak, of which only the trunk remains, which stands on high ground in Charnwood Forest in Leicestershire, was held by tradition to have been a centre of Druidic worship. In the Middle Ages it appears to have been a place where swainmotes, or lordship courts were held.[35] Near Dolgelly, in Merioneth-shire, once stood the haunted oak of Nanneu, held to be the abode of spirits and demons.[36] Other examples of this kind will be instanced when we come to consider the subject of sacred groves. What were known as "Bull oaks" may still be seen in many parts of England. These were very old and hollow trees of which the country folk said that they were so-called because bulls sheltered inside them. That they should have been associated with the bull, the Druidic beast of sacrifice, seems significant.[37] They may have been styled "bell" oaks, as some trees in Ireland and Scotland were. I have already alluded to Herne the Hunter and the oak which he haunted in Windsor Forest. There was formerly in the park of Sir Robert Vaughan in Wales, a celebrated oak tree named "The Elf's Hollow Tree."[38] Oaks such as this were, indeed, regarded as the haunts of spirits, thus revealing that formerly they must have been thought to be ensouled by them and consequently adored or placated. In later times such haunting spirits come to be looked upon as elves, fairies, or demons. An old English folk-rhyme has it:

> "Turn your clokes,
> For fairy folkes
> Are in old oakes."

That is, one must turn his cloak or coat outside-in to neutralize their harmful magic.[39] Such spirits were capable of entering houses through knot-holes in oak timbers, as did an elfmaid in Smaland, who wed with the son of the house.[40] This belief seems to cast some light upon the significance of the Irish female spirit Mess, whose name, as we have seen, implies "timber-knots."

In some districts of Lower Saxony and Westphalia, says Grimm, "holy oaks" were preserved, to which the folk "paid a half-heathen half-Christian homage" until "quite recent times." In Minden, on Easter Sunday, the young people danced a circular dance round an old oak, and a procession was made to another by the people of Wormeln and Calenberg. A memory of the heathen worship of oaks, thought Grimm, was preserved

in the place-name *Dreieich*, that is "Three Oaks."[41] In Brittany and
France oaks are still associated with saints. One finds such names as
"Our Lady of the Oak" in Anjou and the same at Orthe, in Maine, places
famous for pilgrimage. "One sees at various cross-roads in Maine the most
beautiful rustic oaks decorated with figures of saints. There are seen there,
in five or six villages, chapels of oaks, with whole trunks of that tree
enshrined in the wall beside the altar."[42] An oak-coppice or grove near
Loch Siant, in the Isle of Skye, was at one time held so sacred that none
would venture to cut even the smallest twig from it.[43]

The Mile Oak, near Oswestry, in Shropshire, was deemed sacrosanct,
and a local ballad declared of it:

> "To break a branch was deemed a sin,
>   A bad-luck job for neighbours,
> For fire, sickness and the like
>   Would mar their honest labours."[44]

To deface the holy oak at Ragnit in East Prussia boded misfortune
or bodily ailment for the spoiler.[45] On a rivulet between the governments
of Pskov and Livonia, in Russia, stood a stunted and withered holy oak
to which homage was paid until at least the year 1874. At a given
ceremony there, wax candles were fixed to the trunk and branches, and a
priest of the Orthodox Church adjured the tree: "Holy Oak Hallelujah,
pray for us." The people then worshipped the tree and the proceedings
concluded with a drunken orgy.[46]

Old Aubrey tells us that in England "our late Reformers gave order
(which was universally observed accordingly) for the Acorn, the fruit of
the oak, to be set upon the top of their maces or crowns, instead of the
Cross." He alludes, of course, to a supposed Puritan decree, but I can find
no authority for the statement. In this regard, it is amusing to find so
authoritative a student of folk-lore as the late Rev. Sabine Baring-Gould
declaring that "under the name of Methodism we have the old Druidic
religion still alive, energetic and possibly more vigorous than it was
when it exercised a spiritual supremacy over the whole of Britain."[47]
And who shall dare to say that it does not to a great extent survive in
the "Christianity" of Brittany, or remain as an "under-current" to that
somewhat fuliginous faith?

"When an oake is felling," says Aubrey, "before it falls it gives a kind
of shriekes or groanes, that may be heard a mile off, as if it were the genius
of the oak lamenting. . . . To cut oak-wood is unfortunate."[48]

In Balkan story we find a holy oak growing out of a slain king's mouth,
which seems to reveal an association between the tree and the kingship.[49]

In England the oak was believed to attract lightning.

> "Beware of an oak,
>   It draws the stroke,"

ran an old rhyme.[50] This shows that a belief must once have prevailed
that the tree was the abode of the thunder-spirit. The oak tree was

thought to exhibit certain omens on occasion. The change of its leaves from their usual colour was more than once regarded as giving a fatal premonition of coming misfortunes during the great Civil War in England. The Earl of Winchelsea gave orders to fell a curious grove of oaks, whereupon his Countess died and his eldest son was killed in action at sea.[51] I cannot pretend that this category of folk-lore beliefs respecting the oak is either embracive or definitive, but at least it suffices to indicate the survival of religious beliefs concerning the tree.

THE MISTLETOE AS A DRUIDICAL PLANT

Both tradition and literature have inevitably associated the mistletoe plant with Druidism. This connection, so far as its literary part is concerned, has probably emerged from Pliny's account of the Druidic rite in which the plant figures. "The Druids," he tells us, "held nothing more sacred than the mistletoe and the tree that bears it, always supposing that tree to be the oak. But they choose groves formed of oaks for the sake of the tree alone, and they never perform any of their rites except in the presence of a branch of it." Everything which grew on the oak, they believed, "has been sent from heaven." This last sentence, indeed, appears to me to satisfy all doubts concerning the authenticity of Pliny's account, as it certainly agrees with what we know of most tree-cults. The mistletoe, however, is found but rarely upon the oak, he continues, and when it is, it is gathered with due religious ceremony, if possible on the sixth day of the moon, when her influence is already being felt. They (the Celts) call the mistletoe by a name which in their language means "all healing."

After a repast beneath the trees of the sacred grove, they brought forward two white bulls, "whose horns are bound for the first time." A white-robed priest then ascended the tree and cut the mistletoe which adhered to it with a golden sickle, so that when it fell it was received by his colleagues in a white cloak. The bulls were then sacrificed and prayers were offered up to the God of the Oak, requesting that he should render the plant propitious "to those to whom he has granted it." "They believe that the mistletoe, taken in drink, imparts fecundity to barren animals and that it is an antidote for all poisons."[52]

It is not a little extraordinary to discover a similar ritual act in ancient Egypt. At the feast of the first Pachons, associated with the rite of vegetation, the Pharaoh cut *with a sickle* a sheaf of corn and sacrificed thereafter *a white ox* consecrated to Min, the god of fecundating energy. The ox was regarded as one of the forms of Osiris. (J. G. Frazer, *The Golden Bough*, vol. III, pp. 94 ff., and 104 ff.; A. Moret, *Mystères Egyptiens*, pp. 7–8.) The month Pachons fell in summer. The close analogy between this rite and the Druidic one can scarcely be accidental. Probably both cast back to a very ancient ritual associated with the powers of fertility and the rites carried out by a king who represented the earthly form of a god of fertility.

The willow, the poplar and the apple are the trees which chiefly attract the mistletoe as a parasite. Its Druidic name is still preserved in Celtic speech, in words meaning "all-healer" and "sap of the oak," and it is also known more familiarly as *Druidh lus*, or "Druid's weed."[52]

MacCulloch pregnantly criticizes Pliny's account. He thinks that Pliny was "relating something of which all the details were not known to him." The rite "must have had some other purpose than that of the magico-medical use of the mistletoe, which he describes." He is of opinion that the oxen sacrificed may, at a later time, have taken the place of an earlier human victim. Perhaps, according to a more ancient form of the ritual, remarks this authority, a branch of the tree may have had to be captured from its guardian and "king," that is, the personal representative of the God of the Oak, as was the case in the ritual associated with the Golden Bough at Nemi, in Italy.[54]

But long ago Frazer indicated a Roman equivalent to the Druidic rite. For at the Capitol at Rome and on the Alban Mount white oxen were offered up to the earthenware image of Jupiter (originally a god of the oak) by the Roman consuls, and triumphal processions of victors in war were held there.[55]

I may say, in passing, that the circumstance that the sickle employed by the Druids was actually made of gold has been questioned, and it has been suggested that the Latin word *aurea* has been scribally substituted for *aerea* (brass). It is significant that Vergil expressly remarks that herbs used for magical purposes were cut with sickles of brass.[56] Stukeley, alluding to the rite described by Pliny, says: "This mistletoe, they (the Druids) cut off the trees with their upright hatchets of brass."[57] In old-time phraseology the term "brass" usually implies bronze. Towards the end of the eighteenth century a Mr. Philip Rashleigh found a brass sickle at the bottom of a mine near the River Powey.

"The mistletoe or branch," says MacCulloch, "was the soul of the tree, and also contained the life of the divine representative. It must be plucked before the tree could be cut down or the victim slain."[58] This is very well, so far as it goes, but I am of opinion that it is possible to carry the significance of the mistletoe farther. It was, indeed, regarded as the semen or life-essence of the oak, the glutinous matter contained in its berries was thought of as the spermatozoa, or impregnatory fluid of the god, and to such fluid, indeed, it bears a quite remarkable resemblance. This theory is supported by the prevalence of the superstition that the mistletoe was given to barren animals to render them fecund, while the amatory practice of "kissing under the mistletoe" seems to have some tincture of recollection of a rite which might make a union fertile by "sympathetic magic." I think it is further fortified by one of the names conferred upon the mistletoe by the Bretons, *dour-dero*, that is the "pith," "vigour" or strength of the mistletoe, but literally "water of the mistletoe." (J. Cambry, *Monumens Celtiques*, p. 330.) It seems to me that the slaying of bulls, animals notoriously symbolic of sexual vigour, was regarded as compensation to the God of the Oak for the loss of his vigour, thought to be contained in the berries, or seminal vessels of the plant, and for the removal of his male protoplasm. That the mistletoe was thus not so much the "soul" of the oak but rather its life-essence, is, I think, demonstrable. But I refer the reader to my remarks concerning Australian beliefs about the connection of the mistletoe with "spirit children" on a previous page, and I entertain the sentiment that this belief may explain the Druidic reverence for the plant in some degree. The ancient forest folk who adored the oak may well have nourished such an idea concerning the plant which adhered to it, indeed the belief may be so ancient that a universal concept of it may have been entertained in parts of the world very distant one from the other, and it may well have gradually spread from one centre to areas so far apart as Europe and Australia. The Australian belief is that spirit-children are contained in the bunches of mistletoe. There is no evidence that the Druids believed as much; but the two beliefs would appear to have developed from one and the same idea.

That the mistletoe was identical with the silver branch or bough of ancient Celtic tradition, I am also assured. This branch, the especial property of the Irish god Manannan, a deity intimately associated with Druidic art, was cut from a mystical apple tree. It furnished the bearer with food and drink and emanated enchanting music. It led one to the abode of the gods and was the symbol of the divine tree standing in the centre of paradise. It is the equivalent of the Golden Bough mentioned by Vergil as a passport to the Land of the Gods. Indeed, he says that this branch *is* the mistletoe.[59] A correspondent in *The Gentleman's Magazine* for February, 1791, got very near the truth when he wrote that "Mistletoe, a magical shrub, appears to be the forbidden tree in the middle of the trees of Eden." I do not suppose that after what has been said by Rydberg concerning the "mistletoe" with which the Norse sun-god Balder was slain, anyone will expect a dissertation on that legend. The *Mistleteinn* which took his life was the name of an enchanted sword, *teinn* meaning a "branch" or "sword" in the poetic sense, as we speak of a "brand."

FOLK-LORE OF THE MISTLETOE

So far as I am concerned, this concludes the explanatory criticism of Pliny's account. We must now examine what folk-lore has to say upon the question, and whether it supports, or declines to support, my view. Aubrey states that in England a decoction of mistletoe was given to promote the discharge of the placenta in calving cows.[60] In Worcestershire farmers took the Christmas mistletoe bough from the wall and gave it to eat to the first cow that calved after New Year's Day, an act which was supposed to avert ill-luck from the whole dairy, but which must surely have originated in a former notion that it induced fertility in the animal.[61]

Elsewhere, in his *History of Surrey*, Aubrey observes that when an oak tree at Norwood was felled about 1657, the mistletoe it bore was sold to some London apothecaries at "ten shillings each time." The men who cut it were visited with misfortune. One fell lame, "soon after, each of the others lost an eye," while he who felled the tree broke his leg. Sir John Colbatch, in his *Dissertation Concerning Mistletoe*, states that it was used for the cure of animals smitten by various diseases.

In Brittany the mistletoe was believed to give strength and courage to those who engaged in wrestling and athletic sports and this, I think, goes far to reveal that it was regarded as a seminal product. In Scotland it was, for this reason, thought of as a cure in cases of decline. But it well deserved its name of "All-heal," for it was employed as a specific against epilepsy, as a liniment to dispel stiffness, a cure for stitches of the side, a panacea for "green" wounds, that is gangrene, and a nerve-tonic.[62]

In Sweden the mistletoe is the "thunder-besom," or broom, the implement of the thunder-god, which reveals its ancient association with the oak-cultus.[63] Placed on the doors or walls of houses, it protected them from the lightning. A certain oak, entwined with mistletoe, was associated by tradition with the ancient and noble family of the Hays of Errol, in Perthshire. So long as the mistletoe grew on this tree (said a venerable saw, believed to have fallen from the lips of Thomas the Rhymer) the Hays would flourish. But should the oak decay and the mistletoe wither, the grass would grow on the Earl's hearth-stone. It was believed that a sprig of mistletoe cut by a Hay on Allhallowmas eve with a new dirk, and after the gatherer had walked three times round the tree sunwise, was a certain charm against sorcery and fatality in the day of battle.[64]

But we find that quite another vegetable medium had associations with kissing besides the mistletoe. The "kissing-bush," hung up in houses in the Cleveland district of Yorkshire (at Christmas, presumably), was an ornamental bush made of holly and evergreens, with "roses" cut from coloured paper and hung with apples and oranges. When railways made their appearance, the mistletoe was added to the "bush." It had evidently been remembered, but had been unobtainable locally before that time.[65] Stukeley says that mistletoe was carried to the high altar of York Cathedral on the eve of Christmas Day, when a "universal liberty" and pardon was proclaimed to "all sorts of inferior and even wicked people" (thieves, loose women and so forth) "at the gates of the city," and this is corroborated by Leland.[66] Now this was actually the procedure at the Roman "Saturnalia," the festival of the Latin agricultural god Saturnus, held on December 17th to 23rd, during which season no criminals were punished. This festival was held on the Capitoline Hill, the home of Jupiter, God of the Oak, and during its incidence the people gambled for nuts.

I think that on the whole a reasonably good case has been made out for the authenticity of Pliny's assertions regarding the Druidic rite of mistletoe, even though it is not referred to elsewhere in classical literature.

I am not of opinion that the widely diffused superstitions respecting the mistletoe plant were derived from Pliny's account, more particularly that part of them which deals with the exhibition of mistletoe at Christmastide and its tradition as a lovers' plant. That it was also held as sacred is proved by the superstition which averred that bodily misfortune overtook those who cut it from the tree without sanction. That it was thought of as the life-essence of the oak is revealed by the fact that it was given to athletes and consumptives in Britain. Its all-healing character, as recorded by Pliny, is fully displayed in European folk-medicine. That it is associated with the thunder and lightning is made clear by its being affixed to houses in Sweden as a "lightning conductor," or protector against the heavenly fire. The associations of its rite as carried out under official religious auspices at York seem to make it evident that the plant must have received ancient reverence in that city and its neighbourhood, though this last may well be a survival of ancient Roman practice in "Eboracum."

In a tumulus at Gristhorpe, near Scarborough, only a little more than thirty miles from York there was unearthed in 1834 an oak coffin containing a human skeleton which was covered with oak branches and vegetable matter identified, according to one account, as mistletoe. The burial was of the Bronze Age, and thus of a period greatly anterior to that normally connected with Druidic belief. Yet the discovery seems to show that mistletoe and the oak were known as sacred, protective and allied plants in Britain long before historic times.[47]

REPRESENTATION OF GODS

The question as to whether the Druids did or did not fabricate and worship images or idols of their gods is one which has given rise to some controversy. As we have seen, Maximus of Tyre says that the Celts worshipped Zeus in the form of a great oak. Justin states that a statue of a goddess was to be seen in a shrine at Marseilles (lxiii, 5) and the Galatian Celts had images of their deities (Strabo, XII, 5, 2). Cæsar remarked upon the numerous effigies of Mercury in Gaul, and Lucan distinctly states that there were many images in the celebrated Druidic grove at Marseilles.[48] Irish literature almost teems with statements concerning idols. Lucan seems to suggest that the images at Marseilles were tree-trunks roughly carved. Figures of Mercury have been found beneath and upon menhirs or standing stones at Peronne in the Somme country and at Kernuz in Finisterre.

In a well-known essay M. S. Reinach has argued that Druidic sentiment was contrary to the fabrication of idols in human form.[49] On the whole, it would seem that the presentation of the Gaulish deities in human shape was partly an innovation introduced under Roman auspices, as we have already seen in the cases of the god Cernunnos and other deities. Reinach's attitude on the subject is prompted by his theory that the Druids were of pre-Celtic origin and were thus unaware of the use of effigies, and that they favoured Pythagoreanism, which was opposed to the worship of images. But there is no mention of Druidic antipathy to images in classical writings, as surely there would have been had it existed, and animal effigies were certainly adored in Gaul. We read of the image of the goddess Berecynthia in sixth century Gaul, and of the "Venus of Quinipily" in Brittany, which existed, the one in post-Roman and the other in Roman times (although it may be older, even if it bear part of a Latin inscription). Camille Jullian believed that the majority of such images were "unformed trunks, rough-hewn pillars, a kind of sheath in wood or stone, analogous to the most ancient *Xoana* of the Greeks, without any of the features of a man, or those fixed attributes which make it possible to distinguish a Zeus from an Apollo."[70]

O'Curry indicates that in Cormac's *Glossary* there is a passage which mentions that the Druids took idols into their couches at night to influence their visions. There was also an invocation to idols in the rite known as *Teinm Læghala*. He adds: "That the people of ancient Erinn were idolators is certain, for they certainly adored the great idol called Crom Cruach." (A standing-stone.) "But it is remarkable that we find no mention of any connexion between this idol and the Druids, or any other class of priests, or special idol-servers."[71] It is worthy of mention that Tara, the capital of ancient Ireland, was known in St. Patrick's day as "the chief seat of the *idolatry* and Druidism of Erin," although in this instance the term "idolatry" may here be merely a synonym for "paganism."[72] Groups of images existed at Rath-Archaill, "where the Druids' altar and images are" (Ailred, *Vita St. Ninian*, p. 6.) The ancient Irish King MacCuil adored for his god a log of wood. (Keating, O'Connor's translation, p. 108.)

Keating recounts a legend which states that in the days of King Cormac one of the idols of the ancient Irish was a golden calf. On one occasion this effigy was brought by the Druids into the presence of Cormac, who had become a convert to Christianity. The Chief Druid, Maoilogeann, inquired of the King why he did not adhere to the religion of his ancestors, whereupon Cormac replied to him in a scornful manner, saying that the idol in question was merely the image of a beast and not the true god. The Druids removed the idol, only to bring it back later bedizened with jewels and covered with ornamental housings, and once more asked the King if it were not worthy of his devotions. But he refused even more strenuously to bow the knee to the image. Resolved on vengeance, the Chief Druid so enchanted a salmon which had been prepared for Cormac's evening repast that one of its bones stuck in his throat and choked him.[73] Miss Eleanor Hull thought that this story was "a mere adaptation of the Biblical account of the golden calf in the wilderness." It is true that the main idea of a calf of gold inspires both stories, but otherwise I can trace but little resemblance between them.

A strange case of seeming idolatry in Wales, at a period so late as the reign of Henry VIII, is on record. It occurred in the diocese of St. Asaph and is described in a letter from one Ellis Price to Thomas Cromwell, the famous secretary of Henry, dated April 6th, 1538. Price wrote as follows:

"There ys an Image of Darvellgadarn within the said diocese, in whome the people have so greate confidence, hope and truste, that they cumme dayly a pillgramage unto hym, somme with kyne, othir with oxen or horsis and the reste with money; in so much that there was fyve or syxe hundrethe pilgrimes to a man's estimacion, that offered to the said image the fifth daie of this present monethe of Aprill. The innocente people hath ben sore aluryd and entised to worship the saide image, in so much that there is a commyn sayinge as yet amongst them that who so ever will offer anie thinge to the said Image of Darvellgadarn, he hathe power to fatche hym or them that so offers oute of Hell when they be dampned."

This idol was conveyed to Smithfield and incontinently burnt there, along with a "friar" or priest who bore the same name as itself. The general circumstances surrounding the affair yield the impression that the idol was associated with a surviving cultus of the sacred ox. Oxen were offered up to it, and we shall see that the sacrifice of these animals was fairly common in Wales until a late date. An ancient British deity known as Hu Gadarn was said to have drawn souls out of Annwn, or Hell, and "Darvellgadarn" had certainly some reputation in Wales as a "saint." "Darvell" may perhaps be a corruption of *tarw*, the Welsh word for a bull. May he not be the same as Gargantua or Cernunnos? It seems to me not altogether improbable that he was.

Numerous objects resembling idols have been recovered in Ireland, chiefly from bogs. Some are garbed in a short petticoat or kilt and wear forked beards. One such, now in the Dublin Museum, was taken from beneath the root of a large tree in Roscommon. It had formerly been gilt and is about five inches in height. A metal idol weighing twenty-four pounds was recovered from the soil at Clonmel. About 1690 a large wooden image was found in the bog of Cullen, in Tipperary. Pins and pegs were stuck in different parts of it, and gold plates found near it seem to have been suspended from these, evidently as offerings. "The old Tuath, a vaulted stone temple at Knockmay, in Galway, which was afterwards turned into an abbey, had a remarkable figure, like Apollo, *bound to a tree*, pierced by arrows." Strabo, as we shall see, mentions that the Druids sacrificed some of their victims by shooting them with arrows, and indeed shooting at tree-trunks is a feature of tree-worship in some countries, as Frazer observes. It may, indeed, have been a part of the ritual of the forest-god or spirit known to later ages as "Robin Hood," and that of his Swiss "cousin," William Tell.

At Cashel a stone image was discovered late in the last century. It was about two feet in height, the legs taking the form of serpents crossed."[4]

An image of wood about two feet high, in the likeness of a woman, was piously preserved by one of the family of O'Herleby in Ballyvorney, County Cork, and when anyone was smitten by the small-pox they sent for it, sacrificed a sheep to it and wrapped the skin about the sick person, while the family ate the sheep.[15] Tigernmas, an Irish king, is said to have been slain by lightning for worshipping an idol. Petrie, the great Irish antiquary of the nineteenth century, was of opinion that such effigies had replaced the worship of standing-stones in Erin. He alludes to Kerman Kelstach, the favourite idol of the folk of Ulster, which had for its pedestal the golden stone of Clogher, and which may have resembled in its general shapelessness the Greek *Hermæ*. He attributed the introduction of such images to "the Eastern fire-worshippers"![16]

It appears to me as not improbable that some of these effigies at least may have been associated with Druidic worship. That such rude images were actually connected with it in Gaul we have seen, and that they were also adored in Ireland it seems scarcely rash to assume, though a number of them may possibly have been worshipped by the adherents of other cults. Yet this seems hardly possible in view of the very exclusive character of the Druidic faith.

THE DRUIDIC IDEA OF CREATION

We read that the Druids of Ireland claimed that they were the creators of the world. On one occasion King Connla of Connaught convened a great gathering of the Druids, who in the course of the discussion claimed that they were the creators of the heavens and the earth. But their pretensions were scoffed at by the monarch, who challenged them to alter the courses of the sun and moon so that they should appear in the north, to their complete confusion.[17]

But there seems to be a certain degree of truth in the superstition that the Druids believed themselves to have possessed such creative powers. Professor A. M. Hocart has made it clear that the priesthoods of other races indulged such a notion. The natives of Western Vanua Levu, in the Fiji group, hold installation ceremonies or consecration of the chiefs, at such times as the crops do not flourish. These they call "creating the earth." The same ceremony was known in early India, and the book entitled *Satapottia* describes at length the method to be followed in a rite known as "the creation of the world." A piece of clay is shaped "like the world." By this means, imitating the creative process, the priest or enchanter is thought to gain control over the whole earth, he places plants in the clay model, he mimics the sun by holding fire above it. "The whole purpose of the king's coronation is to gain control of the world and thus create abundance and creatures."

The Egyptian Pharaoh did much the same. He "renewed every day the mystery of the creation." The same process was carried out in the ritual of the Eleusinian mysteries. Indians and Germans, Scandinavians and Babylonians knew of a myth which told how a god, a monster, or a man had been slain and dismembered and how the universe was subsequently created from his several parts, the soil being composed of his flesh, the rocks from his bones, the sky and clouds from his brains and the sun and moon from his eyes. In some cases a human sacrifice was performed in order to re-enact the process, which was that of renewing the earth's vigour. The king or chieftain then took mystical possession of the essence of the earth for the benefit of the community.[78]

It seems not at all impossible that a Druidic myth and ritual of a similar propensity and significance lay behind this claim of the Irish Druids, who, after all, were, as we shall see, a body of priests chiefly identified with the cultus of the Sacred King. By the time of Connla the belief in this rite may have waned considerably or grown partly discredited, and only the general memory of it may have survived. But that the survival of belief in the creation of the world by the Druidic caste suggests the former existence of such a myth and rite seems clear enough, for the belief could scarcely have existed unless such a ritual practice had once prevailed.

THE DRUIDS AND WELL-WORSHIP

We find the Druids mentioned in connection with the worship of wells. In the "Annotations" of Tirechan on the life of St. Patrick, to be found in the *Book of Armagh*, and which contains material at least as old as the latter half of the seventh century, we are told that Patrick came to the fountain of Findmaige, which is called Slan, because it was shown to him that the Magi honoured the fountain and made offerings to it "as gifts to God," and that they "worshipped the fountain as a god."[79]

As Whitley Stokes points out, this is the only passage which connects the Druids with well-worship. But it is important, as it indicates their association with such spirits or genii as those who presided over wells. The rather elaborate ritual engaged in at some sacred wells is still mimicked in certain children's games surviving in Britain, and these may possibly represent fragments of ancient Druidic ritual. This cannot actually be proved, but the circumstance that such sacred wells are, or were, frequently to be found in the near neighbourhood of venerable oaks, with which they are associated in local legend, seems to support the idea that they were places of Druidic reverence. Moreover, we find distinct traces of official priesthoods at such wells. At that of St. Aelian, in Denbighshire, a woman resided who officiated as "priestess." Evilly-disposed folk, who wished to bring down a curse on an enemy, resorted to her, and for a small sum she registered the name of the blighted one in a book kept for the purpose. A pin was dropped in the well in the name of the victim.[80]

This recalls a Gascon belief that those who wish to revenge themselves upon their enemies may be able to induce a priest to say a mass to their detriment and injury. This rite, known as "the Mass of St. Sécaire," will, of course, be performed only by a priest of the most abandoned character and such are indeed few. It can be said only in a ruined church at midnight, with an equally depraved woman acting as clerk. A black, three-pointed host is used and water from a well into which the body of an unbaptized infant has been cast. The man against whom the mass is said is supposed to "dwindle, peek and pine" until he dies. (J. F. Bladé, *Quatorze superstitions populaire de Gascogne*, p. 16 ff.) At St. Teilo there is an "oxen's well," formerly tended by a family called Melchior, which, says Sir John Rhys in his *Celtic Folklore*, "may indicate a succession which seems to point unmistakably to an ancient priesthood of a sacred spring."[81]

It is worthy of notice that the tale known as "The Lady of the Fountain," to be found in the Welsh *Mabinogion*, appears to hold a significance connected with the worship of the oak. It recounts how a knight is made aware of an adventure which is to be encountered in the neighbourhood of a tall tree, beneath which stands a fountain, bounded by a marble slab. To this is attached a silver bowl. If water be taken from the spring in this bowl and cast upon the slab, a terrific peal of thunder resounds, and a storm of rain follows, so terrible in its fury as scarcely to be endured by flesh and blood. Immediately after the phenomenon a multitude of birds in the tree burst into songs of rhapsody. Then a champion mounted on a black steed appears, with whom the knight must do combat. This defending champion is slain and the knight who slays him marries his wife and rules over his country. But he must defend the fountain, as did his predecessor, or his lady's right to the kingdom will lapse.

The story obviously contains certain elements of Celtic mythology. Within its compass we are confronted with the thunder-oak and the rain-making well. Is the Lady of the country a goddess or "Sacred Queen"? The combat of the knights under the tree appears as reminiscent of the strife between the priests at Aricia, the shrine of the "Golden Bough," or Nemi, in Italy, and if the interloper conquers the defender, he weds the Queen, or goddess, a proceeding which seems to have been carried out in the ancient ritual connected with the King and Queen of the May, as in that of "Robin Hood." The tale appears to contain some of the factors of the Divine King myth as well as those of the sacred oak and fountain. The fountain seems reminiscent of the shrine of Zeus at Dodona, with its oak tree and sacred spring, its oracular birds and iron basin.[82] Indeed, the resemblance seems too close to be a matter of chance.

DRUIDIC RITUAL

Apart from the subject of sacrifice, which will be dealt with in the following chapter, objective information concerning Druidic ritual is somewhat hard to come by. We find that a rite resembling baptism was performed by the Druids in Ireland. Thus it is said of Conall Cernach that when he was born, "Druids came to baptize the child into heathenism, and they sang the heathen baptism over him." When twins were born to two families, a pair of boys and a pair of girls, the boys were baptized first and later the girls, by the Druids, who acted as officiating priests and duly named the children. Ailill, the husband of the famous Medb, was "baptized in Druidic streams."[**] Druids also seem to have officiated at burials in Ireland. The Druid Dergdamsa recited a funeral oration over the hero Mog-neid, buried him with his arms and chanted a magical rhyme over him, and it seems probable that the Druid priesthood also carried out sacrifices at the grave on such occasions, as for example, at the burial of Fiachin, when fifty hostages were buried alive and the death-dirge was chanted by a bard. "The Druidic or other sacred ceremonies" and funeral games, says O'Curry's editor, "appear to have been included under the collective name of *Nosad*."[**]

DRUIDIC PHILOSOPHY

Doubtless a great deal of extravagance has been indulged in by those writers who made the loftiest claims on behalf of Druidic philosophy. In all likelihood, however, Druidic doctrine was of not less distinction than the thought of Egypt or of Babylonia in the earlier phases of these civilizations, which is not according it a very high position.

The curiosity of Roman freethinkers was aroused by the discovery that the barbarians of Gaul entertained the doctrine of immortality, and probably the intense earnestness of the Druidic caste impressed Cæsar, himself a priest, and indeed Pontifex Maximus in the honorary sense. Their somewhat theatrical anathemas also appear to have scared the Roman men-at-arms, when they confronted them in Anglesea. Indeed, the rather blasé Roman of the last century B.C. felt that he was the spectator of a cultus which must have closely resembled that of his own more simple forefathers and the latent sense of virtue, never to be sought for in vain among the best Roman minds, was probably stirred and quickened by the austere habits and bearing of the Druids with whom they came in contact, until at last the seemingly grotesque magical ideas and fetishistic practices which underlay Druidic "thought" came to be recognized. The ghastly sacrificial system appears to have disgusted Italian sentiment, which properly regarded it as unhealthy and abhorrent. Later, I shall deal more particularly with the theory that certain Druidic ideas had their origin in the Pythagorean philosophy. Here I am concerned merely with the content and nature of Druidic thought, or "philosophy" or theology in general.

In his homily on Ezekiel, Origen, the Christian apologist, who flourished in the third century, remarked that the people of Britain had "worshipped the one God" "previous to the coming of Christ," and in his Commentary on the same book, he says that the island "had long been predisposed to Christianity through the doctrines of the Druids and the Buddhists, who had already inculcated the doctrine of the unity of the Godhead." But although it seems probable that the Druidic system had originally been confined to the worship of one god, that of the sacred oak, we are confronted by a good deal of evidence that other gods, those of the

Celtic pantheon, in fact, were also recognized, if not adored by it. The probability seems to be that Druidism, originally the cult of the god of the oak tree, adopted in the course of its existence a great deal of mythical material concerning other deities. Probably those belonged to the general stock of European nature-gods, as their resemblance to Italic, Greek, Teutonic and Slavonic deities appears to bear out, and we seem to be left with the general impression that the original Druidic cult of the oak came to terms with other prevailing cults, as was the case in Greece, Rome and Germany, but that it still maintained a predominance in the national or tribal worship in certain parts of Gaul, which the oak-worship of Greece and Rome had not succeeded in attaining. The philosophy of Druidism, the spirit which animated it, can, in my opinion, only be surmised from a general review of its history and practice, and this, it seems to me, reveals it as a system in which a mass of myth, magical lore and taboo was slowly being formed into a "wisdom-religion" somewhat resembling that of the early Semites, or that of the "Aryans" of India, and which was beginning to entertain views of a moral character derived chiefly from the circumstances of taboo, distinguishing *fas* and *nefas*, dividing right and wrong, into what was "lawful" and "not lawful." The *geasa*, or taboos, which surrounded the Irish kings seem to reveal such a gradual process.

And as Diogenes Lærtius tells us, the Druids inculcated the observation of a rough general maxim: "to worship the gods, to do no evil, and to exercise courage"—enough, indeed, for a race of men existing in a condition of almost primeval simplicity. It is held in some quarters that the Welsh Triads embrace in their obscure numbers much of the ancient Druidic philosophy and belief. But it is difficult to credit that the remains of a system which had been abolished and evidently extirpated at least seven centuries before the earliest of the Triads was composed could have survived such a passage of time. In any case, the necessity of proof lies with those who infer such survival, and their endeavours to make good their claims impress me as being of about as much value as the reasoning by which their opponents seek to denounce them.

Classical writers speak well of the integrity of the Druidic caste. "The Druids," says Strabo, "are considered the most just of men." "They are of much sincerity and integrity," says Diodorus Siculus, "far from the craft and knavery of men among us, contented with homely fare, strangers to excess and luxury." Where such strict discipline was maintained, it could scarcely have been otherwise, and the circumstance that the Druids were not a celibate priesthood must certainly have helped to maintain a high standard of personal morality among them.

Chapter VII

IDEAS CONCERNING THE AFTER-LIFE, FESTIVALS AND SACRIFICE

A DEEPLY rooted belief exists, not only in the ranks of wayfaring men, but in the mind of a certain type of scholar, that the Druidic caste entertained a belief in the Pythagorean doctrine which held that the souls of men after death entered other bodies either human or animal, as an expiation for their shortcomings during life. This belief is founded on a passage in the fourteenth chapter of the Sixth Book of Cæsar's *Gallic War*, which runs as follows: "They (the Druids) wish to inculcate this as one of their leading tenets, that souls do not become extinct, but pass after death from one body to another, and they think that men by this tenet are in a great degree excited to valour, the fear of death being disregarded." Cæsar does not mention what kind of body the dispossessed spirit passes into, but it could hardly be other than human, having regard to the remainder of his statement.

Diodorus, writing of the Gauls, says that "the Pythagorean doctrine prevails among them, teaching that the souls of men are immortal and live again for a fixed number of years inhabited in another body."[1] Strabo avers that the Druids, and "others as well," "say that men's souls, and also the universe, are indestructible, although both fire and water will at some time or other prevail over them."[2] Pomponius Mela states of the Druids that: "one of their dogmas has come to common knowledge, namely, that souls are eternal and that there is another life in the infernal regions, and this has been permitted manifestly because it makes the multitude readier for war. And it is for this reason that they burn or bury with their dead things appropriate to them in life, and that in times past they even used to defer the completion of business and the payment of debts until their arrival in another world. Indeed there were some of them who flung themselves willingly on the funeral piles of their relatives in order to share the new life with them."[3]

Pomponius here says nothing respecting reincarnation. He is, of course, mistaken in his view that the belief in immortality had been invented by the Druids to encourage the valour of the Gauls and that as a consequence they buried their goods with the dead, as this practice had certainly been in vogue for thousands of years prior to the Roman conquest of Gaul.

The legend, for it is little more, that the Pythagorean doctrine of metempsychosis accepted, though by no means invented by Pythagoras, was a Druidic article of faith seems to have gained a fairly wide currency in the classical world. It appears to have been circulated by Timagenes, in the days of Pompey and Augustus, and is copied from his lost writings in the works of Ammianus Marcellinus, who flourished in the fourth century A.D., and who describes the Druids as "members of the intimate fellowship of the Pythagorean faith."⁴ About a century before Ammianus, Hippolytus circulated a story to the effect that one Zomolxis, a slave of Pythagoras, had journeyed in Gaul, and had inculcated the doctrines of his master among the Druids.⁵ Clement of Alexandria also states that Pythagoras had been in touch with the Celts, who had known his philosophy before it was disseminated in Greece.⁶ Valerius Maximus, who flourished in the early part of the first century, also remarks that one might laugh at the notion of the Gauls that the souls of men are immortal "were it not for the fact that what these trousered barbarians believe is the very faith of Greek Pythagoras himself."⁷

The Zomolxis alluded to by Hippolytus is mentioned by Herodotus, who flourished in the fifth century B.C., as a god of the Getæ, a people of Thrace, and his mythological character seems undoubted. He is mixed up with a strange story of resurrection, and it was probably this which identified him with the notion of immortality.⁸ In any case, the Getæ folk themselves laid claim to immortality, and all this may have connected their god in the mind of the ancients with Pythagoras and his idea.

The doctrine of metempsychosis was known in India and elsewhere ages before the time of Pythagoras, who lived in the sixth century B.C. and who believed that men's souls at death entered new bodies, either human or animal, as an expiation for their sins during life. Proof is utterly lacking that Pythagoras was ever in touch with the Celtic world. The whole question of the transmission of religious and eschatological ideas from Greece to the Celtic peoples was discussed with much erudition by the late Mr. Alfred Nutt in his *Voyage of Bran*, wherein he potently argued the possibility of early Celtic, and particularly Irish Celtic borrowings from Greek philosophical ideas respecting transmigration. That Pythagorean or Orphic ideas found their way to early Ireland seems beyond question. But that they were received there in any manner implying an intellectual acceptance or indeed with anything but the most confused mental recognition, seems to me highly improbable.

Rice Holmes thought it not unlikely that Druidism may have absorbed Pythagorean tenets through the medium of the Greeks of Marseilles, but he thought its hold upon the Celts must have been slight, as their notion of a future life was a form of the "Continuance Theory," an existence in an Elysium of the West, where they lived much as they had done in the world, only without the drawbacks of human anxiety.⁹ But as Kendrick has indicated, it is doubtful whether Pythagoreanism in its original state ever spread far afield outside a limited world of educated Greeks, so exclusive was it and so unlikely to be paraded before barbarians. Nor as an active cult was it long-lived, having arisen in the sixth century B.C. and being suppressed in the following century.¹⁰

Professor Anwyl drew near the heart of the argument when he wrote: "The prominent feature of their (the Druids') teaching which had attracted the attention of other writers, such as the historian Diodorus Siculus and the Christian theologian Clement of Alexandria, was the resemblance of their doctrine concerning the immortality and transmigration of the soul to the views of Pythagoras. Ancient writers, however, did not always remember that a religious or philosophical doctrine must not be treated as a thing apart, but must be interpreted in its whole context in relation to its development in history and in the social life of the community in which it has flourished. To some of the ancients the superficial resemblance between the Druidic doctrine of the soul's future and the teaching attributed to Pythagoras was the essential point and this was enough to give the Druids a reputation for philosophy."[11]

Nor are the resemblances betwixt the Pythagorean and Celtic ideas of reincarnation so remarkable as to invite any theory of the origin of the second from the first. The notion of repaying debts after death, or that associated with the burning or the burying of articles of personal use at a funeral, such as Pomponius Mela tells us the Gauls entertained (to separate these from the other elements of the Celtic idea of immortality) are not in unison with the Pythagorean idea of reincarnation. These Gaulish customs are eloquent of a belief in the immortality of the individual, and his continued identity, whereas Pythagoreanism posits a change into a different body, human or animal. The thought of a secondary existence of expiation did not enter into the Gaulish belief. The theory that Pythagoras received his ideas of reincarnation from Celtic sources is even more fantastic. In short, the Romans would appear to have "combined their information" concerning Hellenic and Celtic notions of rebirth. The conception of reincarnation was novel to them, it was credited by both Greeks and Celts, *ergo* the beliefs of Greeks and Celts regarding it must "naturally" have had a common origin!

Celtic notions respecting reincarnation were dissimilar to the Pythagorean doctrine. "Irish literature," said Sir John Rhys, "preserves traces of a belief in the reappearance of an ancestor in the person of a descendant: in other words, the same person or soul might be expected to appear successively in different bodies."[12] Indeed this belief is identical with that alluded to by Lucan in his *Pharsalia* (I, 450–8) in which he apostrophizes the Druids, saying that they hold that "the same spirit has a body again elsewhere." Wentz remarks that "there was also a belief, probably widespread, among the ancient Irish that divine personages, national heroes who are members of the Tuatha Dé Danann, or *sidhe* race, and great men, can be reincarnated; that is to say, can descend to this plane of existence and be as mortals more than once."[13] The same conclusion was reached by Miss Eleanor Hull, who, writing on the Cuchullin cycle of Irish literature, stated that: "There is no doubt that all the chief personages of this cycle were regarded as the direct descendants, or, it would be more correct to say, as avatars or reincarnations of the early gods . . . there are indications in the birth-stories of nearly all the principal personages that they are looked upon simply as divine beings reborn on the human plane of life."

Dr. Douglas Hyde, another authority of standing on the subject of Celtic belief, has given it as his opinion that there is abundance of evidence to show that the doctrine of reincarnation was familiar to the pagan Irish. But he holds that there is no literary testimony that the belief was ever "elevated into a philosophical doctrine of general acceptance, applicable to everyone," and that there was "no ethical stress laid on the belief in rebirth"—that is it was not regarded as an expiation of one's sins, as in the case of the Pythagorean system of belief. As it has come down to us, thinks Dr. Hyde, we find that the pagan Irish believed that *supernatural beings* could become clothed in flesh and blood, could enter into women and be born again, could take various shapes and pass through different stages of existence as birds, animals or men.[14]

Sir John Rhys and George Henderson indicate that vestiges of this belief survive in Wales and Scotland, particularly as regards the importance of the custom of calling a child after some deceased ancestor. This, in the Highlands, was known as *togail an ainm*, or "raising the name."

But the belief in reincarnation is by no means exclusively Celtic. As Hartland says: "Among many savage peoples the son is regarded as identical with his father, in a sense at least . . . And traces that the child is the reappearance of an ancestor are to be found all over the world." He cites numerous instances of this idea among barbarous races.[15]

Celtic legend, Irish and British, reveals a few cases of the transmigration of souls. One of the most striking of these is the story of Tuan Mac-Carell, a man of Ulster, with whom St. Finnen is said to have forgathered about the middle of the sixth century. The ancient warrior unfolded to the saint the tale of his many previous existences. He spoke of the five invasions of Ireland, of how he had, as a man, been saved from the plague which had attacked the primitive tribe of which Partholan was the leader. In that stage of existence he reached extreme old age, dwelling in waste places and growing almost bestial in appearance. He beheld the Nemedians take possession of the island, but kept away from them. One evening he fell asleep as usual and awoke in the form of a stag, in which shape he was the leader of the herds of Ireland. When the Nemedians perished in their turn, he became a wild boar. Some time after the settlement of Semion and his folk, the progenitors of the Firbolgs, Tuan was metamorphozed into a vulture or eagle—he does not appear to be quite certain which—and during the régime of Beothach, the remote ancestor of the Tuatha Dé Danann, he retained that form. The Milesian Celts then entered the island and during this epoch Tuan became a salmon. After avoiding the nets of fishermen for many days, he was at last caught and taken to the wife of Carell, the Queen of Ireland, who ate him whole. She conceived him as a child and he was reborn of her in the body in which he encountered St. Finnen.[16]

Somewhat different was the process by which the hero Cuchullin, who is obviously the son of the sun-god, and therefore a later avatar of that deity, reached the terrestrial sphere. His mother, Dechtire, was about to be wed to the chieftain Sualtam, and was seated at the wedding feast when a fly fell into her wine-cup. She swallowed the insect at the next draught, and shortly afterwards fell into a profound sleep, in which the sun-god Lugh appeared to her and informed her that it was he whom she had swallowed. He then transformed her, along with fifty of her maidens, into bird-shape. Later her infant was revealed to the men of Dechtire's brother, Conchobar, and was taken to Ulster.[17]

But before parting with Cuchullin I should mention that we discover another reference to that hero which is concerned with the belief in reincarnation. We are told that when he had reached manhood he was yet unmarried. The warriors of Ulster, anxious that he should have an heir, urged him to take a wife, assuring him "that his rebirth would be of himself"—that is, that the son of his body would be in a sense his own reincarnation.[18]

Mongan, King of Ulster, who seems to have been an historical personage, was believed to be the avatar of a god. The Irish annals speak of him as having been slain by a Briton named Arthur, son of Bicur, in the year 625. In another account he is alluded to as a reincarnation of the ancient hero Finn Mac Coul, the chief figure in the Ossianic cycle of legend, who is said to have flourished in the third century. Confusion may have crept in here, or perhaps two separate rebirths are indicated.[19]

We learn, too, in the tale of "The Generation of the two Swineherds," that the bulls alluded to in the great saga of "The Cattle Raid of Cooley," which brought such disastrous consequences to Ireland, had formerly been swineherds respectively belonging to Bodh, King of the *sidhe*, or gods, of Munster, and Ochall, King of the *sidhe* of Connaught. They had successively taken the shapes of two ravens, two sea-monsters, two warriors, two demons, two worms, and, finally, two bulls.[20]

Etain, the surpassingly beautiful wife of Mider, a god of the Irish Otherworld, was also the subject of a tale of reincarnation. Carried off by Angus, the divinity of Love and Youth, from her husband, she was imprisoned in a magical bower of glass, but was freed by a rival lady, who, out of spite, changed her into a fly, in which form she fell into the golden ale-cup of the wife of Etair, one of the vassals of Conchobar, and was reborn as that lady's daughter. In this form she remarried. But Mider was resolved upon her restoration, and by beating Etain's husband, Eochaid, at chess, regained her for himself.[21]

If we turn to the legends of Wales for instances of reincarnation we certainly do not find them so much in evidence, yet they are none the less enlightening. For instance, the manner in which the bard Taliesin was reborn of the goddess Ceridwen. In the tale which refers to him in the *Mabinogion*, Taliesin sings of his adventures in answer to King Maelgwn, who asks him who or what he is. His original country, he says, is the region of the summer stars. Idno and Heinin called him Merddin. "At length every king will call me Taliesin." He was with his lord in the highest sphere, on the fall of Lucifer into hell. He had borne a banner under Alexander of Macedon. He was in the Galaxy at the throne of the Distributor. He conveyed the divine Spirit to the level of the Vale of Hebron. He had been at the Tower of Babel, and with Noah in the Ark, with Moses, Mary, and other celebrities of Christian story. He was Gwion Bach, bard to Lleon of Lochlin, at the court of Cynvelyn, and would be in the world until the day of doom. It was not known whether his body was flesh or fish.[11] Other shapes assumed by him included a sword-blade, a drop in the air, a star, a word in a book, a bridge, an eagle, a boat on the sea, the string of a harp, the foam of water. "There is nothing in which I have not been," he finally exclaimed.

If we try to identify the types of the several Celtic reincarnation stories we have just perused, we find that the first, that of Tuan Mac Carell, is an account of simple transmigration from a human body through stages of brute form into human shape once more. Etain and Cuchullin, again, assume insect form and are then reborn, and much the same may be said of Taliesin, whose metamorphoses through animal shapes in his flight from Ceridwen resemble the transformations of magical shape-shifting rather than the "avatars" of a soul taking up its residence in a series of bodies. I may add that this particular passage recalls the circumstances of the ballad of Tamlane, which I have criticized elsewhere. I should also indicate that the fly-shape assumed by Etain and Cuchullin is a well-known form frequently taken by the soul in folk-lore, more especially in the Balkans and in the case of vampires.

But in the allusion to Cuchullin's marriage we seem to have a direct reference to the belief that the son of a god or supernatural hero was actually none other than that hero in a secondary form, a distinct projection of him, and that it was thought possible that the son of a god could assume a form identical with that of his father and function in the same manner. Indeed, in Irish myth we discover so many instances of this process, particularly in the case of the sun-god, that it has frequently puzzled students of mythology to account for a plurality of sun-gods—a phenomenon with which we meet also in Greek myth and other religious systems. The story of Mongan, again, is one where transmigration appears to take place after the lapse of centuries. The second story of Taliesin's various transmigrations is almost certainly of late origin and reveals alien and imported ideas.

Now as regards these metamorphoses, some are assumed by a well-known folk-lore process of change: that is, first into animal and then again into human shape, while others presume the projection by a sun-god, through the process of birth, of a filial image of himself, ideas, as we shall see, associated with the institution known as "the Divine King."

In these myths we encounter both a tradition associated with the lower cultus and a belief connected with the cult of a solar divinity. But be it specially remarked that most of them are narrated of personages who in one way or another are connected with a solar cult and are, moreover, of royal race—if we except the egregious instance of the swineherds of the rival *sidhe* rulers, who, after all, have a royal association, if it be a remote one.

Perhaps D'Arbois de Jubainville sums up the case for Celtic reincarnation more appropriately than any writer who has approached it. After drawing attention to the fact that at least *two forms of reincarnation* are alluded to in Irish myth, that as found expressed in the story of Etain and that to be observed in the tale of Finn, reborn as Mongan, he describes the first as an example of *divine reincarnation*, and the second as a story of *transmigration*. But the stories of Finn and Tuan MacCarell, he points out, are exceptions to the rule in ancient Irish literature, wherein "it is not usual for the dead to be born a second time." This kind of transmigration, he continues, may have a certain likeness to that of the Pythagorean doctrine, but it is not identical with it. In the code of the Greek philosopher transmigration into the bodies of men or animals is the wages of sin. It is not so in the Celtic system. Tuan and Finn experienced it because they were exceptional. In Celtic doctrine men after death find "in another world the life and new body which their religion holds out to them." And wherefore were Tuan and Finn exceptional? Simply because the composers of the Irish sagas wished to use them as mouthpieces who would, through the circumstances of a reincarnation story, describe the early mythical history of Ireland, and so justify their chronology and statements concerning that history as eye-witnesses of the several invasions of Erin, and so forth.[13]

I think that D'Arbois is justified in his general conclusion, although I feel he has put the cart before the horse, the tale of Etain being obviously a transmigration story, while that of Finn is one of reincarnation. "Transmigration" myths are the exception which prove the general Celtic rule that it was only individuals of divine or royal origin who underwent *reincarnation*. The Egyptian equivalent circumstance that only the Pharaoh had such an experience practically clinches the matter and reveals that the theory of the Divine Kingship was associated with both the Egyptian and Celtic ideas of reincarnation as apart from the Pythagorean view.

But—for the science of myth bristles with that preposition, and here I may say I do not quote the French Celticist—in later Egyptian belief the idea came into force that most people, if not all, might undergo reincarnation. This belief was certainly an extension of the idea of the pharaonic process of reincarnation. Because the Pharaoh underwent the process, so might or must, the wealthy and powerful. And that such a process also took place in ancient Ireland we know. For, when the divine race of the Tuatha Dé Danann was dispossessed of its godlike status and was reduced to the condition of mere fairyhood, dwelling in the mounds and raths, *reincarnation became its general lot*. The *sidhe*, or fairies, the "dead" god-kings, came to be regarded as the spirits of the dead awaiting reincarnation in human bodies, reincarnating, indeed, again and yet again. What had been thought of as happening in the case of the king-gods now happened to all as the dead. I have frequently described the process, and need not do so again in these pages.[14] In this sense, then, we are justified in saying that reincarnation came to be a later general belief among the Celts, though in such a form it certainly did not partake of the Hellenic idea of an expiatory process. And, indeed, it was almost certainly a recrudescence of a much older and more primitive native doctrine. It is, I think, associated with that alluded to by Diodorus, and by Lucan and Cæsar. The statement of Valerius Maximus, it has not yet been made clear, is obviously erroneous. He confuses the Celtic idea of immortality, pure and simple, with that of Pythagoreanism, as is very plain.

It would seem, then, that the Pythagorean origin of Celtic and Druidic ideas respecting reincarnation cannot be upheld and that among the Celtic peoples it arose out of primitive notions concerning the secular return of the spirits formerly inhabiting human bodies into those of newly-born children, such as obtains to-day among some of the native tribes of Australia and elsewhere. That is, the spirit of the ancestor, on the alert to return to the human sphere, enters the body of a woman as she passes its haunt and ensouls her unborn infant.[15] These Australian spirits so closely resemble the *sidhe* or fairies, or mound-spirits of the Celtic peoples as to permit of no question that the belief concerning them originated in an entirely similar train of primitive thought.

This is the authentic type of Celtic belief in the reincarnation of souls, and those instances of it of which we read in Irish and Brythonic myth are merely late and confused versions of the primal doctrine concerning the "facts" of reincarnation. But such beliefs were obviously powerfully affected by notions regarding the reincarnation of kings induced by the doctrine of the Divine King, which may have existed contemporaneously with the original Celtic idea of rebirth, or have been influenced by it at a later period as we conceive it as one of equally ancient acceptance by the Celts or as a more novel introduction. The idea of the reincarnation of the Divine King can only have arisen by virtue of the tenet that he is the son of a solar deity, and it is thus manifestly due to the notion of the rebirth of a "new sun," projected from the "old sun." The king, son of the sun, was therefore also "projected" from his father, the older king, as was the sun.

The conception of the reincarnation of the ancestor by his ensoulment of an unborn child may, perhaps, have originated in the solar myth. The latter appears to have been entertained in respect of Celtic royalty, the former concerned the general commonalty. But, as was inevitable, the two notions became confused to some extent, though it is equally clear that the conception of royal transmigration was separately maintained in a sense, and recurs from time to time in Celtic story as explanatory of the reappearance of certain monarchs and heroes.

THE DRUIDS AND THE CELTIC FESTIVALS

It is essential that the question of the association of the Druids with the several Celtic festivals should be discussed with care. If it can be proved that the Druids officiated at these festivals or were in any way connected with them, it not only shows that their status as a priesthood was no merely fallacious notion of the eighteenth century, but that it was indeed identical with Celtic religious practice itself.

As in the case of Mexican and other primitive time-systems, it is easy to see that the Celtic year was in the first instance regulated by the solar round and not by a calendar-system composed by reference to the seasons. Indeed, as Rhys remarks, it was "more thermometric than astronomical," that is, more related to the incidence of actual solar heat than to the solstices and equinoxes induced by solar movement. The calendar, or time-count, again, as far as it is known to us, seems to have been devised on a lunar basis, and time was measured by the moon. It is probable that, as in the case of the Mexican calendar, the lunar round was the elder and that attempts were made to adapt it to solar time measurement.

There were three outstanding festivals, *Samhain*, that is Hallowe'en, held on November 1st; *Beallteinn*, or Beltane, on May 1st, and *Lugnassad*, on August 1st. Midsummer day was also observed, and its ritual is obviously the same as that celebrated by other European peoples at this date; but in later times it came to be confused with *Beallteinn*. The Celtic year began with *Samhain*, when "the powers of blight were beginning their period of ascendancy, yet the future triumph of the powers of growth was not forgotten."[16] Originally it seems to have been a harvest festival, associated perhaps with threshing rather than the cutting of the grain. On the introduction of Christianity, *Samhain* was certainly confused with Yule or Christmas, and some of its rites were transferred to Yuletide.

It would be little to the purpose to describe and explain the rites and ceremonies of these festivals other than in a summary manner, as they have already been explained by more than one able writer.[17] In any case, what I am most concerned with presently is the question of Druidic association with them. The outstanding feature of *Samhain* was the burning of a great bonfire. The old fires were discarded with the old year, and the domestic hearth was replenished from the new sacred flame. But *Samhain* was also a festival of the dead, whose spirits at this season were thought of as scouring the countryside, causing dread to the folk at large. To expel them from the fields and the precincts of villages, lighted brands from the bonfire were carried round the district. Animals were slaughtered for winter consumption and their flesh "salted down." There are traces of sacrificial custom in this act, as in Ireland a beast was offered up at this season to St. Martin, who in this connection is rather obviously confounded with an ancient deity whose "fair" or "market" (Gaelic *malairt*) was held at the beginning of November, festivals of all kinds being associated among the Celts with large fairs for the barter or exchange of goods.[18] Indeed, this festival came in Christian times to be known as "Martinmas," and in the Highlands of Scotland the cow, or ox, slaughtered at this time for family provender was until recently known as "the mart-beast."

Samhain, in a word, was the old winter festival of the Celts, held on the approach of winter, when divinations for the fate of the individual throughout the new year were engaged in. In ancient Ireland, the great assembly or parliament of the provinces was held at Tara on this date with much solemnity. A sacrifice was offered up to the gods at Tlachtga, in Meath, "at which it was the custom to assemble the Druids of Ireland on the eve of *Samhain* to offer sacrifice to the gods. At that fire they used to burn their victims."[19] Tuathd, an Irish king, we are told, ordered a fire to be kindled annually on the eve of *Samhain* at Tlachtga for the purpose of summoning the Druids to consume the sacrifices offered up to the gods. It was said that on November 1st the Druids sacrificed a black sheep and offered libations to the spirits of those who had died during the year.[20]

The festival of *Beallteinn*, a name which, according to Cormac's *Glossary*, implies "a goodly fire," was intended to promote fertility. "On this occasion," says Keating, "they (the Druids), were used to kindle two fires in every territory in the kingdom" in honour of the pagan god Beul. Cattle were driven between these fires as a preservation against the murrain. In the *Tripartite Life of St. Patrick* it is mentioned that the *Beallteinn* fire could be lit by the chief Druid only. A fair for the barter of goods was held at this time.[21] Sometimes the *Beallteinn* fire was kindled beneath a sacred tree, or a pole covered with greenery was surrounded by the fuel, or a tree was burned in the fire. This suggests the survival of the burning of the oak, already alluded to as a part of ancient tree-worship. One of the spots where this rite appears to have taken place in Ireland was Cloghaunnatinny, in Clare, which is still known as Clochin-bilé-teine, "the stepping-stones of the fire-tree," from a large tree under which May fires used to be lighted, while another was situated at a place called Creeve, in Westmeath.[22]

In Scotland in the eighteenth century a cake or "caudle" (custard) was made and cut up, and a portion of it blackened or burnt. He who received this piece was known as "the Beltane carle," or "the devoted," and he had to leap through the Beltane fire three times. During the festival he was spoken of as "dead." The whole proceeding is racy of the symbolic survival of human sacrifice by burning, such as the Druids were wont to celebrate, according to Cæsar and Strabo.

The Maytime revels exhibit traces of Druidic belief. The May King and Queen, and Robin Hood and Maid Marian, represent earlier tree-spirits who were regarded as embodying the powers of vegetation and fertility at this festival. Their marriage and union were believed to magically assist growth and fertility, as did that of Zeus with the Oak Queen and that of the Irish kings with the woman known as "the Sovereignty of Ireland," later to be described. I must not press analogy too far, or I might adduce many instances of folk-lore practice which seem to support the theory of the survival of Druidic seasonal rites. But I do not wish to include any rite or custom which does not reveal a quite distinct trace of Druidic association, for indeed this kind of licence is frequently more damaging than otherwise, and certain writers on the subject have employed it more extravagantly than prudently.

Having identified *Samhain* and *Beallteinn* with Druidic practice and rite, is it possible to effect similar proofs of the association with the festival of *Lugnassad*? This festival, held on August 1st, was celebrated at Tailltenn in Ireland in honour of the sun-god Lugh, just as the Gauls had met at Lugudunum, or Lyons, to do homage to his Continental equivalent, Lugus. Lug was the god of light and knowledge. Cormac explains the *Lugnassad* as a festival of Lugh, while the "Rennes Dind-senchas" explains it by the statement that Lug established it in memory of his foster-mother Tailltiu, who died on that day and whose demise was thus annually recalled. The festival is, indeed, closely associated with the cult of the dead, and of the "dead" or "dying" sun of summer, when magical devices were employed to ensure the sun-god's existence for another year. Games were held as at Olympia, in Greece, wrestling, horse-racing and so forth, and it has been assumed that the intention underlying these was to select "one who for a year should be a god on earth," as in the Olympic Games. It may be so, but elsewhere I have endeavoured to make it clear that the emanations of physical strength and effort put forth in such games were regarded as giving new strength to the god of the place (in this case the sun-god), enervated and weakened by his labours during the year that was past.[13] The celebration of the *Lugnassad*, we are told, had a distinct bearing upon the yield of corn, fruit, milk and fish throughout Ireland, and evil results would follow if its rites were neglected.[14] Marriages on a popular scale formed a special feature of the fair which followed the festival, and the phrase "A Tailltenn marriage" is still used in Ireland as signifying a hasty or casual union.[15]

Tailltiu, in whose honour the Tailltenn games were founded, seems to have been a goddess resembling the Greek Kore, or Ceres, a spirit of fruitfulness, a nourisher of both men and gods. Indeed, Tailltiu seems to have been an old goddess of the soil. In this rite she was associated with her "foster-son" Lug, the sun-god, after whom, indeed, the festival was named. The myth about her was probably "explanatory" to account for the acceptance of the god of a solar cult within the ritual of a grain-goddess. But *Lugnassad* means "the marriage of Lug," for at this ceremony he was supposed to take the land of Ireland as a bride, to wed the kingdom itself. This circumstance was actually made clear by the god

Lug himself to King Conn of the Hundred Battles *and his Druid* on one occasion when, overtaken by a magical mist, they entered a glorious mansion and beheld, seated on thrones, the god Lug himself and a beauteous princess crowned with a golden diadem, whom the deity introduced as "the Sovereignty of Erin till the day of doom." She was indeed the immortal bride of Lugh, and she appears to have been ritually married to him at the *Lugnassad*, the annual festival of the newly-risen sun.

The earthly monarch of all Ireland was regarded as the worldly representative of Lug and was, judging from the evidence, literally married to this goddess-consort, or to a woman symbolizing her, in his character of the god Lug on earth, as were the kings of Rome to a goddess of vegetation, the intention being, as we shall see when we come to discuss the subject of the Divine King, that such a union would consummate the connection between him as Son of the Sun and the Lady Erin as the representative of the soil, so that the land of Ireland might yield plentifully as a result of their combined connubial and deific might.[36] The idea of the existence of a potent essence in the oak, which made for a heavy crop of acorns, was passed on to the later agricultural régime and, like Jupiter, originally a deity of the oak, its god became a god of agriculture. The oak was the reservoir of the fire which fed the sun, as Frazer remarks, therefore it had a solar connection.

The association of a Druid with King Conn in his explanatory interview with the god Lug,[37] seems to make it plain that the Druids were connected with that deity, and therefore with the festival of the *Lugnassad*. And, as Professor Macalister indicates, the assembly at Tailltenn, and other Irish gatherings of the kind, must have been of the same type as that held by the Druids of Gaul at Chartres of which Cæsar wrote.[38] We know that the coronation ceremony of the kings of Ireland had Druidic implications. It seems to stand to reason, therefore, that the ceremony at Tailltenn, which was so closely connected with the kingship, was also under express Druidic supervision. The topic of "the Sovereignty of Erin" survived in ancient English and Scots literature and folk-lore, as I have shown in the work referred to under note 33.

Mr. Kendrick has given it as his view that "an agreement between druidic observances and widespread Keltic customs is suggested by an examination of the pagan festival days that are still, or were until recently, celebrated in France and Great Britain by the lighting of bonfires and kindred demonstrations. . . . It is exceedingly interesting," he says, "to find that in Scotland and Ireland there are also instances of a very ancient tradition that the ceremonial fires were lit on ground associated with the druids, or actually by the druids themselves."[39] John Ramsay of Ochtertyre wrote in the eighteenth century of Beltane fires being lit on an artificial mound, surrounded by a low circular wall and surmounted by an upright stone, which was traditionally a site of Druidic worship.[40]

In Dartmoor, young men met on May 1st, or Beltane, at a menhir, or rough stone monument, selected a ram lamb from an adjacent flock, and after running it down, fastened it to the pillar and sacrificed it, after which they roasted it whole. The rite was followed by dancing and wrestling-matches and was known as "the Ram Feast."[41] We have already seen that the Druids sacrificed a sheep in the same manner.

The Scottish Highlanders nourished a superstition that the May sun gave them a new lease of life, until the next autumnal equinox. In Scotland the Lammas celebrations survived until last century as did those of the *Lugnassad* at Tailltenn at the same season. The rites of *Samhain* seem to have left their mark upon the harvest customs of Britain, although it is impossible at this great distance of time definitely to associate these survivals with Druidic practice. Higgins in his *Celtic Druids*, mainly an imaginative work, asserts on the authority of Hayman Rooke, that "so late as the year 1786 the custom of lighting fires was continued at the Druid Temple at Bramham, near Harrogate," on August 1st. *The Lanercost Chronicle* of the year 1268 alludes to a practice which "certain bestial persons, monks in garb, but not in mind," indulged in. They extracted fire from wood by friction, and set up a priapic idol to protect their cattle from disease. MacLauchlan, in his work *The Early Scottish Church*, remarks that "there are places in Scotland where, within the memory of living men, the *teine eigin*, or 'forced fire' was lighted once every year by the rubbing of two pieces of wood together, while every fire in the neighbourhood was extinguished in order that they might be lighted anew from this sacred source."

This, of course, is in consonance with what I have said regarding the re-lighting of domestic fires at *Samhain*. The *teine eigin* may indeed mean "the oaken fire." In Mull it was made by turning an *oaken* wheel over nine oaken spindles. Thus it seems to be associated with a cult of the oak and perhaps with the solar wheel of the Druid Mog Ruith, and we know that the Celtic Midsummer festival had wheel ceremonies. (E. Hull, *Folklore of the British Isles*, pp. 184–5.)

The association of the Druids with the seasonal festivals of the Celts is therefore pretty clearly demonstrated. As Mr. Kendrick remarks: "It is significant that the Druids of Ireland were servants of the primitive Keltic festival-system in its Central European form."[42] That the Druids of Gaul also filled a like office scarcely seems a matter of doubt. In Brittany, Midsummer Day, or St. John's Day, the Christian substitute for the old pagan festival was celebrated by the burning of Bel-fires round which the peasantry danced all night in their holiday attire to the strains of the *biniou*, or bagpipe. In many parishes the local Catholic priest went in procession to light the sacral fire, a brand of which, if placed in a house, preserved it from lightning, as did a piece of the Yule log (I. Taylor's translation of Villemarque's *Ballads and Songs of Brittany*). In June, the unmarried young people gathered round a dolmen, the lads sporting green ears of corn, the girls flowers of the flax. These were deposited on the dolmen and so long as they remained fresh, the affections of any given pair were thought to last. A dance round the dolmen was then engaged in, which was locally believed to have descended from the Druids. The rites of Maytime in modern France so closely resemble those of Britain as scarcely to be discernible from them.

We find Eligius, Bishop of Noyons (A.D. 640–685) imploring his hearers not to observe the month of May (the season of *Beallteinn*) or the pagan feast of St. John (Midsummer's Day). In Brittany St. John's Eve and Hallowe'en are still regarded as days sacred to the dead and feasts are celebrated thereon. (A. Le Braz, *Le Legende de la Mort*, XL, pp. 283–4.)

HUMAN SACRIFICE

Certain writers on Celtic history have indignantly denied that the Druidic caste ever practised the horrible rite of human sacrifice. There is no question, however, that practise it they did. Tacitus alludes to the fact that the Druids of Anglesea "covered their altars with the blood of captives." If the words of Cæsar are to be credited, human sacrifice was a frequent and common element in their religious procedure. He tells us that no sacrifice might be carried out except in the presence of a Druid. Those persons who suffered from painful diseases, or who found themselves in danger of their lives in the day of battle, made a vow that were their sufferings mitigated or their lives spared, they would sacrifice a human victim to the gods, making the Druids the *performers* of these sacrifices.[48] To this Cicero refers in his Oration for Fonteius as to a well-known fact, and the reader may be reminded that he had personally known the Æduan Druid Divitiacus, who had indeed been the guest of his brother Quintus Cicero. Cæsar adds that it was thought essential that the life of one man must be offered up to save another, and many illustrations of this practice are to be found in British folk-lore. In 1590, for example, Hector Munro, Baron of Fowlis, who was sick, was informed by a witch that "the principal man of his blood must die for him."

It is in this same passage in his *Commentaries* that Cæsar introduces the famous topic of the huge wicker-work images in which the Druids were said to burn scores of people alive. "Others," he says, "have figures of vast size, the limbs of which, formed of osiers, they fill with living men, which being set on fire, the men perish enveloped in the flames." Victims, he tells us, were mostly criminals, who were more pleasing to the gods, although when such were scarce the innocent were victimized in their places. Strabo avers that the greater the number of criminals sacrificed, the greater the yield from the land.[44] In a later passage Strabo tells us that the Druids "having devised a colossus of straw and wood, throw into the colossus cattle and wild animals and human beings, and then make a burnt-offering of the whole."[45]

That these holocausts were held at the spring festival of *Beallteinn* (May 1st) appears highly probable, and that they were thought to have had a definite effect upon the fertility of the soil is certain. In all likelihood at the original *Beallteinn* rite human victims were passed through the fire in order that they might furnish the sun-god with renewed power to carry on his arduous labours in respect of growth and fertility, as in ancient Mexico, where human sacrifice was believed to refresh the solar, rain and maize-gods. A similar rite at May-time seems to have been celebrated in nearly all parts of Europe. That such notions lingered on in England until a comparatively late date, is revealed by the circumstance that at the burning of the hapless Bishop Latimer in 1554, some of the barbarous onlookers were heard to remark that it was unfortunate that it had not taken place earlier in the season, as then it might have saved the crops! We are informed by Keating that the Irish Druids on the eve of *Samhain* burned their victims in the holy fire. (*History of Ireland*, Vol. II, pp. 133, 247, 251.)

In many parts of France until the eighteenth century, the local officials burned baskets filled with wolves, foxes, dogs and cats at the feast of St. John, that is Midsummer Day, June 24th. It has also been remarked that the Basques burn vipers in wicker panniers. The above custom prevailed at Paris until the beginning of the reign of Louis XIV." It seems to me that it could scarcely have been other than a popular survival of the ancient Druidic practice.

The circumstances connected with this abominable rite seem puzzling and contradictory. It would appear to be impossible to burn human beings in what seem to have been wicker-work cages, which themselves must have been highly inflammable unless they were put together from green withes, or osiers, which, on the other hand, would scarcely take fire readily. We must suppose that the unfortunate victims were bound hand and foot, otherwise their tortured writhings would quickly have set them free from the flimsy and fire-crumbled cages. The same applies even to the destruction of animals by this means. Were these "images" set upright, or laid flatwise on the soil? In any case, to be effective, the images must surely have been surrounded by large bundles of blazing firewood, to step into which would have meant destruction. The amount of coal and firing essential to a witch-burning in the middle-ages is usually reckoned by waggon-loads, as the contemporary accounts of these horrid proceedings reveal. To pursue such a subject is unpleasant, but I do so merely on behalf of accuracy and because this feature of Druidic practice has always appeared to me as obscure and highly confusing. I may add here that, in connection with a cairn in the parish of Latheron, in Caithness, legend avers that when the chief Druid of the district grew old and infirm, he was burnt alive on this altar, his successor circling the spot in order to watch his fleeting spirit. (M. MacPhail, *Folklore*, Vol. IX, p. 87.)

Diodorus Siculus alludes to another species of human sacrifice practised by the Druids. He says: "When they attempt divination upon important matters they practise a strange and incredible custom, for they kill a man by a knife-stab in the region above the midriff (diaphragm) and after his fall they foretell the future by the convulsions of his limbs and the pouring of his blood, a form of divination in which they have full confidence, as it is of old tradition."⁴⁷ Strabo, referring to this type of sacrifice for the requirements of auspices, states that the victim was slain by a sword-stroke in the back.⁴⁸ The former was the method employed in sacrifice in ancient Mexico.

Strabo also alludes, in the same passage, to the practice of shooting sacrificial victims to death with arrows. This is the only reference to such a method of immolation in connection with Druidic rite. It finds a curious parallel in ancient Mexican sacrifice. In connection with the rites of the god Xipe, the deity of seed-time and the planting of the maize, a captive was secured to a scaffold and shot at with darts, so that his blood might fall upon the ground. This usage may be regarded as of the nature of sympathetic magic to secure rainfall. The earth-goddess Tlazolteotl seems to have been regarded as the inventress of this especial mode of sacrifice. She and her sisters, the Ixcuiname, after they had invaded Mexico, says her myth, gathered together their war-captives and explained to them how they were to be disposed of, saying: "We wish to couple the earth with you, we desire to hold a feast with you, for till now no battle offerings have been made with men. We wish to make a beginning of it and shoot you to death with arrows." The late Professor Seler was of the opinion that the sacrifice was meant to symbolize a sexual connection between the victims and the earth-mother; but I prefer to think that it was intended to induce rainfall, rain being regarded by the ancient Mexicans as human blood transformed.⁴⁹ Some such ceremony, I believe, is hinted at in the legend of Robin Hood. In the reign of Henry VIII his festival was regarded as an archery shooting-match pure and simple.

But I feel that a more ancient rite associated with him ended with the sacrifice of a man who personified the forest spirit Robin of the Wood and who was despatched by a flight of arrows, symbolizing a shower of fertilizing rain, for in all parts of the world the primitive arrow of flint is the emblem of rain. And it is to be remarked that Robin Hood's legend avers that he "bled to death."⁵⁰ The same may perhaps be said of the legend of William Tell, and of that of Egil, brother of the mythical Velundr, in the Norse saga of Thidrick. There are also Finnish and Persian stories of the same kind.⁵¹ The legend of the martyrdom of St. Sebastian, who was shot to death with arrows, may have had its origin in some ceremony of the kind. "The Ostyaks are said never to have passed a sacred tree without shooting an arrow at it as a mark of respect."⁵² It seems to me more probable that they did so for the reason that the arrow symbolized rain and that they sought by the act to refresh the tree by means of sympathetic magic. I think it probable that the Druidic act of shooting a man to death by arrows holds the significance of a rite associated with the desire for rainfall.

Strabo mentions casually in the above-mentioned passage the horrid fact that the Druids were in the habit of impaling certain of their victims in their "temples." We should have heard no more of this particular abomination in classical writing had it not been for the allusion of Cassius Dio to the horrors perpetrated by Boadicea, Queen of the Iceni of Norfolk and Suffolk, when that injured but revengeful lady made the Romanized folk of Londonium pay all too dearly for the cruelties perpetrated upon her daughters and herself by the Roman tax-gatherers. Dio says: "They (the Iceni) hung up the noblest and most distinguished women . . . afterwards they impaled the women on sharp skewers run lengthwise through the entire body. All this they did to the accompaniment of sacrifices, banquets and wanton behaviour, not only in all their other sacred places, but particularly in the grove of Andraste. This was their name for Victory, and they regarded her with most exceptional reverence."[53]

Now nowhere, either in Dio's account of Boadicea's rising, or in the much more detailed record of it by Tacitus, the only classical narratives which deal with the rising of the British warrior queen, do we discover the slightest allusion to the Druids, save the passage concerning those whom Suetonius overthrew in Anglesea, to which I have already referred.

Indeed, before her last battle with the Romans, Boadicea appears to have acted as a priestess herself. Her "native" name "Boudicca," and that of her husband Prasutagus, are almost certainly Gallo-Brythonic in origin (though not necessarily Belgic) as was the general culture of their court near Norwich. As regards the name and functions of the goddess Andraste, to whom Dio says she offered up her wretched Romano-British victims, we have no positive information. The Vocontian Gauls of the south-east of ancient France (the modern Dauphiné) worshipped a goddess whose name was Andarta, which, like that of Andraste, was translated as "Victory" by the Romans. We also find the form "Tutela Boudiga" on a Gaulish altar discovered at Bordeaux, which was erected by a certain Marcus Aurelius Lunaris, a British soldier of the *coloniæ* of York and Lincoln in A.D. 231, to celebrate a prosperous voyage from York to Bordeaux. Professor Paul Courteault describes Tutela Boudiga as "the Phrygian Magna Mater, transformed under the Empire into a guardian goddess of the Cæsars and of the Roman arms" as a giver of victory.

He says that by this era the cult of the Great Mother had spread to Britain and had been assimilated in the native beliefs.[54] The matter, I feel, is one of coincidence, the British Queen and the Gallo-Phrygian divinity having been known by the same name, the word "Boudiga" in the case of the latter being merely an epithet. Nor does Courteault identify the Vocontian Andarta with the "Tutela Boudiga" of Bordeaux, though he indicates that their names had the same significance. But Andarta of the Vocontii was not identified with the Phrygian Mother until nearly a century after Boadicea's time. Boadicea, before her last battle, is represented as praying to Andraste for victory over the Romans. We may be fairly certain that the Vocontii lived under a Druidic dispensation, as there was a powerful Druidic centre not very far off, at Marseilles. If so,

Andarta, who was the chief divinity of the Vocontii, may well have been an especial object of Druidic adoration, and it would seem to follow that she might also have been a divinity of the British Druids, if any there were. In making these later remarks, I need scarcely observe to the reader that I am walking on the sands of surmise and not the soil of fact.

A method of the Irish Druids to promote fertility in vegetation appears to have been (according to traditional Irish writings) to mingle the blood of a slain victim with earth which bore no fruitful thing, and with withered trees. Such a course was advised by them when a blight fell upon Ireland consequent upon the ill-advised marriage of King Conn of the Hundred Battles with a fairy woman. But a cow was sacrificed in the victim's stead, a Christian interpolation in the text, possibly.[55] At Highland funerals in the old times the friends of the deceased fought until blood was drawn, the drawing of blood being held essential. This was most certainly a relic of the sacrifice of a human victim to the *manes* of the newly buried dead.[56]

M. A. Bertrand conceived the opinion that the Druids did not originate, but merely tolerated and sanctioned human sacrifice, which he believes to have been a survival of prehistoric times.[57] He remarks that it was unknown in Ireland—"the country pre-eminently Druidic"—but we have already seen that good proof of a tradition that it was practised there actually exists, as mentioned on this page and in discussing the festival of *Samhain*. The offering up of children to the idol Cromm Cruaich at Mag Slecht, however, cannot allude to Druidic procedure, as that stone was the chief feature of a stone circle, while the first account of the sacrifice in question derives from a period when Druidism could hardly have been an established force in Ireland.

That human victims were in primitive times sacrificed to the spirit of the divine oak tree seems more than probable. Speaking of the mistletoe rite, as described by Pliny, Canon J. A. MacCulloch remarks that "it must have had some other purpose than that of the magico-medical use which he describes, and though he says nothing of cutting down the tree or slaying a human victim, it is not unlikely that, as human sacrifice had been prohibited in his time (by the Romans) the oxen which were slain during the rite took the place of the latter."[58] At least an animal sacrifice was made to the oak.

Survivals of sacrifice to the sacred oak lingered in Europe until nearly the close of the middle ages. The chronicler Wilibald, writing in his *Vita Bonifaci*, of the adoration of a sacred oak at Geismar, near Fritzlar, in Hesse, tells us that at some time between the years A.D. 725 and 731, the people of Hesse sacrificed to this tree and drew omens from it, calling it "the Red Jove." First-fruits of the chase were hung on oaks by the heathen Thuringians and Saxons in the thirteenth century. To the Old Prussians the forest of Romove was the most sacred spot in the land. There stood their pagan images on a holy oak, hung with cloths. Such cloths or rags found at a spot once sacred are undoubtedly to be regarded as relics of ancient sacrifice, or "the substitution of the part for the whole," of a person's clothing for his body. The *Vita St. Germani of Autisio-dorensis*, written in the fifth century, reveals how widely the custom prevailed of hanging the heads of sacrificed animals on trees.⁵⁹ "Men," says Frazer, of the Lithuanians, "sacrificed to oak-trees for good crops . . . and in time of drought, when they wanted rain, they used to sacrifice a black heifer, a black he-goat and a black cock to the thunder-god . . . god of the oak."⁶⁰

At Loch Maree, the reputed shrine of the "saint" Mourie, also locally called "the god Mourie" (that is "Mo Righ," or "my king") is to be found a sacred well, near which stands an oak into the trunk of which visitors still drive nails and coins. To each nail was originally attached a piece of the clothing of each pilgrim who had visited the place—"substitution" tokens.⁶¹ The oak-leaf must have been regarded as a life-giver, as holding the essence of the tree's holy potency. The Romans considered a wreath of oak-leaves as the due of the military hero, and even to-day it figures in the insignia of British field-marshals.

SACRIFICES OF ANIMALS

The overwhelming nature of the evidence which reveals that cattle were "sacrificed" for one reason or another in Britain and Ireland until times comparatively recent, seems to make it positive that this practice must have descended from a very ancient and time-honoured custom, and as it corresponds with what we know of Druidic rite, it seems worthy of the closest consideration. In Carnarvonshire bullocks were offered up to St. Beyno even as late as the year 1589 and no one might cut the trees of his adjacent grove. Beyno's saintship is dubious. He is probably one and the same with the giant-god Benlli, the mythical parent of Beli, a horned British deity, the patron of cattle and perhaps the god who presided over the *Beallteinn* festival, or its "Welsh analogue." Benlli is almost certainly that "Robin the Bobbin, the big-bellied Ben," who, nursery rhyme informs us, "ate more meat than fourscore men," that is, he was a deity who "devoured" the cattle which were offered up to him in sacrifice.⁶²

Reginald of Durham tells us that in the year 1164, St. Aelred interfered in the sacrifice of a bull at Kirkcudbright. In the seventeenth century numerous bulls were sacrificed to St. Mourie at Gairloch, to the scandal of the Presbytery of Dingwall.⁶³ These sacrifices were made to the spirit of the murrain or cattle-plague, and were accompanied by the pouring of oblations of milk on the hills, while one of them at least was for the purpose of restoring a sick woman to health. Professor James Y. Simpson, the inventor of chloroform, tells us that within twenty miles of Edinburgh a relation of his had offered up a live cow as a sacrifice to the spirit of the murrain.⁶⁴ In Mull, in 1767, a heifer was burnt alive as a protection against cattle disease, an old man from Morven muttering incantations the while.[65] The ritual of "needfire" to cure cattle was the subject of a grave reprimand by the Presbytery of Strathbogie.[66] This fire was lit by rubbing pieces of dry wood together and was then used to fumigate the cattle-stalls. In 1850 a farmer in the parish of Dallas, in Moray, sacrificed an ox to the spirit of the murrain.[67] In the nineteenth century an Orkney farmer burnt a live cow in a kiln as an offering to the disease spirit.[68] There can be no question, I think, that the Druidic fires at *Beallteinn* were lit to avert the spirit of the murrain from the cattle which were driven between them, but at an earlier time they may well have been directly sacrificed, and indeed Keating's notice seems to show that they were.

Much the same custom was in favour in Wales.[69] Here the victim was carried to the top of a precipice and cast down. In Cornwall, in the year 1800, a calf was burnt to arrest the murrain.[70] Such instances could be multiplied *ad nauseam*. It will be seen that in nearly all these cases the intention was to provide a 'scape-beast, which must perish for the good of the whole herd. But the practice may be connected with an older form of the sacrifice of a divine animal the death of which was supposed to benefit all the cattle in the neighbourhood, an animal prototype, which represented the god of the oak. And that the bull was regarded as symbolic of the god of thunder, the spirit of the oak, is amply proven. Jupiter, the God of the Oak, *par excellence*, is represented as a bull, while Parjanya, the old Indian god of thunder and rain, was compared with a bull.[71] In England, as we have seen, certain oaks are still known as "bull oaks," tradition asserting that the animals "take shelter within their hollow trunks" on the occasion of a thunderstorm. If so, why not cows as well? The spirit residing in the oak must have taken taurine form.

But evidence is not lacking that on occasion a human being might even be sacrificed to save cattle from the plague. The Rev. K. Macdonald recounts a legend to the effect that a farmer in Kinlochewe, whose beasts were stricken, was informed that could he procure the heart of a man who did not know his parents and dip it into a tub of water, the liquid, if sprinkled over his herds, would drive away disease. In order to obtain a human heart, he took the life of a travelling pedlar and resorted to the ghastly expedient mentioned. His cattle were cured indeed, but the disease was transferred to his family.[72] A tradition exists in Breadalbane that once, when pestilence took toll of the local herds on the south side of Loch Tay, the folk laid violent hands on a poor "gangrel bodie," or tramp, bound him hand and foot, and then placed him in a ford, where all the cattle in the neighbourhood were driven over his body, so that he perished.[73]

The first of these expedients recalls the story of Merlin as told in the Irish edition of Nennius, for the counsellors of King Vortigern advised him to "seek a son whose father is unknown, kill him, and let his blood be sprinkled upon the Dun," or castle of the chieftain, which might not otherwise be built.

A priestly association with the bull seems to be indicated by the use of its hide in Scottish popular rite. In the Christmas or New Year ceremony of *caisean-uchd*, a strip of skin from the breast of a sheep, or the neck of a cow, is set on fire, and is given to each member of the family so that they may inhale the smoke, which will "keep spirits away." It was borne from house to house by a procession of young people. Round the head of one of the men or youths the hide of the cow slaughtered at Martinmas for family use was wrapped, and he kept on striking it with a stick. This recalls the Roman *Luperci*, who, at the festival of the *Lupercalia*, dressed themselves in goat-skins and struck all women who approached them with thongs made from the skins of their dead victims.[14]

This is by no means the only instance of British people wearing skins on ceremonial occasions. The "Penitential of Theodore" devoted to the description of heathen practices, and composed by Theodore, Archbishop of Canterbury, who died in A.D. 690, relates that on the second week of the season of Yule the people dressed themselves in skins and masks to imitate various animals.[15] In the Highland rite of *taghairm*, or prophecy in sleep, the seer wrapped himself in a bull's hide.[16] Some information concerning the man in a cow-skin is given by Ramsay of Ochtertyre in his *Scotland and Scotsmen in the Eighteenth Century* (Vol. II, p. 438). To attire oneself in an animal's skin, in the belief of primitive folk, is to become the animal itself for the nonce through the power of sympathetic magic, and consequently to acquire any supernatural knowledge it may possess as a divinity. The fact that the *taghairm* seer wrapped himself in the hide of a *newly-slain* bull seems to indicate that at one time the sacrifice of the animal preceded the act of prophetic slumber.

Now Keating says that the Irish Druids actually made such a sacrifice in order to procure omens. They "slew a bull and spread out its hide on round wattles made of the quicken tree, putting the side that had been next to the flesh uppermost," relying on spirits to answer their questions. This was certainly an Irish form of *taghairm*, and was known as "the wattles of knowledge." As we have seen, too, a story in the Welsh *Mabinogion* alludes to a hero having a symbolic dream while sleeping on the skin of a heifer. (E. Hull, *Folklore of the British Isles*, p. 300.)

In Dorset there appears to have prevailed a popular rite in which a person wore a head-dress representing a bull. This head-dress was known as "the Ooser" and was made of painted wood, the wearer donning at the same time the skin of an ox.[17] The name "ooser" is obviously cognate with the Scottish word "ouse" meaning "an ox" the Flemish *osse*, and the Gothic *auhs*.

At the Godiva ceremony at Southam, a village near Coventry, in which a *black* Godiva figured, the procession was headed by a personage known as "Old Brazen Face," who wore a mask representing a bull's head, with horns complete. The name appears significant of a sun-god, and sun-gods, as we have seen, are frequently represented in tauric shape. Again and again we read in the accounts of the old witch-trials that the "Black Man," or Governor of the witches in any district, either "transformed" himself into a bull, or had the appearance of one. Doubtless he was occasionally dressed in a bull's hide. There can be little doubt that the devil, as pictured in popular belief in bygone Britain, was derived from the memory of an ancient British deity who was thought of as taking the form of a bull—the spirit of fertility and of the oak cultus, later identified with the sun.

HERDS OF WHITE CATTLE

The former existence of the bull-cult and the sacrifice of cattle in Britain suggests a reason for the presence of those herds of wild white cattle which have been preserved with so much care in certain parks in Scotland and England. An extraordinary fascination cleaves to the wild white cattle of Britain, those waifs and strays from the ancient forests of our island, which now exist only in a few depleted herds, scattered, but still revealing a decided unity of type. The question of their origin has been debated so frequently, and by so many erudite naturalists, that there is scarcely any need to-day to discuss it further. What I am more particularly interested in is the possibility of probing to conclusions which might supply us with the reasons for the preservation of these herds. Other kinds of wild animals, their contemporaries in prehistoric times, have vanished, but these white cattle, of a breed generally admitted to be most primitive, have been conserved with a care which appears to the student of folk-lore to savour of that pious solicitude which formerly cleaved to things sacred. Are our white cattle the remains of herds once sacred and employed only for sacrificial purposes, and is the jealousy with which they are still protected a traditional memory of pagan piety surviving with all the strength of hereditary custom to a later time ?

Whether the wild white cattle of the ancient British breed which still remain are descended from the Urus, which became extinct in England in the prehistoric period, but survived longer in Scotland, or from the Celtic shorthorn, known to have been the prevailing type in Roman times, does not concern me here. But it seems capable of proof that genuine wild cattle existed in several parts of Britain until a comparatively late period. They are alluded to in the forest laws of Canute, promulgated in the first third of the eleventh century, as cattle which live "within the limits of the forest," but which must be distinguished from "wild bulls" or "buffaloes." The Welsh laws of Howell Dda, enacted about a century earlier, speak of wild white cattle with red ears, and Matthew Paris tells of the existence of forest bulls in the Chiltern woods in the early thirteenth century, while William Fitzstephen records the presence of wild bulls in Epping Forest at a date still earlier.

For the fullest account of the wild cattle of Scotland in early times we are indebted to Hector Boece, the historiographer, who provides us with a useful paragraph concerning them in his *Scotorum Historiæ*, published in 1526. He tells us that in the great Caledonian Forest there were to be found white bulls "with crisp and curling manes, like fierce lions." "These appeared meek and tame, yet were more wild than any other beasts." They feared the presence of man so greatly that they shunned all woods and pastures frequented by human beings, nor would they crop any herb near which they had passed. It was almost impossible to capture them alive, so cunning were they, and should they be taken they soon died "from importable dolour." If attacked, they rushed fiercely upon their assailants, nor were they afraid of hounds or lethal weapons.

On the occasion of the baptism of James VI at Stirling in 1566, a hunting party was arranged in honour of the Earl of Bedford, the English ambassador, when "the wild bull" was hunted in Stirling Park in the presence of Queen Mary. Four years later it is recorded that some retainers of the Regent Lennox were charged with destroying "the white kye and bulls" of Cumbernauld Forest in Dumbartonshire. The account of this outrage adds that "that kind of kye and bulls has been keipit this mony yeiris in the said forest and the like was not mentenit in ony other partis of the ile of Albion, as is well knawn."

The prolonged existence of a herd of white cattle in the ancient policies of Cadzow Castle, which lie in the gorge of Avon Water about a mile and a half from Hamilton, is a household word in Scotland, and in the popular belief this herd is unique save for that of Chillingham. But, as we shall see, this is, or was, by no means the case. The two enclosures known as the Upper and Lower Oaks, comprising about a hundred and fifty acres, are the last remains of an old forest, the oaks which it contains being famous for their lack of height and great girth of trunk. The brothers Sobieski Stuart, those strange and unaccountable figures in British social history, described the herd in 1848 as about sixty in number, of a pure white colour, with dark blue eyes, black noses, the ears tipped and lined with black, and the "feet" speckled. Only the vestiges of manes were apparent in the bulls, while the cows included both horned and "humble" specimens. They were a degree larger than Highland cattle, the biggest bulls weighing from fifty-five to sixty stones, and full-grown cows from twenty-eight to thirty-five stones. The bulls were fierce when pursued, and "at all times shy."

Other investigators have described their habits. In browsing, they invariably keep close together, as wild cattle everywhere do, and never straggle. They are always to be found in the same part of the park at the same hour of the day. At sunset they return to the north side of the park and sleep there, and at sunrise begin to work their way southward in grazing. The bulls are generally good-tempered but, if vicious, reveal themselves as "cunning and revengeful." When approached, the herd toss their heads and scamper off. They follow a single leader, an old bull, and the cows, when alarmed, conceal their calves in the thickets.

Dr. John Alexander Smith, in his *Notes on the Ancient Cattle of Scotland*, gave it as his opinion that the Cadzow or Hamilton cattle were "an ancient fancy breed of domesticated cattle preserved for their beauty in the parks of the nobility." But, as will be seen, this by no means explains certain circumstances associated with their type or preservation. In the 'thirties of last century a herd of wild white cattle, with black ears, muzzles and hoofs, was kept in a park near Blair Castle, Perthshire, the seat of the Duke of Atholl. It is unknown for what length of time they had been there. For some reason the herd was disbanded in 1834, being divided between the Marquis of Breadalbane and the Duke of Buccleuch, who settled the two portions of it at Taymouth Castle and Dalkeith Palace respectively. Neither moiety, however, was preserved for long, but some of the animals were conveyed to Kilmory House, Argyllshire, where they were mingled with other herds.

Until 1780 a herd of wild white cattle was kept at Drumlanrig Castle in Dumfriesshire, a seat of the Queensberry family. But in that year it was found necessary to dispose of them, on account of their ferocity, to an English nobleman. Pennant, in his *Tour*, written in 1772, described this herd as being "derived from the native race of the country," and as "still retaining the primeval savageness and ferocity of their ancestors." They were, he says, "more shy than any deer," and galloped off at the approach of man. In summer they kept apart from all other cattle, but in the winter months they haunted the out-houses in search of food. They were "of a middle size" with very long legs, and the orbits of the eyes and the muzzles were black. The bulls were lacking in mane.

A similar herd was brought to Ardrossan Castle in Ayrshire by the tenth Earl of Eglinton in 1750. It was probably because of their extreme wildness that they were gradually reduced by shooting to some twelve cows and bulls. In 1820 the twelfth Earl gave orders for their destruction, and this was carried out. About the same time a herd of white cattle was brought to Auchencruive, Ayrshire, but on the purchase of the estate by a Mr. Oswald in 1763, he found it necessary to destroy the herd owing to its dangerous tendencies.

The white herd at Chillingham is much too well known to necessitate any prolonged description of it. The park in which it dwells is mentioned in records as early as the beginning of the thirteenth century, and the herd is known to have existed there from the end of the fifteenth century at least, though almost certainly it is very much older. It is strange to think that this celebrated herd should have been preserved in a wild tract of Cheviot country, scarcely twelve miles from the bounds of Scotland, throughout the perilous days of the Border reivers, who could surely not have left it in much peace—though perhaps it was too ferocious to attract the Scots! Pennant says distinctly that the Chillingham cattle are of the same kind as those he saw at Drumlanrig. They then numbered between thirty and forty. One authority describes them as "invariably white, muzzle black, the whole of the inside of the ear, and about one-third of the outside from the tip downwards, red, horns white with black tips, very fine, and bent upwards; some of the bulls have a thin upright mane about an inch and a half or two inches long." A modern naturalist has classed the Chillingham white cattle as of the species of *bos longifrons*, a very ancient type indeed.

Other herds of wild white cattle are, or were once, to be found in England at several centres. That at Chartley Park, Staffordshire, roams in a park formed from a part of Needwood Forest, and it appears to have been driven into this enclosure from the surrounding forest when this park was first formed in 1248. The birth of a black or parti-hued calf in the herd was formerly supposed to be a certain omen of death in the family of the Earl of Ferrers, their owner. In Lyme Park, Cheshire, a herd of wild white cattle, similar to that at Chillingham, existed from time immemorial up to 1890, though I cannot discover whether it is still located there. In his *British Animals Extinct within Historic Times*, Mr. J. E. Harting gives particulars of other places in England where herds of wild white cattle were to be found. These were Neworth Castle, Cumberland; Gisburne Park, Yorkshire; Whalley Abbey, Lancashire; Wollaton Park, Nottinghamshire; Somerford Park, Cheshire; Woldenby Park, Northamptonshire; Leigh Court, Somersetshire; Barnard Castle, Durham; Bishop Auckland, in the same county; Burton Constable, Yorkshire; and Ewelme Park, Oxfordshire. We have also seen that Scottish herds existed in Stirlingshire, Dumbartonshire, Lanarkshire, Perthshire, Dumfriesshire, and Ayrshire.

Now, with one exception, that of the herd at Blair Atholl, every one of these herds of white cattle are, or were formerly, established in areas inhabited by people having a Brythonic culture and speaking the ancient British tongue until well into the historic period. In Scotland, there is only one exception to this circumstance among the six localities in which these animals were to be found, and indeed it may scarcely be called an exception, as Perthshire was anciently a Celtic area where customs similar to those of the Brythonic folk were maintained. All the other localities in Scotland in which wild white cattle were or are to be found are situated within what was once the British Kingdom of Strathclyde, which stretched from the Firth of Clyde to Cumberland, and from the Ayrshire coast to the Pentlands. Only a part of this tract was covered by the ancient Caledonian Forest, which, according to Skene and Rhys, stretched from the district of Menteith, near Loch Lomond, across country to Dunkeld, near which the Blair Atholl herd was to be found, although at one time its area may have been greatly more spacious. And as for the English localities where herds of white cattle were preserved, with two exceptions only, these were formerly within the bounds of those ancient British kingdoms and principalities which were among the last to come beneath Saxon influence, maintaining their independence and racial customs in some cases until the seventh century, or even later.

Enough has been said above to make it evident that the sacrifice of cattle in connection with pagan ceremonies in Britain was not only a most ancient usage, but one which survived in a vestigial state until a comparatively recent period. That it did so in those parts of the country which had maintained their Celtic characteristics most strongly is also plain enough.

In Druidic times the beasts sacrificed at such ceremonies must inevitably have been preserved in sacred enclosed herds from which such victims as were necessary would have been selected as occasion required. That such cattle employed for sacrifice were, in ancient times, invariably of a white colour is clear, not only from Celtic but Roman accounts. Is it not possible that herds of these white cattle would be preserved after the introduction of Christianity, at first because of their sacred and inviolable character, and later because of that strong hereditary sentiment of preservation of ancient things which insists upon the upkeep of forms, ceremonies and their associations, long after the reason for their very existence is forgotten?

Several circumstances connected with these herds appear to me as corroborating such a theory. The white colour of the animals concerned is perhaps the most outstanding among these. The most meticulous care has been taken to keep these herds free from admixture with ordinary breeds, to preserve them untainted. This deliberate policy, I feel, could only have been handed down from one generation to another in respect of a tradition originally powerful and inspired by sacred sanction and pious intention.

The spirit in which these herds were preserved inviolate and rigidly enclosed for centuries is eloquent of a deliberate policy, the reason of which may have been forgotten, but which was none the less fixed in its purpose. Hundreds of antique local ceremonies still persist amongst us, the original significance and intention of which have long been lost in oblivion, and the mere suggestion that they should be dispensed with arouses an irritation which anyone but a student of folk-lore will be at a loss to account for. Few would be so hardy as to hint to the owners of our herds of wild white cattle that they serve no adequate purpose, or that their upkeep is not dictated by any sound economic reason. The reply that their preservation is dictated by sentimental reasons, for which their proprietors could not well account, would certainly be forthcoming, and it would be as surely added that their very antiquity furnished perhaps the best reason for their future existence.

The scribal statement that the white cattle of Cumbernauld had existed there for a great length of time, and that they were unique "in the ile of Albion," reveals that the spirit of pious pride which maintained and guarded them existed nearly four centuries ago, indeed, it still exists to-day. Assuredly, too, it is allied to that sentiment which has inspired the maintenance of a herd of bison in the Yellowstone Park in America—that is, an intention to preserve an ancient breed well-nigh extinct. Possibly a more searching examination of the folk-lore of the several areas in which these herds are kept might reveal the existence of beliefs or customs associated with the sacrifice of cattle in the past. However that may be, it appears to me incredible that a tradition of solicitude so extraordinary should exist in connection with their upkeep, unless it had been dictated by a primary sentiment associated with their sacred character.

Chapter VIII

PLACES OF WORSHIP

Tradition that the Druids were associated with Stone Monuments

For nearly three centuries a tradition has been in vogue among the general public of this and some other countries that the megalithic monuments, single standing stones and circles, cromlechs and dolmens, to be found so plentifully in Western Europe, were the handiwork of the Druidic caste and were its "temples" or places of worship. The genesis of this tradition is not in doubt. In his work *The Druids* Mr. T. D. Kendrick has furnished what is by far the best account of the manner of its inception and progress. To a great extent it owes its origin to the efforts of the older school of antiquaries to explain the significance of Stonehenge. James I became interested in this particular monument and the enquiries which he set on foot as to its nature and beginnings issued in reports which in some cases gave rise to the current notion that it had been built by the Druids. From this it was only a short step to the belief that every rude stone monument was the work of the Druidic brotherhood.

The first writer who appears to have alluded to a Druidic origin for Stonehenge was Inigo Jones, last of the great Elizabethan architects, and the casual manner in which he put forward the theory provides a speaking commentary on the ease with which tradition or legend can gain ready currency and achieve popular credence. But almost at once he summarily rejected it. The next to allude to it was the celebrated John Aubrey, whose brief statement appeared in a later edition of Camden's *Britannia*. Yet Aubrey's more extended essay on the subject of Stonehenge was never given to the public. In any case, his suggestion that Avebury, Stonehenge and other rude stone monuments were temples of the Druids was put forward as a probability only, indeed he lays some stress upon the unlikelihood of his surmise.

John Toland, who composed the first general work in English upon the Druids, *A Critical History of the Celtic Religion and Learning, containing an account of the Druids, or the Priests and Judges*, written in 1718-19, did much to strengthen the popular notion that the erection of rude stone monuments was due to the Druids, yet even he maintains that they "were commonly wont to retire into grots, dark woods, mountains and groves."[1] The famous works of the antiquary William Stukeley on Stonehenge and Avebury written about the middle of the eighteenth century, composed with a muddle-headed fervour which has rarely been surpassed in the whole history of crankhood, achieved more than anything else to convince an uncritical public that the rude stone monuments of Britain and France were of Druidic origin.

As time proceeded, the legend loomed ever larger upon the archæological sky, but those who wish to follow its course must betake themselves to the excellent and tolerant account of it in the pages of Mr. Kendrick's delightful and knowledgeable work.[2] Here it is more to my purpose to record that the notion of a Druidic origin for the stone monuments having achieved a powerful hold upon public favour, it was carried into all parts of the country by the dilettante antiquary and the enthusiastic tourist, two types of person who have done more to add to the stock of sham folk-lore and legend than any, unless perhaps, the local parson or schoolmaster.

By this means, aided, of course, by that most flourishing plant of propaganda, the "grape-vine," the notion spread apace, and in the early years of the nineteenth century had obtained so strong a hold upon the rural mind as to be impregnable in many districts, surviving in some localities even to the present day. Nay, I can assure the reader that I have heard a version of it unctuously delivered by a uniformed official guide on the classic soil of Stonehenge itself! And here I may briefly and regretfully remark upon the endless damage done to such remains of folk-lore as may seem legitimately to point to a Druidic connection by this thoughtless and foolish tradition, and the consequent and understandable nervousness which the mere name of Druidism has awakened in the minds of serious archæologists. Much the same process occurred in France, the notion of a Druidic origin for the great stone circles of Brittany being maintained in such works as that of the *Monumens Celtiques* of J. de Cambry, published at Paris in 1805.

PROOF THAT THE DRUIDS WORSHIPPED IN GROVES

Here I cannot do better than set forth the evidence furnished by classical writers that the shrines of the Druids were chiefly situated in groves and afforested localities. Lucan, in his *Pharsalia* (I, 450–8), apostrophizing the Druids, says: "The innermost groves of far-off forests are your abodes." Pliny tells us that "they choose groves formed of oaks for the sake of the tree alone." (*Natural History*, XVI, 249.) As we have seen, the sacrifices of Boadicea to the goddess Andate or Andrasta took place in a grove. Tacitus (*Annals*, XIV, 3c) says that the groves of the Druids of Anglesey were devoted to their inhuman superstitions.

Apart from classical allusions, we have the statement in Irish literature that sacred groves existed in Ireland.[3] As Mr. Kendrick remarks, "Until Aubrey's time it never occurred to anyone to suppose that they worshipped elsewhere."[4] The name *Nemeton*, says Miss Eleanor Hull, was employed for a sanctuary of trees "and in Central Asia Minor about 280 B.C. the Gauls established a central council at a place called Drunemeton, the chief *nemeton*, or sacred place . . . Nearly every tribe in Gaul seems to have had a *nemeton* or sacred place, combining religious worship with the promulgation of justice . . . An eighth century list of superstitions and pagan rites speaks of 'shrines in groves which they call *nimidæ* ' ".⁵ M. Camille Jullian, writing on the religion of the Celts, says that "the majority of consecrated places were simply open spaces limited by ritual, but not by material boundaries, spaces where fragments of the precious metals, destined for the gods, were accumulated. There were also clusters of trees, spaces reserved in the great forests, or even lakes or marshes, like those of Toulouse." Jullian gives it as his opinion that "the true Gauls" were more attracted by the worship of mountains than by that of springs. But the Ligurians, Aquitanians and Germans cared more for that of forests and trees, though all the Gallic peoples were acquainted with the same gods. It is, he says, possible to distinguish between deities of the whole forest, most plentiful in the North, and those which inhabited a single tree, such as the *Deus Fagus*, god of the beech tree, or the *Deus Sexabores*, which inhabited a group of trees, such as we hear of in Irish myth.⁶ The Scholiast of Lucan tells us that "the Druids worship the gods without temples in woods."

In Scotland certain groves were regarded with superstitious awe until modern times, and it is not improbable that these may have been connected with Druidic rite in the distant past. Such a grove is to be found at the Chapel of St. Ninian in the parish of Belly, and another, the branches of which must not be cut, formerly existed in the Isle of Skye; while still another stood near Ellery, at Loch Caolisport, Knapdale.

Such woods in Scotland are known as "Bell trees."⁷ The name is derived from the Gaelic word *bilé*, "a tree." Sacred plantations of this kind were also known in Ireland by the same name.⁸ As late as the year A.D. IIII the men of Ulster came in a host to Tullabogue, the inauguration place of the O'Neills, and cut down the ancient trees there, for which they had to pay the heavy fine of 3,000 cows.⁹ According to Mrs. Bray, Wistman's Wood, in Dartmoor, in Devon, had, in her time, always been considered "as the *posterity* of a Druid grove." In 1832, it was found from the manuscript known as the "Perambulation of the Moor" preserved in the office of the Duchy of Cornwall, that the wood was, at the date of the composition of this MS., in nearly the same state as at the time of the Norman Conquest, and as it was also when Mrs. Bray wrote. The grove was of oak trees, though rather stunted. This appears to be an authentic tradition of a Druidic grove.¹⁰

The survival of a similar tradition relating to a Druidic grove may possibly be indicated by the children's game of Doagan which was played in the Isle of Man about a century ago. A rude human effigy was affixed to a cross and sticks were thrown at it, while certain words in Manx Gaelic were recited. These, translated, run:

> "This to thee, the Doagan,
> What says the Doagan,
> Upon the cross, upon the block,
> Upon the little staff, straight or crooked,

In the little wood over yonder.
If thou wilt give the head of the Doagan,
I will give thy head for it."

Kelly, in his *Manx Dictionary*, says that Doagan was a play, and that it refers to Dagon, god of the Philistines, alluded to in the Old Testament, whose idol was shattered by Jehovah. The allusion to "the little wood over yonder" seems to me to be to a sacred grove, and I think the game is a survival of that sacrifice by shooting with arrows which I have already sought to explain. "Doagan" is probably the Celtic god Dagda, as in two passages in the *Book of Leinster* that deity is spoken of as Dagan.

Before concluding the subject of Druidic groves it is necessary to mention the problem presented by the site which has come to be known as "Woodhenge," a monument which stands not far from Stonehenge and which was discovered by air-photography. A wide circular ditch about 250 feet in diameter, contains six concentric rings of holes which formerly held wooden posts or tree-trunks. Mr. Kendrick believes this was "a druidic grove of the La Tène period."[11] Of course it must have been an artificial "grove," and it seems not improbable that the construction of such a shrine in a treeless countryside may have been regarded as essential. The La Tène period in Britain flourished from 400 B.C. to the first century of our era, so that Woodhenge may possibly represent a phase between the grove proper and those more elaborate roofed temples in stone which the Celts erected in the Roman period, or, as we shall see, even before it, according to some authorities, though some writers think it was a forerunner of or model for Stonehenge. The circle at Arminghall, near Norwich, was also discovered from the air, and consisted of eight pillars made from large oak trees let into the soil. It is of the same period as Woodhenge and is interesting as relating to the region of the Iceni, whose goddess seems to have been Andate, who had a grove at London.

The great Druidic grove at Marseilles is described by the poet Lucan as a gloomy wood whose priests bedewed the tree-trunks with human gore. No birds nested therein nor did wild beasts make their dens within its bounds. Black streams divided the ground and horrid idols of hideous aspect grinned out of the darkness. These were adored by the ignorant multitudes. Even the priests themselves were wary of treading this dreadful ground. Of course we must make allowances for poetic licence, but it is well to remember that Lucan, who died in the year 65, was practically a contemporary of the last Druids.[12]

ERA OF THE STONE CIRCLES

Were the stone circles the work of the Druids? What is their date of construction? If modern authorities are vague concerning anything it is about this. The matter is still one of obdurate debate. In general they are classed as Neolithic, or New Stone Age, which may signify anything from

10,000 B.C. until the beginning of the present era, or, perhaps more definitely from the beginning of the manufacture of polished stone artifacts to the age of Bronze, which in Britain made its first appearance about 2000 B.C. The modern view is that about 2500 B.C. certain East Mediterranean influences had reached Southern Spain and that these had resulted in the erection of the large corbelled tombs there. The type spread into Portugal, Brittany, Britain and Scandinavia. The Beaker Folk, who came from Spain and perhaps from North Africa, about the beginning of the Bronze Age (2000 B.C.), seem to have constructed the *later* stone circles proper.

STONEHENGE

The latest of these circles is Stonehenge, the several parts of which date from various periods. The functions of these monuments have been warmly disputed, but as many of them have been proved by excavation to have been the sites of sepulchral practice, this may be recognized as one of their definite purposes, although it has been all too readily assumed to be the principal and only one. It may be said in passing that the popularly received belief that stone circles are of Druidic origin is rendered highly improbable by reason of chronology. If the date of erection of Stonehenge, the latest among the circles, be taken as 2000 B.C., as authority suggests, it is eighteen centuries older than the first literary allusion to Druidism, that of Sotion of Alexandria, which dates about 200 B.C. And the stone circles of Asia could scarcely have been "Druidic." The evidence seems to show that the ditch and bank are of Beaker or Early Bronze Age construction (*ca.* 2000 B.C.), that is of the same period as Avebury. The great sarsens and trilithons and the "Blue Stones" belong to a later phase of the Early Bronze Age. The circles of holes known as "Z" and "Y" seem to belong to a still later age, that is about the beginning of the Christian era.

But Colonel R. H. Cunnington, in his work *Stonehenge and its Date*, has argued that Stonehenge cannot be dated earlier than about 400 B.C., that it is La Tène I, and that the technique of the central structure of sarsen and blue stones with tenon-and-mortise fitting and curved lintels bespeaks this much later origin. If this be so, it probably brings its period within that of fully established Druidism in Gaul. This later dating attributed to Stonehenge fortifies the theory of Mr. Kendrick that Stonehenge may have been a Druidic temple. There is, Mr. Kendrick avers, a more severe precision of outline, the area of the enclosure is sacrificed to increase the height and dignity of the pillars. "The technique of tenon-and-mortise fitting of the cross-pieces appears to have been learned at secondhand from those who had some knowledge of the temple-masonry of Greece and Rome. It is, in principle, the ordinary classical method of assembling the members of a column."[13]

But Stonehenge, as I have said, was by no means the erection of a

single age. Its inner ring is composed of certain "blue stones," which are
known to have been of much earlier provenance. In 1923 it was definitely
proved by Dr. Thomas of H.M. Geological Survey that these stones, about
thirty in number, can have been taken or quarried only from the comparatively limited area of the Prescelly Range of Hills in Pembrokeshire.[14]

In the opinion of the present writer they are the ancestral or
spirit-stones of an early tribe which, for some reason, changed its habita-
tion from Pembrokeshire to Salisbury Plain, and which it was necessary
to convey to the new home for reasons of tribal good fortune and
prosperity. These Blue Stones, I think, were believed to embody the
spirits of its ancestor-gods, just as trees were thought to embody the
spirits of the dead, or to be the abodes of godlings. The evidence goes to
show that the "Blue Stones" were erected within the greater circle
immediately after it was built, that, indeed, it was built, or re-edified,
expressly for their reception. It is, of course, not impossible that the folk
who built Stonehenge had originally arrived from the Prescelly area
long before the era of its construction to Salisbury Plain, and moved by
the circumstance that their ancestral "idols" remained in the ancient and
revered home, had sent an expedition thence for their removal.

The venerable legend alluded to by Geoffrey of Monmouth, that
Stonehenge had been brought wholesale from "Ireland," may have been a
memory of such a proceeding. Merlin, he tells us, magically transported it,
"the Choir of Giants," to Salisbury Plain.[15] According to Geoffrey, the
stones of the Giants' Choir could heal diseases, precisely as certain menhirs
are thought to be able to do among the French peasantry to-day, and
were thought by the Irish, Scots and Welsh peasantry to do not so very
long ago. Rhys believed that Stonehenge was "the original of the famous
temple of Apollo in the island of the Hyperboreans, the stories about
which were based in the first instance most likely on the ground of
Pytheas' travels."[16] The version is to be found in Diodorus and this
brings it down almost to the beginning of the Christian era, although of
course it was much older in its original form.

WORSHIP OBSERVED AT STONE CIRCLES

What type of worship was observed at stone circles? I believe that
these were formerly regarded as the shrines or temples of spirits or gods of
an ancestral character and that the stones were intended as rude
representations of these dead chiefs or deities. The term "false men," still
used of such standing stones in Ireland and Scotland, as well as the far-
flung tradition that they are the habitations of spirits, seems to me to make
this perfectly clear. Concerning this I have afforded the fullest proof
elsewhere.[17] It was a simple worship of the dead, who were later transformed into "powers" or "gods," and were regarded as the agents of
vegetable, agricultural and animal fecundity.

Worship at megalithic centres was associated with the idea of seasonal growth and the regulation of agricultural operations. That the dead were thought of as among the agencies of growth, that they acted as "Chthonic," or underworld powers who superintended the magic or alchemy of growth, and that, in such a character, they in time took on the shape of divinity itself, or were amalgamated with it, is a theory too well established to require more than passing mention. This phase of megalithic worship would appear to have been a later superimposition upon the earlier cult of the dead as the powers behind vegetable growth pure and simple. It could not, indeed, have made its appearance prior to the practice of agriculture, and it seems to have been accompanied by certain devices associated with stone circles, which tended to regulate the times of the sowing of seed and the reaping of grain, according to the manner in which these were indicated by the phases of the sun appropriate to them.

At this later stage of things, the stone circle was orientated by the accurate placing of additional stones which marked either the beginning or end of the sun's annual journey, so that the approximate seasons for ploughing or planting, sowing or reaping, might be gauged from them. These "calendric" solar positions would, of course, also indicate the incidence of seasonal festivals associated with agricultural rites, and it seems unnecessary to discover in such apparatus and practice a more intricate or mystical character.

In a word, this "worship" of stones bears such a strong similarity to that of trees that I feel one can only with difficulty be distinguished from the other. The underlying belief in both cases was the same—to obtain aliment through the benign agency of the spirit animating the stone or the tree. The old Stone-Age worship seems to have resembled that of the Druidic and other tree-worship so closely that I, at least, am unable to differentiate between them. Is there any proof of the relationship between the two cults, of the passing of tree-worship into that of stones, or vice-versa? It may be as well to mention here that the worship of stones, trees and wells survived in Britain for centuries. (See Thorpe's Laws, Vol. I, pp. 298, 378; E. Hull, op. cit., pp. 95–108.) Frazer has provided quite a number of instances in which stones are employed to make crops and plants grow by homœopathic magic.[18]

"The general probability," says Mr. Kendrick, arriving at a conclusion concerning the stone circles, "is plainly that the bulk of the stone circles in the druid area were erected many hundreds of years before the druids themselves were heard of. But this does not by any means dispose of the subject, and we must not suggest without further reflection that these priests had nothing whatever to do with their so-called temples."[19] He adds that Professor Garden of Aberdeen, who in 1692 made a study of the circles in his neighbourhood, reported that tradition in Scotland associated them with worship and sacrifice in heathen times. But Garden could not trace any connection with Druidic worship. For my own part, the fact that a people went to the length of transporting the "Blue Stones" from

Wales to Salisbury Plain, reveals that they regarded them with profound sanctity and that they were objects of worship; but that they were "Druidic" we have no evidence. Mr. Kendrick concludes his survey with the observation that it seems almost certain that *some* of the circles were known to the Druids because of their continued use by the native population into the Iron Age, as at Stonehenge, and that being so, the Druids may have appropriated certain of them for their own ceremonies.

THEORIES THAT STONE CIRCLES WERE DRUIDIC

M. Salomon Reinach was of the opinion that the dolmens, chambered tombs and standing stones of France were erected under the influence of the Druids. He felt that it was impossible to explain their presence otherwise than by the assumption of a religious aristocracy exerting absolute control over a numerous population. Who can doubt it? But was such a religious aristocracy necessarily Druidic? Judging from its funerary remains, it would appear to have been composed mainly of chieftains of the military class rather than priests, though these, too, may have exercised priestly functions.[10]

The argument of Mr. A. Hadrian Allcroft in connection with the claim that Druids were responsible for the great stone circles is an interesting one. If these circles be really as old as the Bronze Age, as most archæologists maintain, it is strange, he thinks, that they should be so largely confined to Brythonic areas, the Brythons having entered this island only about 450 B.C. The notion of their Bronze Age origin, he maintains, is based mainly upon the fact that they are built of unhewn stones and that no iron is found within the area of the circles. But such negative evidence is of dubious value. It may, he thinks, have been taboo to bring metal of any kind within the circles. This is in itself negative evidence with a vengeance! That so many of the circles remain in a complete state is, he believes, good evidence of their comparatively late date. Indeed the fact that ingenious mechanical skill was employed in placing the stones in position argues a late erection for the megalithic rings. The argument that they had an "astronomical" significance, he feels, cannot be employed except in relation to an elementary knowledge of the sun's yearly course. In brief, he is of the opinion that the circles, as found in Britain and Brittany at least, were constructed by people of Brythonic race between the fourth century B.C. and the ninth century A.D.[11]

Long before Mr. Allcroft's views concerning the late character of the stone circles appeared, Mr. James Fergusson had asserted a similar belief in their comparatively modern construction. Fergusson possessed an intimate knowledge of the circles and of architectural art in general. He gave it as his belief that these monuments "belong to a style, like Gothic, Grecian, Egyptian, Buddhist, or any other. It has a beginning and an end," and it belongs to "true historic times." In a word, he claimed that "they were generally erected by partially civilized races after they had come in contact with the Romans, and most of them may be considered as belonging to the first ten centuries of the Christian Era."[11]

Professor R. A. S. Macalister summarizes the position relative to the age and purpose of standing stones with that neatness and lucidity which might be expected of him. No specific date can be assigned to them and no specific purpose. Indeed they served a variety of purposes. "Some were grave-marks; others were land-marks. Others were figures of deities, or did duty as such, taking the place which statues would have taken, had the preparation of such been possible in the state of art at the time." Stone circles were either employed to fence a grave-sanctuary, or were formed of standing pillar-stones set in a circular ring, sometimes with an extra stone standing outside the circle, rarely inside. An instance of the latter type appears in the Patrician legend of Cromm Cruaich already alluded to. The central stone, that of Cromm Cruaich, was that of the chief god of a pantheon surrounded by the "effigies" of other and subordinate deities. Burials found within the area of such circles may be those of sacrificial victims. Professor Macalister has "no faith" in deductions respecting astronomic phenomena drawn from the orientation of rude stone monuments of any kind.[12]

There are not wanting modern authorities who believe that the Druids were in one way or another connected with the stone circles. The late Miss E. Hull indicated that Keating mentions in his *History* (as we have seen) that the dolmens were called "idol-altars," and that this belief had a firm hold upon Irish opinion in his day, the seventeenth century, and she mentions place-names which, for her at least, maintain a tradition of Druidic association.[13] M. L. Siret believes that certain Oriental voyagers and prospectors introduced a tree-worship into Western Europe in early times and that this was connected with the early megalithic monuments of that area. This worship, in a word, was Druidism. "We are now obliged," he says, "to go back to the theory of the archæologists of a hundred years ago who attributed the megalithic monuments to the Druids. The instinct of our predecessors has been more penetrating than the scientific analysis which has taken its place."

A similar view is that maintained by Dr. W. J. Perry, who believes that "ruling groups" were gradually spreading across Europe, beginning in Egypt and moving out by way of Crete and Mycenean Greece, from the period of the first Egyptian dynasty (i.e., *ca.* 3400 B.C. onward) in search of precious metals, and that such migrants may have been responsible for the Neolithic culture in Western Europe. He does not associate this culture with the Druids. But it is beside my purpose to follow his arguments here, as they scarcely trench upon the question of Druidic origins.[15]

THE CIRCLES PRE-DRUIDIC

Mr. Kendrick reviews the whole subject of megalithic monuments in the Druidic area with characteristic care and impartiality. He distinguishes between "altars" and "temples," that is dolmens and the like and stone circles. He lays stress on the important circumstance that monuments of precisely the same type as those found in the area in question have a wide distribution elsewhere and that this does not appear to have been appreciated by the older antiquaries. Those of what he calls the "altar" class, that is, dolmens, and grave-chambers or barrows, were certainly used for sepulchral purposes. There is no evidence that Druids worshipped at such sites, but the construction of such chambers may have been continued until Druidic times. Generally speaking, the whole series is, however, manifestly pre-Druidic and there is a great gap between the two cultures. Nor is there any actual proof that the Druids were in any way connected with these monuments.

So far as the "temples" or stone circles are concerned, the lesser of these, thinks Mr. Kendrick, are occasionally of a sepulchral character. The larger, again, were religious centres and were erected many centuries before the advent of Druidism. It seems reasonably clear that these latter were not burial places. If human remains are found within them they are most likely due to sacrifices. Some were probably places of popular gathering or observatory posts for determining the movements of the heavenly bodies for agricultural purposes, though this latter view has in some cases been "pressed to absurdity." "Elaborate astronomical measurements" are out of the question. Like Professor Macalister, Mr. Kendrick regards the legendary story of the Cromm Cruaich circle as a possible tradition of former worship at such places. But the actual temples of the Druids were natural groves. *Some* of the megalithic graves and *some* circles were known to the Druids because of their continued use by the native population right into the Iron Age, and they may have appropriated certain circles for their own ceremonies.[16]

Canon MacCulloch says definitely that "the old idea that stone circles were Druidic temples . . . must be given up," along with the "astronomic lore associated with the circles." But some of the Celtic gods were worshipped at tumuli and the *Lugnassad* was commemorated at burial places, though these were mounds and not circles.[17] An Irish poem by Cinaeth O'Hartigain (A.D. 973) preserved in the *Book of Ballymote* (folio 189 b) alludes to "The Mound of Finn, the Mound of the Druids." As I have said in the section on the Isle of Man, a tradition of Druidic sacrifice is associated with a stone circle in that island known as the Lonan, or Cloven Stones.

Macbain was undisguisedly hostile to the notion of Druidic association with the stone circles. "Popular tradition," he says, "knows nothing of the Druids in connection with these circles. The nearest approach to the Druidic theory is where, in one case, the popular myth regards the stones as men transformed by the magic of the Druids." Such legends are nearly always "late" in origin, as I have recently revealed in my *Minor Traditions in British Mythology*. Macbain believed the stone circles to have been erected by the Picts—a dark saying, though popular tradition makes them the builders of nearly every structure of antiquity in Scotland, down to Edinburgh Castle and Glasgow Cathedral! This seems all the more amusing when his nervous anxiety to share the official view respecting these monuments is taken into account.[18]

LATER DRUIDIC TEMPLES

But that the Druidic "cult" could boast at a later period of temples in the true meaning of the term appears as not at all improbable, though the likelihood is that most of these were erected under Roman auspices and at a period when the Gallic religion had been Romanized. Of course those Celtic peoples who dwelt at no great distance from the Latins would be the first to accept the roofed temple. Polybius, the Greek historian who flourished in the second century B.C., says that the Celtic Insubres, who dwelt on the right bank of the River Po, adored a goddess whom he describes as "Athena."[19] The Boii, who bordered upon the Helvetii, whose territory to some extent was commensurate with that of Switzerland, had, according to Livy, a temple in which they heaped up spoils of war.[20]

But in Gaul proper it seems unlikely that temples were introduced before the collapse of Druidism as an official faith and the adaptation of Gallic belief to Roman forms. Jullian thinks that "*all* the temples and altars without exception, which were consecrated to Gallic gods, date from the period of the Roman Empire, and by that time the Roman architects and priests had invaded the land with their stereotyped buildings and their customs, the *templum* and *ara*. This does not imply that it is impossible to discover in these constructions a trace of indigenous survivals. Thus a great many temples in Gaul are constructed on a square plan (as for instance that of Champlien in Normandy) and this architectural type is hardly to be found in the Græco-Roman world, therefore it may possibly recall some sacred custom of the Gauls."

Jullian thinks it possible, too, that in the time of independence the Gauls must have possessed a few temples like that of the Isle of Sena, to which I have alluded, "complete buildings with walls and roofs," doubtless made of wood.[21] But Sena is a poor exemplar, and half-mythical at that, resting as it does upon Pomponius Mela's adaptation of Pytheas' account, and even Eratosthenes gibes at it. Diodorus speaks of treasure collected in "temples and sacred places," but the allusion may well be to groves, where, as we have seen, offerings were certainly suspended.[22]

Gildas, the British exile who wrote so feelingly on the misfortunes of his country as it languished after the departure of the Romans, refers to its "deserted temples," where "diabolical idols" could still be seen in his day, the middle of the sixth century, "with stiff and deformed features, as was customary." Inferior as Romano-British art was, it could scarcely be so characterized and it seems probable that the reference is to British native shrines and sculpture.[22]

CHARTRES

I have already alluded in passing to the great centre of Druidic convention, which, as Cæsar tells us, was "a consecrated place in the territories of the Carnutes, which is reckoned the central region of the whole of Gaul." It was at or near Chartres, or according to some authorities, in the neighbourhood of Dreux, more than thirty miles northward, where, it is said, traces of these assemblages may still be found. At Chartres there is a local tradition that the Cathedral stands upon the site of a Celtic temple where the worship of a "Black Virgin" was celebrated, whose figure is situated in the crypt, a mere substitution for the original, which was destroyed during the French Revolution and which was possibly a relic of paganism.[24] It is claimed that certain grottoes or caverns beneath the Cathedral have existed there since the time of the Druids.[25] MM. Bosc and Bonnemère, in their *Histoire Nationale des Gaulois* (p. 48), give it as their impression that the meetings were held in an "impenetrable thicket" in the vicinity of Chartres—a concession to Gallic romanticism. Pomponius Mela states that the Druids of Gaul instructed their noble pupils in caves or "secluded dales."[26]

CONCLUSIONS

In reviewing the evidence, I think that it has been plainly proven that the era of the large stone circles and the worship celebrated within them was greatly anterior to that of Druidism as we find it described. But, as Kendrick and others aver, it appears as not improbable that the Druids may in some instances have made use of the Neolithic circles as religious centres at a later date. Writing as a student of folk-lore rather than as an archæologist, I am compelled to the conclusion that a strong similarity existed between the cultus engaged in at the stone circles and that of Druidism.

Although we cannot be said to know much concerning the former type of religion, we now possess at least a solid outline of its form and tendency, and that it consisted of a worship of the dead, who were identified with the forces of vegetable, cereal and human fructification and growth, is manifest. The godlings representing these forces were certainly symbolized in the pillars of the stone circles. That Druidism was in all its essential doctrines a religion which had sprung from a similar conception is also scarcely to be questioned. Its chief elements are represented by the oak as a food-giver, the sacred tree inhabited by a spirit or godling, precisely as the stone pillar was ensouled by that of a god or a dead chieftain. But this important question will receive fuller consideration

in the latter chapters of this book in which the origins of Druidism will
be reviewed.

More to the point here is the fact that stone monuments had little
or no association with the Druidic cult. In most of the lands where the
ancient oak-cult held sway, it had been preceded by the cult of the stone
circle or menhir. Indeed, when the antiquity of the oak-cult falls to be
considered, the probability is that the twain may have been contemporary
for many centuries, but probably in different regions.

The strong probability, to speak generally, is that the cult of the
worship of the oak originated in a thickly afforested region and that it
had its inception in those parts of Eastern Europe where oak forests were
of the longest duration and where a tradition of reliance on the oak tree
as a food-provider and fuel-giver had had sufficient time for its development into a religious or quasi-religious cultus. From thence it may well
have been gradually imported into Gaul. The oak, we know, appeared in
Europe, or in the more northern parts of that continent, at a later period
than the pine, the birch, willow, hazel, elm and lime, although local
variations are large and significant, and the prevalence of Pre-Boreal
and Boreal phases has to be taken into consideration along with increases
of rainfall and wind-storms. In Britain, for example, these latter agencies
brought about widespread deforestation until the course of the Atlantic
storms shifted again.[17] But when the oak tree found a firm footing in
Europe, so did the germ of that faith which later came to be known as
Druidism.

Chapter IX

DRUIDISM AND THE DIVINE KINGSHIP

In more than one passage in this book I have alluded to the association of the Druidic cult with the institution which has come to be known to students of tradition as the Divine Kingship. I now desire to stress this connection, to establish it, indeed, beyond doubt. It is the association of the Divine Kingship with Druidism which provides the best proof for the existence of the latter cultus in some Celtic lands, and had the value and nature of the evidence concerning this been recognized by enquirers at an earlier phase, the stupid and even foolish hypothesis which held that Druidism never existed, or that, alternatively, it is a subject of no importance in folk-lore and history would scarcely have intruded itself. It is, of course, perfectly clear from the evidence that the idea of the Divine Kingship had associations with primitive religious cults other than Druidism; but the nature of the idea underlying all of these was, it is clear, homogeneous. All of them, without exception, were cults of fertility, in which cereal and vegetable growth was regarded as a magical process which emanated from the Divine King, and which was due to the indwelling vitality of the monarch.

THEORY OF THE DIVINE KINGSHIP

The institution of the Divine Kingship is now so widely known and comprehended in its principles that only a general review of its significance and circumstances seems to be necessary in this place. I have already given a summary account of this cult, the history and development of which has been so completely and admirably set forth and illustrated by Frazer, Hocart, Hooke and Perry, and, as regards its Irish associations, by Miss Eleanor Hull and Professor Macalister. Hocart claimed that "the earliest *known* religion is a belief in the divinity of kings," the earthly representatives of the gods, though it is not necessarily the most primitive. That this was certainly the case in Egypt and Sumeria has been proved beyond question, and the same holds good of early Greece, while the kings of Rome were also regarded as of divine descent.[1]

In Egypt kings were regarded not only as the sons of the sun-god Ra, Osiris, or Ra-Osiris, but as being actually that deity in his earthly form. Perry believes that this doctrine was established about the year 2750 B.C., when the dynasty associated with Heliopolis and its solar religion gained possession of the throne of Egypt. "When the god (of the sun) procreated a king," he writes, "he gave him the gift of life, strength and duration in the form of a magnetic fluid, so that in his veins ran 'the liquid of Ra, the gold of the gods and goddesses, the luminous fluid from the sun, source of all life, strength and persistence.' This fluid the King transmitted to the

Crown Prince, who was associated with him." In the first phase of this doctrine the Pharaoh, in the priestly belief, exercised full powers over the water supply and the growth of vegetation and all fertility. At a later time, the solar idea mentioned above superseded this view. Or, perhaps, the older became merged in the newer solar doctrine. The entire significance of the Pharaoh, his business in life, was the prosperity of the land and the people thereof, the magical fertilization of the soil, the flocks and the folk by the sun, as represented by himself. The punctual appearance of the Nile floods which fertilized the soil of Egypt, the fertility of women and animals, the presence of fish in the rivers were all due to his personal vigour and magic as the representative of the sun on earth.[1]

It was naturally believed that this exhausting office exercised a tremendous strain upon the Pharaoh, and the appearance of lean years or poor crops must certainly have been regarded as due to a partial failure of his powers. There are hints that in early times this was obviated by the sacrifice of the King and his substitution by his son, whose strength was unimpaired. But by degrees this practice seems to have been abandoned, in favour of a change of monarchs every seven or eight years.

"The belief that kings possess magical or supernatural powers by virtue of which they can fertilize the earth and confer other benefits on their subjects would seem to have been shared by the ancestors of all the Aryan races from India to Ireland," says Frazer. "It was the belief of the ancient Irish that when their kings observed the customs of their ancestors, the seasons were mild, the crops plentiful, the cattle fruitful, the waters abounded with fish, and the fruit trees had to be propped up on account of the weight of their produce."[2] The king was therefore priest, king and god, or demi-god in one and the same person. Indeed, in early times the line of demarcation between the king and the priest is so thin as scarcely to be discernible. At a later time the priesthood makes its appearance as a separate institution, but it invariably remains in the closest possible association with the kingship. "In Ireland," says Rhys, "druidism and the kingship went hand in hand, nor is it improbable that it was the same in Gaul, so that when the one fell, the other suffered to some extent likewise."[4] After the fall of the royal power in ancient Rome, it was found necessary to appoint a "King of the Sacrifices," that is, a priest who had to perform certain religious rites connected with the name of king.[5] The priest of the "Golden Bough" was also known as *"Rex Nemorensis,"* "King of the Forest," and we still have our "King" and "Queen" of the May.

EXPANSION OF THE IDEA OF THE DIVINE KINGSHIP

The doctrine of the Divine Kingship came by degrees to find acceptance over a very wide area. In Europe, it penetrated to Greece, Rome, Scandinavia and Ireland. In Egypt it composed the entire national religion. In other lands, it appears to have associated itself with many fertility cults. These primitive faiths connected with food-yielding trees, such as the oak, the hazel and the apple seem to have accepted it naturally.

In all likelihood they contained within themselves the incipient germ of such a belief. The doctrine of the solar king would help to explain their terms to the primitive people who maintained such cults. Wherever agriculture spread (and that it had its beginnings in the Nile country and was disseminated from that area is not now in doubt) the doctrine of the Divine Solar King was certain to accompany it. It rationalized the more ancient cults connected with the food-yielding trees, to some extent at least. In the case of Druidism, the oak was associated with the heavenly fire in the more primitive sense. The proof of this is that the ancient oak-cults of Zeus in Greece and Jupiter in Italy were most certainly sophisticated by the solar doctrine. Zeus, the ancient god of the oak tree, became "the bright sky," and in consequence was regarded as a solar deity.

The same may be said of Jupiter, who became "Lucetius," that is, "light" and its cause. In much the same manner, the Gallic deity Taranis, associated with the Druids by more than one classical writer, and equated by them with Jupiter, and who was almost certainly developed from the thunder-spirit resident in the oak, came in later times to be regarded as a sun-god and had as his symbol the solar wheel concerning which we hear so much in Irish lore and legend. The unwritten and undeveloped myth inherent in the ancient belief respecting the food-giving trees found in the later solar doctrine a larger fulfilment and justification of the primitive notions which slumbered within it.

THE DIVINE KINGSHIP AMONG THE CELTS

Writing on the subject of the Celtic priesthood, Mr. Kendrick remarks that the Celts, like the Greeks and Latins, were ruled by kings and princes invested with a spiritual as well as a temporal authority, who performed the ordinary functions of the priest. Celtic legend in Ireland reflects an ancient belief in the divinity of kings. But there must have been a tendency, even at an early period, "to distribute temporal and spiritual functions that had hitherto devolved upon the king alone and so to pass into the stage in which the conduct of religious affairs is entrusted to those who were purely and simply priests." "A Keltic divine king preceded in point of time the Keltic priest pure and simple."[6]

Were the first Druids therefore priest-kings? When one considers the close relationship of sacred food-yielding trees with officials known as "kings," as found in Italy and elsewhere, the ascription would, I feel, seem to be a more than conjectural one, and so would appear to imply that the idea of the kingship in connection with the worship of such trees was coeval with the inception of such worship. But the adoration of food-yielding trees must indeed have been of extremely ancient provenance and doubtless in its first stages must have been the care of chiefs or of a caste who would later develop a regal position. That it would be regarded as of the utmost importance to the community is obvious. If it preceded the introduction of agriculture, it might seem to remain doubtful whether the ideas connected with it were importations from the East, unless they were of the nature of adaptations to the cult of oak, hazel and apple-tree of "religious" ideas associated with Oriental food-yielding trees, such as the palm or the date—a contingency suggested by M. Siret, as we have seen. On the other hand, it appears to me more probable for many reasons that the folk of Europe alone may have been responsible for the religious ideas they entertained respecting the food-bearing trees they adored. Indeed the likelihood is that the oak, once accepted as a symbol of vegetational increase and fertility, continued to be so regarded long after the adoption of the agricultural mode of life. That it actually was so among the Romans is clear.

Its Connection with Druidism

In Ireland the Druidic caste was closely associated with the kingship. The monarchy was connected with a cult of royal or famous ancestral spirits identified with the god-race of the Tuatha Dé Danann, who were from time to time reborn as kings. Some of these were solar gods, indeed the entire race of the Tuatha Dé appears to have had a solar connection, so that the position in Ireland reveals a similarity to that in ancient Egypt. The ceremony of the coronation of an Irish king makes it plain that it signified "not only his admission to the sovereignty of Ireland, but his reception into a higher sphere of action as a divine being endowed with superhuman qualities and capabilities." The king was surrounded by restrictive taboos, lest the powers that were incarnated in him, and in whose preservation the well-being of the people was involved, should suffer injury. These early Irish monarchs exercised a priestly as well as a kingly office and may well be described as priest-kings.' There were even Druid kings. Ailill Aulomon, King of Munster, who flourished in the first century A.D., was such a one, while three Druid-kings ruled in "the Isle of Thule" and there were other instances of royal Druids in Ireland.'

Dion Chrysostom makes the association of the Druids with the kingship clear enough. Writing of the Druids of Gaul about A.D. 100, the Greek sophist remarks: "Without their advice even kings dare not resolve nor execute any plan, so that in truth it was they who ruled, while the kings who sat on golden thrones and fared sumptuously in their palaces became mere ministers of the Druids' will."' That this was also the case in Ireland is certain, as many passages in early Irish literature proclaim. The *Táin Bó Cualnge* says that the men of Ulster must not speak before the King, and the King must not speak before his Druid. The King was attended by ten officers, one of whom was always a Druid.

The Divine King in Ireland

Irish myth and legend are also eloquent of the belief that the king was responsible for the success of the crops and for the food supply in general. Some Irish kings were "pledged" to rule for seven years in rotation, along with others, in order that their magical powers of production might not be over-strained. To ensure that they would keep faith, the three kings of Emania, in Ulster, who ruled thus by rotation, gave as hostages seven chiefs who were liable to death by fire if the king for whom they were security did not resign at the end of his septennial term.[10] The burning of such hostages may have been a relic of the sacrifice of kings, a substitution of less important lives for the royal person, such as is thought to have been the rule in early Egypt. We have already seen that a tradition existed in Caithness that Druids were burnt when too old to exercise their office. As revealing the power of the Druids in Ireland in connection with royal privileges, we discover a tradition that a Prince of Leinster, who sought to hold court at Tara, was informed by a senior Druid that he might not do so, as he had not been admitted to the order of Knighthood, which was the passport to such a privilege.[11]

If the crops failed and famine supervened, the King was held responsible. And were the King maltreated, the harvest failed. When the vassal clans revolted in Ireland in the reign of Tuathal Teachtmhor, in the first century A.D., says tradition, famine followed, and the people were informed by the Druids that the failure of the crops was due to the manner in which they had murdered the sub-King of Connaught.[12] In the reign of Cairbre, a bad king, "there was not one grain in the ear, one acorn on the oak, or one nut on the hazel," the earth withholding her fruits for five years. In the days of the good King Conaire, again, fish were plentiful in the streams, there was abundance of everything and fair weather prevailed.

But if a king were not free from all bodily blemish, his reign would be marred. And were his consort not equally virtuous with himself, the earth might not yield. The Queen, it may incidentally be remarked, had Druids of her own. So long as Conn, King of Tara, was married to the virtuous Eithne, all went well. But on her death, he espoused a fairy wife, and during the year they dwelt together there was neither corn nor milk in Ireland.[13] The Druids sought for a human victim, but a cow was offered up in his stead. Even the great King Conchobar, who was "wiser than any creature," was not permitted to tender advice, lest he might deliver a false judgment, a proceeding which would have had an evil effect upon the crops.[14] Irish kings were, in some cases, probably sacrificed before they became too frail to exercise their magical powers of fertility, and this may account for the wistful exclamation of King Ailill: "If I am slain, it will be for the redemption of many."

THE ASSOCIATION OF KINGS WITH SACRED TREES

Now, as we have seen, it was believed that tree-spirits made the crops to flourish. These tree-spirits became gods such as the Greek Zeus and the Roman Jupiter, originally gods of the oak. Ancient Greek kings mimicked the functions of Zeus and made mock thunder and rain so that vegetable fertility might follow.[15] Irish kings did likewise. The king's life appears to have been connected with a certain tree, perhaps that species of tree in which the spirit of an ancestor was supposed to lurk, who, at the due season of his reincarnation, left his place of immurement and entered his mother's body, to be born again as a man. His life was bound up with this tree, as is that of the Australian aborigine with his *okanikilla*, the tree or rock in which his spirit resides until it is due for reincarnation. Such trees were represented in Ireland by the *bilé*, or sacred tree. Some of the tribes of Gaul appear to have taken their names from trees. Thus the Eburones, dwelling in the north-east of Gaul, were "the yew-tree tribe," and their surname *Vivisci*, implies that they were "Mistletoe Men," as the Druids were "Oak Men," a circumstance which might lead to the conclusion that the name of "Druid" also once had a tribal as well as a religious significance. "Names borrowed directly from trees are also found —*Eburos*, or *Ebur*, 'yew,' *Derua*, or *Deruacus*, 'oak,' etc."[16] I have already alluded to the existence in Scotland and Ireland of ancient groves the branches of which must not be cut or broken.

RITUAL MARRIAGE OF THE DIVINE KING

By the exercise of his marital functions the Divine King promoted the fertility of his country. I have already alluded to the circumstance that at the festival of the *Lugnassad* the Irish kings, as Rhys suggests, seem to have gone through a species of ritual marriage with a woman representing the realm of Ireland. This was, indeed, the marriage of the sun and the soil, and was one and the same with the Roman and Egyptian idea of the ritual marriage between the Divine King and Queen.

We find such a royal ritual marriage described in Frazer's *Golden Bough* (the classical instance of it indeed) in connection with the cult of Diana near the modern Nemi, in Italy. The priest of this grove guarded a certain tree there jealously, but should he be overcome by a rival in combat, he lost his office and his life, and his conqueror took his place. Such a candidate must break a branch of a certain tree in the grove before he could do battle with the guardian priest, "the King of the Wood." Diana, like the Irish goddess of the soil, was not regarded as a mere deity of trees alone, but was also a goddess who gave fertility to the crops and to humans, and according to some Roman authors she annually went through a ritual of marriage with the King of the Wood, a living woman probably enacting her part in this ceremony.[17] We see, then, that the self-same rite of a marriage between persons representing the sun and the soil (for Virbius, or "the King of the Wood," was merely a surrogate of Jupiter) took place in Italy and distant Ireland alike. The tree at Nemi from which a branch was plucked was certainly an oak.[18] Its branch equates with the "Golden Bough" of Latin and Hellenic legend.

TRACES OF THE KING'S TREE IN CELTIC STORY

We find no sacred tree figuring in the ritual marriage at the Irish *Lugnassad*, the wedding of the sun-god Lug. That is not to say that the guarded tree of the grove finds no equivalent in Celtic myth. Davies, no very good guide, certainly, but here, I think, trustworthy enough, quotes an ancient Welsh poem, "The Avalenau," which tells how the bard Merddin, or Merlin, armed himself with sword and shield and lodged in the Caledonian wood, guarding a tree in order to gratify the goddess Bun, "the Maid," who seems to have been the nymph or patroness of the tree in question.[19] What is this, if not a parallel to what took place at Nemi? Merddin alludes to himself as "a wild and distracted object," thus heightening the resemblance to "the ghastly priest" of the Arician grove. And here Avallon, the mysterious, the otherworld of the Brythonic Celts, takes the place of that sacred Irish land in which stood the "Silver Branch." The writer of "The Avalenau" could not have invented this parallel with Arician practice. The mythic implications behind "The Golden Bough" story were unknown in his day.

But Professor Macalister, alluding to the myth of "The Golden Bough," as set forth by Frazer, has made it clear that "as in the sacred grove of the Golden Bough at Aricia, the King of Tara reigned, as a rule, by virtue of having slain his predecessor." The ancient Irish historians knew of this custom of the slaying of predecessors, but did not understand it, or had forgotten its purport. They connected it with the idea of a blood-feud. In any case, they allude to a series of kings who were slain by their successors. When the king began to lose his faculties, he was slain in a ritual combat.[20] As I have shown, the lives of Irish kings were mystically connected with trees. It seems, therefore, not improbable that some such ritual proceeding took place in Ireland as in the Arician grove. Miss Eleanor Hull, it should be noted, did not take Macalister's contention seriously. She did not believe the royal lists upon which it was founded to be authentic. "It was an obvious device to make the successor to the kingship the slayer of his predecessor." It does not seem to me "an obvious device," and it is evident that Miss Hull was unaware of the passage in "The Avalenau," and of other Celtic allusions to sacred trees in their association with royalty.[21]

IRISH KINGS AND MAGICAL TESTS

The connection between Irish royalty and the Druids is further illustrated by the nature of some of the magical tests to which the Irish kings were subjected before coronation. One of these at least is specifically associated with Druidic belief. The candidate must drive in his chariot to two stones called Bloc and Bluicne, which opened up sufficiently to allow him to pass between them were he accepted, but closed before him were he rejected. These in some way were the memorials of certain Druids who may have been buried alive at the spot. The story concerning them is obscure. It may have been that the boulders in question were of that class of stone which was believed to enshrine the spirit of a dead man. Bloc and Bluicne appear to have been the proto-Druids of Tara. The entrance to a megalithic shrine was usually regarded as of great sanctity, and it may be that the stones Bloc and Bluicne formed such a boundary. To pass between such stones was regarded as a test of worthiness. By passing betwixt them the candidate is "reborn."[22] Some idea concerning ritual rebirth seems then to have been associated with Druidic belief, some such notion as was connected with the "rebirth" of kings in Egypt. In the Egyptian mysteries at the point when the Pharaoh was reborn, the *dad* or sacred pillar of Osiris was erected. The ceremony seems to have been of the nature of what has been called a *"rite de passage,"* the inauguration into a new life, were the candidate worthy. Needless to say that in the case of a divinely descended monarch it could seldom have remained unaccomplished.

THE LIA FAIL

The magical stone of the kings of Ireland which was situated at Tara and which recognized the true High Kings of Ireland by emitting a loud shriek when they placed their feet upon it, has also Druidical associations. Legend avers that one morning King Conn, "the Hundred Fighter," repaired at sunrise to the battlements at Tara, accompanied by his three Druids, Mael, Bloc and Bluicne, and his three bards, for the purpose of watching the firmament, so that no hostile being from the air might suddenly descend upon Erin. In the course of his inspection, Conn chanced to tread upon a stone which immediately shrieked under his feet so loudly as to be heard all over Tara and throughout the bounds of East Meath. He asked his Druids to explain the omen to him, and so profound was its significance that they required fifty-three days to arrive at a decision respecting the same. At length they informed him that the name of the stone was Fal, and that its cry was ominous of the royal descent of those who trod it.[23] Professor Macalister is of opinion that its shriek was produced by a "bull-roarer."[24] The Stone of Fal was evidently that in which the spirit or protectress of Ireland was thought to reside. It is not the same as the British coronation stone, now in Westminster Abbey.[25]

Lastly, in Britain we discover at least one myth which has a relationship with the Divine Kingship. I allude to the myth of the Waste Land of Logres, in the pseudo-Chrestien portion of the "Conte du Graal," which recounts that in the wells and springs of Logres, which is either the South-western or Central part of England (for authorities differ as to this), certain damsels dwelt who regaled wayfarers with pasties, meat and bread. But Amangons, King of that land, did wrong to one of them and purloined her golden cup, so that "nevermore came damsels out of the springs to comfort the wanderer." Worse still, the king's men followed his evil example. Thereafter the springs dried up and the grass withered and the land became waste and the Court of the Rich Fisher disappeared. This is certainly a myth of a flourishing land which prospered until a sinful king offended its presiding genii, when it was given over to a condition of devastation. I believe, as did Alfred Nutt, that the tale "embodies a genuine tradition," and I am inclined to think that it has a British origin, though it appears for the first time in a French setting.[16] Amangons has been identified by Rhys with the British deity Gwynn ap Nudd.

Summarizing the evidence for the connection between the cult of Druidism and the institution of the Divine Kingship, we find that:

(*a*) All those cults which adopted the idea of the Divine Kingship in Europe were cults of fertility.

(*b*) In Ireland, Druidism and the kingship were inextricably associated. It would seem that when the kingship disappeared in Gaul, Druidism lost its power and significance in that area.

(*c*) The solar doctrine would appear to have given those tree or fertility cults which embraced it in Europe a larger fulfilment and justification of the primitive notions which their worshippers had previously entertained.

(*d*) Certain Druids in Ireland functioned as kings, as priests of tree-cults in Italy seem to have done, although the royal status of the latter appears to have been of a ritual character only.

(*e*) The monarchy in Ireland was connected with a cultus of ancestral solar gods who were thought to be reincarnated in the kings from time to time. These kings might not function without the assistance of the Druids, nor might they even venture an opinion on any matter of discussion before the Druids had spoken.

(*f*) The Irish kings were associated with certain sacred trees, the life of which was coeval with their own. This was a belief connected both with Druidism and with the cultus of the Divine King.

(*g*) Some of the magical tests which proved the fitness of an Irish king to reign are associated with the Druids.

(*h*) The "coronation stone" of the High Kings of Ireland at Tara was connected with a Druidic myth.

There is, I am convinced, a sufficiency of evidence to make it plain that Druidism and the Sacred Kingship in Ireland were institutions which had come to be so closely amalgamated that they might not well have been separated without results fatal to both. The same certainly holds good respecting similar conditions in Gaul, and, as has been seen, vestiges of the association of a kingship with tree-cults have been found in Italy. But that some tree-cults have existed without kings is certain, and I think that, judging from this, an amalgamation of cults must have occurred, though gods may have taken the place of kings in those arboreal cults in which no regal figure makes its appearance.

Chapter X

INFLUENCE OF OTHER CULTS ON DRUIDISM

T HE scholarship of the eighteenth and early nineteenth centuries appears to have been convinced that Druidism had its origin in the Orient. This notion survived well into the latter half of last century and is even not without its supporters to-day. Reuben Barrow, for example, boldly averred "that the druids of Britain were Brahmins is beyond the least shadow of a doubt."[1] Borlase traced a surprising uniformity between the cults of the Druids and the Persian Magi, a theory in which he was supported to some extent by the imaginative General Charles Vallancey, who believed that the Celtic priests flourished first as Brahmins, then as Chaldeans and lastly as Magi. Faber, in his *Cabiri*, compared the beliefs of Brahmanism and Druidism, and Franklin, in *Tenets and Doctrines of the Jaynes and Buddhists*, followed suit. This kind of theory almost certainly had its origin in the ideas concerning the migration of races which were current a century or more ago, in connection with which ethnological hypotheses were fabricated on a Scriptural basis. Those who had taken refuge in the Ark of Noah were still regarded as the several parents of the races of man, a notion which found its climax in the wild but widely accepted "Arkite Philosophy" of Jacob Bryant.

But in sober truth one religion of Asiatic provenance appears to have exercised a certain influence upon the Druidic faith in the period of its decline. After the conquest of Gaul and Britain by the Romans, these lands certainly became the theatres of rival cults, as indeed Rome herself was at that period, the first century of our era. Towards the end of that era the cult of Mithraism made its appearance in Europe, and this particular faith succeeded in making considerable headway both in Gaul and Britain, flourishing in these regions almost until the close of the first century.

In our own country the remains of the Mithraic religion are easily traced. Between Poultry and Cannon Street, in London, a carved relief of the god Mithras slaying a bull was unearthed at a depth of twenty feet. It had been dedicated by a retired soldier from the Second Legion at Caerleon at some time in the second century and must have stood in some Mithraic shrine contiguous to the city. Other sculptures of the same type have been discovered at York and Housesteads, Rutchester and Burham, and when we recall the importance of the bull in Druidic rite, it does not seem improbable that a fading Druidism may have seen in Mithraic rite, as practised by considerable numbers of Roman soldiers, a religion kindred in its ideas and its practice.

Mithraism was the cult of Mithras, the Persian god of light, the sun-god. It spread to Rome as early as the beginning of the first century and by the dawn of the second century had established itself almost throughout the Roman Empire, more especially among the military class. It was a mystery religion in which candidates had to pass through numerous degrees. It made no appeal to women but appears to have had a powerful fascination for the masculine sense of sodality. It constituted, indeed, a male brotherhood closely resembling Freemasonry. It also had associations with the cult of the Divine King, for one of its doctrines held that the King or Emperor received his power from the sun and was the earthly representative of that luminary. Military Commanders in Britain were among its more important converts.[a] The Magian priests of this faith must closely have resembled the Druids in their attitudes, both mental and physical.

But its sacred books have vanished, its ritual is unknown, and we are aware only that it was carried out in a cavern, the Mithræum, with considerable secrecy, and that its chief rite was the *Taurobolium*, or sacrifice of the sacred bull, the animal endowed with all the potencies of life, whose immolation indeed had created life in the world, and whose sacrifice at stated intervals ensured the continuance of existence, securing fertility to the fields and immortality to individuals. One of its rites was an oblation of bread and water, of which Justin remarks that it was similar to the Christian sacrament. Another part of its ritual consisted of a baptism of blood, in which the candidate crouched in a pit beneath the sacrificed bull and bathed himself in its gore. Its several degrees of initiation were associated with various animals. The spirit which infused it was intense and full of mystical emotion.

The Hon. Algernon Herbert, a scholar of great attainments, if of somewhat eccentric views, advanced the theory that Mithraism was a parody of Christianity and that it had been accepted by certain Romanized Britons in the reign of Julian the Apostate, Emperor of Rome in the middle years of the fourth century A.D., by which time Christianity had been established in Britain. The descendants of the Druids, he averred, were well adapted to its reception, more especially those of the old Welsh bards who flourished at this period. In short, Mithraism in Britain gave a fillip to a dying British Druidism.

This late renascence of paganism, he held, "was the mongrel produce of Druidism, Mithraic heresy and modern Free-Masonry, kept up under the name of those people (the bards) whose ostensible office was only musical." If this were so, the Druidism which composed a part of the *mélange* must indeed have been of a late and highly artificial character, and although it is not altogether improbable that such a *pastiche* of the old religion may have lingered in some parts of South Britain, as the unaltered Druidic faith certainly did in Scotland and Ireland until the period in question, the evidence that it actually did so is, as we have seen, anything but convincing. At the same time we are certainly faced with certain references in the Welsh triads which seem to preserve in places veiled allusions to ideas not unassociated with the lore of the Neo-Platonic schools of Alexandria, if not of Mithraism. It is, however, essential that we should wait upon approved translations of them by trusted Cambrian scholarship, a condescension for which we can scarcely hope at the present juncture and from the present mood of a body of experts who appear to be either unfriendly to or disinclined for a task which they frankly admit to be beyond their critical capacities owing to the intractable nature of the ancient texts with which they are confronted. That being so, we must extend to them a large measure of sympathy and forbearance.

As we have seen, the tomb of the priest Chyndonax reveals him as a servant of the god Mithras, though not as a Druid, while seemingly Mithraic references occur in Arthurian literature. But none of these can relate to any intermingling of Mithraism with the *original* Druidism and must refer to an admixture of the Asiatic faith with late survivals of Druidism of a more or less fragmentary character.

DRUIDISM AND CHRISTIANITY

Certain writers on Druidism, as, for example, Stukeley and Richards, have created an impression that the Druids eagerly and almost joyfully accepted the Christian faith on its appearance in Ireland and Scotland and that they even regarded it as the fulfilment of their own. But the very reverse appears to have been the case. The Irish Druids appear to have been strongly opposed to St. Patrick and his coadjutors, while those of Scotland revealed the most vigorous hostility to Columba, deriding his powers and seeking to neutralize his conversion of the people. In all likelihood, Patrick took up a position analogous to that assumed at a later date in South Britain by Augustine, engrafting his primitive Christianity upon the body of Druidic paganism. Dr. O'Donovan, editor of *The Annals of the Four Masters*, remarks that: "Nothing is clearer than that Patrick engrafted Christianity on the pagan superstition with so much skill that he won the people over to the Christian religion before they understood the exact difference between the two systems of belief."

Sir John Rhys says that: "Irish Druidism absorbed a certain amount of Christianity, and it would be a problem of considerable difficulty to fix on the point where it ceased to be Druidism and from which onwards it could be said to be Christianity in any restricted sense of that term." The Irish Goidel's faith in Druidism was never suddenly undermined. In the saints he beheld only more powerful Druids and Christ, in his eyes, took the place of the Druids.[3]

The struggle betwixt the early Christian missionaries and the Druids, thought Miss Hull, "was a real and long one." The Druids fought a bitter fight against the new faith. "It is likely that as time went on the Christian teachers felt it necessary to pretend to all the qualities and powers possessed by the Druids."[4] But it is too frequently forgotten that early Christianity, especially in its "Colonial" forms, was often in itself of a

very debased type, such as would readily fuse with a faith like Druidism
and indeed it appears to have been chiefly because their miraculous powers
as enchanters surpassed those of the Druids that its ministers prevailed.
One sometimes wonders how the modern Christian would regard the faith
of his distant predecessors could he behold it in actual practice and it is
probably as well that in the majority of cases he knows little or nothing
about that phase of it! When the Druids of Ireland chanted their charms
against St. Senan, and environed him in mists and horrid darkness, he
exclaimed: "Stronger is the spell that I have brought with me, and better
is my lore."[5]

As we have seen, Columba's strife with the Druids of Caledonia
was one prolonged struggle of magic against magic. Nor may numerous Celtic "Saints" be classed otherwise than as pagan deities with
all the marks of their heathen origin vividly upon them. "St. Molling"
is a character out of the Fenian saga, and "St. Brigit" merely a
Christianized version of the pagan deity of the same name. The plea that
there were "two separate Brigits," one a pagan divinity and the other a
Christian saint who actually existed, may be politic divinity, but it makes
bad reasoning in folk-lore.

In Guernsey a legend is told of "Le Petit Bon Homme Andriou,"
an Arch-Druid who was the last to hold out against Christianity. His
brethren had all accepted the new faith, so in high dudgeon he retired
to a cave at the extremity of Jerbourg Point. Here he would stand for
hours at a time gazing out to sea. One day, during a violent gale, he
perceived a ship labouring heavily in the trough of the waves, so he
interceded with his pagan gods for those on board her. The inattentive
or callous deities whom he petitioned disregarded his prayers and the
vessel was driven almost upon the dangerous rocks on which he stood.
In despair, he supplicated the God of the Christians, and vowed that if the
ship were spared he would become a Christian and dedicate a chapel to
the Virgin. As he wrestled in prayer, the storm abated and the ship came
to harbour. So Andriou embraced Christianity and dedicated a chapel,
as he had vowed, to the Mother of God.[6]

The Hymn of Fiacc tells how the Druids foretold the coming of
Christianity to Erin:

> "For thus had their prophets foretold that the coming
> Of a new time of peace would endure after Tara
> Lay desert and silent, the Druids of Laery
> Had told of his coming, had told of the Kingdom."

Canon Warren, writing on the conversion of the Irish Celts, has
commented upon "the curious policy of the Druids concerning the advent
of St. Patrick, betraying in its language some acquaintance with the
ritual of the Christian church."[7] That there were Christians in Ireland
before Patrick we know from the Chronicle of Prosper of Aquitaine, but

that the Druids of Ireland, in the fifth century, knew all there was to know concerning Christianity is scarcely to be gainsaid.

But we have also to consider the theory that the Druids of Ireland and Scotland carried on a Christianized form of their faith under the name of "Culdees." The name "Culdee" seems to be derived from *céle dé*, "servant of God," and we may safely ignore the more fanciful etymologies of it. A tradition existed that "the Culdees succeeded the Druids at no great distance of time,"⁸ and a good deal of evidence of a certain kind has been amassed which might seem to support the belief that they were persons of Druidic faith who had adopted the Christian doctrine and life. In Scotland we find them established at Dunkeld in the first quarter of the ninth century, carrying on a ritual which appears to have been derived from the rite of the Oriental Church, and we also hear of them as established at St. Andrews. Skene alluded to them as an ascetic order who adopted the solitary service of God in isolated cells, and who later became associated in communities of anchorites or hermits, and he seems to have held the opinion that they succeeded the Columban monks and were finally absorbed among the secular clergy.⁹

The Culdees seem to have recognized the old Celtic form of the tonsure. The Second Council of Chalons denounced them as heretics in the year 813 and the fifth Canon of the Council of Ceol-Hythe decreed in 816 that they were not to be permitted to function as priests in England. They seem to have worshipped in a part of the Church of St. Regulus at St. Andrews until the year 1124, when this privilege was withdrawn from them. At Ripon and York they flourished in the eighth century, and may have held sway for some considerable time in Iona, though this has been denied. In Ireland they functioned at Clones and Armagh and it is even held that in that land they survived the Reformation, as in 1628 a deed was executed by Burton, prior of the Cathedral Church of Armagh, "on behalf of the vicars choral and Culdees of the same."

Bishop Worth, in his rental of Killaloe, drawn up in 1667, adds as a note on the thirty-three canons: "Those in Ulster are called Culdees."¹⁰ But, as Skene remarks, the term "Culdee" appears later to have taken on the significance of "Canon." Pinkerton dismisses the Culdees as "corrupted monks." In my opinion they were the servants of the early British Celtic Church who stood apart from the pretensions of the Roman bishops to hegemony over the Christian Church as a whole. Indeed, they appear to have behaved in this respect much as did Nectan, King of the Picts, and the clergy of Wales. Beda regarded the Culdees of his day as heretical, and Archbishop Lanfranc was horrified because they did not pray to the saints and refused to recognize the Roman service. St. Bernard stigmatized them as "beasts, absolute barbarians . . . Christian in name, but really pagans." They actually committed the unspeakable crime of marriage! Perhaps, the Culdees preserved a tincture of Druidic superstition, but this was surely no more "pagan" than that of Rome, which nourished a tradition of Egyptian doctrine and actually accepted the beliefs of Egypt neatly disguised.

> "O wad some Power the giftie gie us
> to see oursels as ithers see us!"

Wonderful it is indeed to read of and witness the follies of men who know all that is to be known concerning the faith they profess excepting the very articles of its origin and those distortions of thought and superstition which transformed its original purity into the semblance of that very paganism which they abhor!

Chapter XI

DRUIDISM AND THE MAGICAL ARTS

THE title of this chapter has been specifically framed to make it clear beyond peradventure that its contents deal exclusively with such illustrations of the magical art as seem to have been practised by the Druids. It is thus not descriptive of Celtic Magic as a whole, and indeed I have already provided an embracive account of the occult arts as known to the Celtic peoples in a recent work, *The Magic Arts in Celtic Britain,* to which the interested reader is referred.

More than one of the greater writers of the Classical period has laid stress on the association of the Druidic caste with the occult sciences. Pliny alludes to the great popularity of magic in Gaul until a time within his own recollection, and adds that it was only during the reign of Tiberius (d. A.D 37) that a decree was issued against the Druids "and the whole tribe of diviners."[1] It is necessary, too, to indicate this author's somewhat neglected allusion to the Druids as "magicians" ("The Druids—for so their magicians are called") which will be found in his *Natural History* (XVI, 249). It is curious to find this well-informed collector of traditions seemingly referring to the Druids as though they were sorcerers and nothing more, but this is in fact due to his translators, for the Latin term *magus* which he employs in describing the Druid priests has not originally or appropriately the meaning of "magician," but rather that of "wise man," or, as we might say, "philosopher," being derived from the Zend *maz,* "great," and having also the significance of one who interprets dreams. It is in this latter sense, I believe, that Pliny makes use of it rather than as implying an enchanter or wizard. Indeed the whole trend of the passage which follows—that which deals with the culling of the mistletoe—is eloquent of the art of auspices or omen, rather than of crude sorcery.

Dion Chrysostom's allusion to the Druids would appear to bear out this view of their general character as practitioners of auspices, and indeed it is only in legend and folk-lore that we find the Druids alluded to as associated with the cruder forms of magic. Dion tells us that the Druids "concern themselves with divination and all branches of wisdom," without whose advice even kings dared not resolve upon any course of action. Nowhere, indeed, in classical literature have I been able to discover any reference to the Druidic caste as practitioners of what might be described as the lower forms of occult usage, of that sort which we associate with the shaman or the medicine-man, and it would appear that less worthy occult practices began to be indulged in only after the official caucus of Druidism was dispersed by persons who had possibly only a passing acquaintance with Druidic wisdom, "spaewives" and peripatetic conjurers. The position, indeed, seems to have approximated to that which followed upon the breakdown of the Egyptian religion, when the priests of inferior orders repaired in crowds to Rome and the West, acting as mere jugglers and charlatans, as Origen and Plutarch both testify.[2]

The more modern use of the Celtic word *druidheachd*, indeed, reveals the truth of this, meaning, as it does, "magic," or "sorcery," and makes it plain that degeneracy had taken place in Druidic occult custom. Yet, in a poem in the *Book of Taliesin* we discover the Welsh term *derwyddon* employed for the Magi or Wise Men who came with presents to the infant Jesus, showing that in this case, as in the Irish "Leabhar Breac," it was used in precisely the same sense as by Pliny. In Irish, too, *drui* was usually rendered by the Latin *magus*, as in Pliny's text.[3] *The Book of Armagh* also applies the term "Magi" to the Druids in the same sense.

In this chapter I will essay to describe within small compass the several departments of the occult arts as practised by the Druids: their magical system in general, their use of enchantment and transformation; the nature of the spells, charms and incantations employed by them; their methods of augury and system of omen; their prophetic pretensions and knowledge of Astrology. In the first five of these sections we shall find that the main sources of our information proceed from Irish records. As regards their augural lore, the greater part of this has also come down to us through Irish literature, but not a little from classical sources and folk-lore. For their prophetic knowledge we are also chiefly indebted to Irish records.

MAGIC

It is almost impossible to find a page in early Irish literature which does not contain a reference to the Druid in his character of a wielder of magic power, and it is as well to remark that the sources of these references are mainly traditional. In order to conceal himself from his enemies he would cast a dense fog over a landscape. To cover their approach from the sea such a method was employed by the Druids of the Tuatha Dé Danann when they first invaded Ireland, then inhabited by the Fir Bolgs. But these also had Druids, who dispelled the exhalations thus magically engendered.[4] When the Tuatha Dé themselves were at a later time beset by the Milesians they sent a "Druidical" tempest against the invaders which made it impossible for them to reach the shore, until Donn, one of their leaders, prayed "the power of the land of Erin" to cause it to subside.[5]

The Druids of King Loegaire persecuted the early Christian missionaries by sending heavy snowfalls and thick darkness upon them.[6] In like manner, Broichan, the chief Druid of King Brude of the Picts of Scotland, raised a terrific storm accompanied by fell darkness over Loch Ness, so that St. Columba had need of all his faith to withstand the same.[7] The Druid Mog Ruith of Munster, opposing King Cormac and his magi, drove them out of his province by depriving them of water by the simple expedient of drying up the wells. He discharged an arrow into the air so that where it landed a spring was found which provided the men of Munster with the water they needed. They then fell upon the enemy and routed them.[8] The Druid Mathgen threatened to overwhelm his enemies by casting mountains upon them and other Druids transformed trees and stones into the semblance of armed men to destroy their foes.[9]

Almost a compendium of the factors of this species of Druidic magic is supplied by the tale which recounts the manner in which St. Patrick overcame the Druids of King Loegaire at Tara, and which is included in the Tripartite Life of the saint in question. At Slane, Patrick lit a paschal fire to celebrate Easter. But it clashed with the *Beallteinn* fire of the Druids, who proceeded to the spot where it burned. A magical contest followed, and the chief Druid plunged the landscape deep in winter's snowfall. This was dispersed when Patrick made the Sign of the Cross. The king then commanded that each of the representatives of the warring sects should cast his book into the river, so that he in whose volume the letters remained undimmed might be declared the minister of Truth. To this, however, the Druids would not consent. It was agreed that the chief Druid and St. Benin, who accompanied Patrick, should each enter a bower, which should then be set on fire. It is perhaps unnecessary to add that the missionary came out unscathed from this ordeal while the Druid was consumed to ashes.

A strange story of Druidic magic is recounted of the beautiful Mughain, Queen of Ireland, who was unable to present her husband with an heir. In her vexation she betook herself to Finnen, "a Druid of Belus," who consecrated a draught of water of which she drank. As a result she brought forth a white lamb and was naturally much mortified. But the creature was sacrificed, she drank once more of the magic draught and in due time a son was born to her.[10]

In *The Chronicles of the Picts and Scots* (p. 31) we read that when the Picts came to Ireland, the King of Leinster offered them land to settle on if they would expel a people known as the Tuatha Fidhbha. When they met this folk in battle and it became known that they employed poisoned weapons, one of the leaders of the Picts, a Druid named Drostan, ordered that the milk of seven score white cows should be poured into a great bath and that every Pict who was wounded should bathe therein. The new milk neutralized the poison in their wounds, so that none of them was injured. From these folk, we are told, "is every spell and every charm and every *sreod* (sneeze) and voices of birds and every omen."

THE DRUIDIC WAND

The magic wand wielded by the Irish Druids is alluded to frequently in Celtic legend. It was generally made from the wood of the yew tree and sometimes took the form of a symbolic branch of crescent shape from which little tinkling bells depended. Such a wand, it may be said, was probably an imitation of the "silver bough," the magic apple-branch borne by the god Manannan, which acted as a sesame to the land of the immortals. It had the property of causing a great peace to descend even in the midst of battle, for we read in the passage known as "the Inebriety of the Ultonians" that when Sencha, the Chief Bard of Ulster, waved his wand, the roar of battle was hushed. In the piece entitled "The Dialogue of the Two Sages" we are informed that a Bard, Neidha, carried such a silver branch, and that the poets of the second order bore silver branches, while the chief poets carried a branch of gold, the inferior bards being contented with a branch of bronze.[11]

The Druidic wand, as we shall see, was employed in transformations. In Gaul, it was formed of the wood of the oak, while in Ireland hawthorn and rowan wood were in use as well as yew.[12] In Wales, according to a song in *The Myvyrian Archaiology* (p. 62), mention is made of "the magic wood of Mathonwy, which grows in the wood, of more exuberant fruit, on the bank of the river of spectres." Mathonwy was one of the rulers of the British Underworld and thus a master of magic.

We find Mathonwy's son, the celebrated Math, using such a magic wand as a means of divining whether the lady Arianrhod was a virgin or otherwise. He insisted that she should step over it with results disastrous to her reputation. In Yorkshire they still say that "if a girl strides over a broom-handle she will be a mother before she is a wife," and elsewhere of a woman about to bring forth an illegitimate child that "she has jumped over the besom."

I have already fully described and explained the myth of the Silver Bough in a previous work, *The Magic Arts in Celtic Britain* (pp. 28-9).

ILLUSION AND TRANSFORMATION

The art of illusion was a prominent feature of Celtic Magic, but, in the main, it seems to have been the province of the fairies. So far as I am able to discover, this does not appear to have been among the Druidic magical arts. I am, of course, alluding to that species of glamour which transformed a bleak moorland locality into a palace of faerie and withered leaves into pieces of gold.

But in the art of transformation the Irish Druids were certainly not inferior to the elves. Not only could they wield that power of magical disguise which is more exactly defined by the term "shape-shifting," that is, the ability to assume any shape they chose, but they could also bespell others so that they appeared in forms unlike themselves, or in animal or even inanimate shapes. The Irish Druid Fer Fidail assumed the appearance of a woman, the better to permit him to abduct a certain maiden, while another Druid deceived Cuchullin, the Irish Achilles, by taking the form of the Lady Niamh. The Druid Fear Doirche, indignant with the maiden Saar, transformed her into a fawn, in which guise she became the mother of Ossian. When the unhappy children of Lir were transformed into swans by the enchantments of their stepmother Aoife, they said to her: "Thou shalt fall in revenge for it, for thy power for our destruction is not greater than the Druidic power of our friends to avenge it upon thee."

The Welsh Bard Taliesin vaunted that he could assume the appearance of any given object or element, a vulture upon a rock, an eagle, "the fairest of plants," the wood in the covert, the word of science, the sward itself.[13] Whilst in Ireland Mr. Wentz collected a strange tradition concerning a menhir which formerly stood on the coast opposite Inishmurray. It had been frequented by Druids who enchanted each other with brass rods into "stone and lumps of oak." They still haunted the spot in spirit-form, smiting man and beast, seemingly by casting certain objects at them. One of these objects was found. "It wasn't stone, nor marble, nor flint, and had human shape." The man who owned it decided to "blast" it open, and found the enchantment in its heart—"just like a man, with head and legs and arms." A Catholic priest took it away and pronounced it to be "a Druid enchanted."![14]

Canon MacCulloch states that the spell known as *fith-fath* was employed by the Druids to cause invisibility.[15] But I cannot discover or recall any particular instance in which this spell was used by a Druid. I have described and explained *fith-fath* elsewhere.[16] Interesting is the incantation by means of which the Druids formed a "hedge," the *airbe druad*, round an army, thus making a magic circle through which it could not penetrate. If one of the enemy thus surrounded could leap over this "hedge" the spell was broken, but the successful warrior perished instantly.[17] At the famous battle of Culdreimne, we are told in the *Annals of Ulster*, such a hedge was contrived by Fraechan, son of Temnan, "who made the Druids' *airbe* for Dearmait." But it was overthrown by Tuatan, son of Diman.

DRUIDIC SPELLS AND CHARMS

Here I shall deal only with such spells and charms as are known to have had a definite association with the Druids. We read in *The Sick-Bed of Cuchullin* that, on being deserted by the lady Fand, that champion fled to the mountains in a delirious fury. Druids were sent from Ulster to bring him to Emania, whereupon he attempted to slay them. But they pronounced "Druidic orations" against him and when these had rendered him powerless, the Druids administered to him a magic drink which caused him utterly to forget Fand.[18]

In the *Life of St. Senan* allusion is made to the use of spells by the Druids. Coel, a brother of St. Senan, was sent on an errand by MacTail, King of Hui Figente, to command that monarch's brother to quit his lands. In doing so he lost his life, much to the wrath of the King, whom his Druid comforted with the words: "Fear not, for I shall take a charm to thy brother so that he shall either leave thy land or die"—a boast

which was not fulfilled. Regarding the nature of this charm we are not enlightened.

I have already drawn attention to the spells employed by the Pictish Druids against St. Columba. It has been said that in order to pronounce a Celtic spell or incantation a special posture was adopted. The speaker balanced himself on one leg, with one arm outstretched and one eye closed to concentrate the power of the spell.[19] Druidic spells were perhaps associated with indwelling genius on the part of those who wove them. In the story of Deirdre, for instance, we read that when the Sons of Usnach were prevailing over the warriors of King Conor, the King went to Cathbad, his Druid, and said to him: "Go, Cathbad, to the Sons of Usnach, and play Druidism upon them." Whereupon Cathbad "had recourse to his intelligence and art to restrain the Children of Usnach, so that he laid them under enchantment, that is, by putting around them a viscid sea of whelming waves."

In the tale of "The Fair of Carman" we are told that three magicians and their dam who hailed from Greece, landed in Erin and caused widespread devastation by the power of their spells and incantations. But the native Druids, along with the poets and witches of the country, were sent against them and so wrought upon them by their sorcery that they forced the three men across the sea, leaving their mother, Carman, behind them as a hostage that they would never return to Erin.

The Irish Druids pronounced an incantation over a wisp of straw, hay, or grass, which they cast into the face of anyone when they wished him to take leave of his senses and become lunatic. Such a wisp was known as *Dlui Fulla*, or "the fluttering wisp." A Druid, jealous of the hero Comgan, whom he suspected to be his wife's lover, cast the *Dlui* at him, so that he became insane.[20]

A magical force was believed to reside in satirical incantations which enabled the Druid bards of Ireland to disfigure their enemies by the utterance of venomous jibes. If a king did not reward a bard for laudatory poems, he might lay himself open to what was known as the *Glam Dichinn*, or Satire from the Hill-tops, the procedure of which was as follows: the poet fasted upon the king's lands along with six other bards of varying status and, at the rising of the sun, betook himself to a hill which must be situated on the boundary of seven farms, or holdings. Here each poet must turn his face to a different land, the chief among them setting his countenance toward the land of the king about to be satirized. The backs of the party must be turned to a hawthorn tree growing on the top of the hill, while the wind should be blowing from the north. Each man was to hold a perforated stone and a thorn from the hawthorn in his hand, and each of them should sing a verse satirizing the king. These stones and thorns were then to be placed under the stem of the hawthorn. If the bards were in the wrong, the earth of the hill would rise and swallow them up; if the king were blameworthy, he and all his family would similarly be engulfed. This custom, we are informed, survived the introduction of Christianity and was even countenanced by its ministers.[21]

In Cormac's *Glossary*, we find satire explained as *Gairé*, that is "short life." He adds a tale to the effect that a certain Caier who had been satirized found his face covered with blisters raised by the invective. A satire of the bard Cairpre brought out blotches on the face of Bres, while another of his lampoons caused the Fomorians to become powerless. Queen Maeve of Ulster assured a hero that if he refused combat with Cuchullin her bards would so transform him by their satires that he would perish from shame.[22]

Miss Eleanor Hull remarks that: "there is no break between the ancient semi-magical formulæ chanted by the Druids and the later incantation of the wizard and the 'wise-woman.' They both arose in the Veda-like sacred hymns which formed the depository of the learning professed by the body of the druidical teachers and diviners and taught orally in the druidic schools. Most of them were never written down, and the fragments that we possess in writing are probably only the remains of a considerable body of oral literature." In course of time these forms became antiquated and were unintelligible even to the bards themselves.[23]

Peculiarly powerful as a system of incantation was the *Teinm Laegha*, a verse which conferred upon the Druid the power of understanding any hidden or mysterious set of circumstances. The name means "the Illumination of Rhymes" or "the Analysis of Song," and it appears to have been accompanied by a sacrifice to, or an invocation of, certain idols. It was put into practice on every occasion of importance, such as the choice of a chief, the choice of a plan of campaign, and so forth. It is said to have been wielded by Fin Mac Coul, who could exercise it by placing his thumb between his teeth. When the skull of the first lap-dog to enter Ireland was found many years after its death and its origin aroused controversy, a bard, Maen Mac Etnae, settled the point by recourse to *Teinm Laegha*, which seems to have been a charm in rhyme by which it was thought that the rhymer could discover that which he sought by magical inspiration.[24]

Another and equally important Druidic charm, which indeed almost achieved the status of a rite, was that known as *Imbas Forosnai*, that is "Illumination by the Palms of the Hands." It is described in the glossary of the pseudo-Cormac, King and Bishop of Cashel, who wrote towards the close of the ninth century. It was evidently a means by which the Bard or Druid discovered the significance of anything puzzling or mysterious. He chewed a piece of the raw flesh of a pig, a dog or a cat, and then retired to his bed, where he offered the morsel to his idol-god. If, before day, he had not received illumination concerning the point on which he desired information, he pronounced incantations upon his two palms and took his idols into his bed "in order that he might not be interrupted in his sleep." He then placed his two hands on his cheeks and fell into a deep slumber in which he received an intimation respecting that about which he wished to receive enlightenment. During his sleep four Druids chanted over him "to render his witness truthful." The ceremony was employed in discovering the rightful King of Ireland upon the death of a monarch, the new king being beheld in the Druid's vision.[15] A similar result was obtained by the ritual sacrifice of a white bull, the flesh and blood of which were partaken of by the priest.[16] In the "Leabhar na-h-Uidhre" we read how, when it was necessary to find a king for Ireland, the throne having been vacant for seven years after the death of Conaire Mor, the four provinces met and a bull-feast was made by them at Tara so that they might discover the man destined for the sovereignty. A bull was slain and a man partook of its flesh and broth. "And he slept under that meal, and a true oration was pronounced by four Druids upon him, and he saw in his dream the appearance of the man who would be made king of them, his countenance and description, and how he was occupied." This was Lugaidh, who was duly proclaimed King.[17]

Remarking that Gallo-Roman sculpture ignores the Druids, Mr. Kendrick suggests that it is possible that a group depicted on an altar found at Mavilly, near Beaune, may represent certain Druidic personages. One of these, he says, is holding his hand over his eyes. But he seems rather to be holding his hands upon his cheeks and it has occurred to me that not improbably the group represents the rite of *Imbas Forosnai*, which may well have had its Gaulish counterpart, although we have no information respecting the prevalence of this custom in Gaul.

THE MAGICAL SUN-WHEEL

In Chapter V I alluded to the Druid Mog Ruith, his magical wheel and the legend of his association with Simon Magus. Here I should like to discuss more particularly the nature of the wheel with which he is connected. It was, as the reader will recall, known as the *Roth Fáil*, that is the "Wheel of Fál," or "Wheel of Light," and occasionally *Roth Rámach*, or "the Wheel with Paddles," or as O'Curry calls it, a "Rowing Wheel" or "Oar Wheel." This wheel enabled Simon Magus to sail through the air, with what result we have seen. But another version of its myth foretold how it would prove a calamitous possession to Ireland and indeed to Europe, as it was in some way connected with a baleful scourge or plague which would decimate the people as far as the Tyrrhenian Sea.

A prophecy, erroneously attributed to St. Columba, told how the Wheel was a vast ship crowded by thousands of warriors and navigating on both land and sea. This latter legend appears to link up with those weird tales which were current in the France of the early ninth century concerning ships which put out from an aerial region known as Magonia. Agobard, Archbishop of Lyons, tells how he had seen several people who were said to have fallen from such vessels, whom he protected from the vengeance of a hostile crowd.[18] Gervase of Tilbury recounts a similar story about a rope having an anchor at its extremity, which anchor had become fixed in a hillock. One of the aerial crew of the vessel to which it belonged clambered down the rope, but was choked by the terrestrial air, which proved too dense for him. The rope was then released from above, and the unseen aerial craft proceeded on its way.[19]

I am of opinion that these stories are the memorials of Druidic belief which survived into a later age. Indeed the name of Magonia, which occurs in that related by the Frankish cleric Agobard, appears to make this clear enough when we compare it with the Celtic appellations of mystic lands such as Mag Mell and Mag Mon, revealing, I think, that Druidic beliefs survived in those areas in which Druidism had formerly flourished.

The *Roth Rámach*, says the prophecy falsely attributed to Columba (which is contained in the *Book of Leinster*[30]), was a ship containing one thousand beds, with a man for every bed, which would be wrecked on the pillar-stone of Cnomhchoill (near Tipperary), whose chief would slay every warrior it contained. Simon Magus, its inventor, because of the Christian tales concerning his journeys through the air, came to be associated with the Irish myths of the *Roth Rámach* and with the Druid Mog Ruith, who was also addicted to aerial flights, and at last an Irish ancestry was claimed for Simon, and he was regarded as a "Druid." The wheel itself, I believe, was the disc of the sun.

We encounter a similar set of circumstances in British mythology. Bladud, King of Britain, the son of Hudibras, according to Geoffrey of Monmouth, was a very ingenious monarch and a teacher of necromancy, who invented a winged apparatus with which, like Simon and Mog Ruith, he "attempted to fly to the upper region of the air." But he "fell down upon the Temple of Apollo in the city of Trinovantum (London) where he was dashed to pieces."[31] It was appropriate enough that he should crash on the temple of the sun-god, so that the myth appears to relate to the setting of the sun in his own appointed place of rest. The names Bladud and Apollo appear to me to have been derived from the Celtic word for "apple," the divine solar fruit, *abal*, as is also the name "Avallon."[32]

The myth is that of the solar wheel, with which, says Miss Eleanor Hull, Mog Ruith is certainly associated. "His position as Votary of the Wheel probably denotes some official position in the wheel ceremonies of the Midsummer festival. That the myth of the *Roth Rámach* survived for a long time in Ireland seems to be proven by the belief that a fiery bolt and dragon would pass through the land on a St. John's Eve that falls on a Friday, St. John's Eve being connected with Mog Ruith, who is said to have decapitated John the Baptist. The Midsummer rite, Miss Hull thought, "could have had no other meaning than that of the sun at the solstice, so frequently represented by a moving wheel." Rolling a wheel

was, too, part of the summer festivities at Mentz, and near Clarmont, in
Aquitaine, at least up to the fifteenth century. "Rolling a blazing wheel
down a hill-side seems a very natural imitation of the passage of the sun
through the sky, especially appropriate to Midsummer day, when the
annual declension of the sun begins. The Celtic solar deity holds a wheel on
his shoulder or beside him on the ground."[33]

Here I may indicate that the Gaulish god Taranis, so closely identified
with Druidic belief, bears a wheel symbolic of his solar associations.[34]
Many wheels of the kind are depicted on ancient British coins of the
Celtic period, and I would draw attention to that symbol found so
frequently on the sculptured stones of Scotland, the double disc with
sceptre, which would seem to depict the older and younger suns, the
sceptre perhaps being illustrative of the lightning, which was believed by
the Celts to be a spark from the sun.

THE DRUIDIC SYSTEM OF AUGURY

That the Druids were in possession of a system of augury or auspices
is evident not only from classical references to the same but to passages
in ancient Irish literature which make allusion to it. But regarding the
precise nature of this system we remain in ignorance. That it must have
had the same origin as that in use among the augurs of Rome—a most
venerable one—it is difficult to deny. The chief duty of the Roman augurs
was to watch the omens given by birds and to fix the *templum*, or
consecrated space within which the observation took place. This was a
rectangular piece of ground which included the sky immediately above
it. The augur looked south, with the east on his left and the west on his
right, the former being the propitious side, the other the inauspicious.

The birds which he observed were divided into *alites* and *oscines*, the
former including eagles and vultures, which provided omens by their
manner of flying. The *oscines*, again, were birds which gave signs by
their cry as well as by their flight—ravens, owls and crows. Other birds
were thought of as representative of particular gods and thus as symbolic
of their nature and character. The proceeding was known as *auspices*,
a word signifying "observations of birds" (or perhaps, "the watching of
signs given by birds"), the intention being not to forecast the future but
to ascertain whether a particular proceeding was or was not acceptable
to the gods, to divine the will of a god, or of all the gods, in respect of
some human proposal. Besides the signs given by feathered creatures,
others might be gleaned from thunder and lightning, from the behaviour
of domestic fowls while eating, signs given by the cries or motions of
animals, or those given by noises, stumbling, any disturbance or an
epileptic seizure in a public place. No important public or national act
might be entered upon without auspices first being engaged in.

Diodorus Siculus expressly states that the Druids predicted the future
from the flight of birds.[35] But divination of this species was also carried

out by means of the casting of bones or omen-sticks, dreams, crystal-gazing, and so forth. To deal first with that part of divination which is associated with bird-song and flight, we learn from O'Curry that a tract preserved in the library of Trinity College, Dublin, contains material explanatory of the croaking of ravens, the chirping of wrens, and such omens. This appears to have been acquired from birds domesticated for the purpose. If a raven called from above the bed in a house, a distinguished and ancient guest would visit it. If it called *bach*, the visitor would be a monk; if *gradh, gradh*, twice, it would be one of the clergy; if a soldier, *grog, grog*. If it called from the north-east of the dwelling, robbers would raid the place, if from the door, strangers or soldiers would visit it. If it chirped with a small voice, *err, err*, sickness would come upon the inmates.[36] These observations, though of comparatively modern date, may, I believe, be referred to Druidic custom for their origin.

The Celts believed that the crow revealed where new settlements should be situated and that it was able to arbitrate in private negotiations.[37] An ancient poem quoted in the Irish *Nennius* (p. 145) tells us that "six demon-like Druids" who had settled in Breagh-magh practised "the watching of birds." St. Columba repudiated knowledge gained from "the voice of birds."

Folk-lore has preserved numerous illustrations of the survival of bird-augury in more modern times. Among the more important of these I must indicate what in Ireland and the Highlands of Scotland was popularly known as "Raven-knowledge," which appears to have been a direct inheritance from the Druidic period. It is referred to in a poem entitled "The Massacre of the Rosses," and is described by Toland in his *History of the Druids*. At the village of Finglass, near Dublin, he tells us, in the year 1697, he fell in with two gentlemen "of the old Irish stock," who were engaged in private business. They assured him that the affair in which they were concerned would proceed favourably because they had observed on their path a raven with some white feathers in its plumage, nor would they proceed on their journey until they had seen in what direction the bird would fly. When it disappeared southward, their certainty regarding the success of their mission was confirmed. They told the historian of the Druids that a raven so pied with white and flying on the right hand of anyone, croaking the while, was an infallible omen of good presage, and it was with satisfaction that the modern Druid recalled how Pompeius Troganus, a Roman historian of the first century, had pronounced that "the Gauls excel all others in the skill of augury.[38]"

In Wales it was believed that "the descendants of a person who had eaten eagle's flesh to the ninth generation possessed the gift of second sight."[39] In the reign of Henry I, Gruffyd ap Rhys ap Tudor, the rightful Prince of Wales, was alone able to cause the birds on Llangorse Lake in Brecknockshire to sing, aware, as he was, that only the natural Prince of that region would be obeyed by them.[40]

The Wren as a Druidic Bird

The history of the wren as a Druidic bird demands some special consideration. I have already mentioned that its name has been cited as a possible source of the derivation of the word "Druid" by Mr. Whitley Stokes, although I feel the reverse is the case and that it is more probable that it received its Celtic appellation from its Druidic associations. "The Pseudo-Cormac Glossary," says George Henderson, "explains it as *drui-en*, a Druid bird," and this appears to me as the most satisfactory explanation of its name.[41]

That the little wren must at one time have been the central object of a rather widespread worship in some parts of Britain is certain. In Scotland, Ireland and the Isle of Man, as well as in Essex, Devonshire and Ireland, it was hunted on St. Stephen's Day (December 26th) and slain with peculiar rites. The fullest information concerning this practice hails from the Isle of Man. Waldron, one of the historians of the isle, informs us that a legend was current there which ran that a fairy maiden of great beauty had lured certain Manxmen into the sea, who perished therein, but that a youth had laid a snare for her, to avoid which she took the form of a wren and that a spell was cast upon her by which she was compelled on every successive New Year's Day to assume this form. (The rite had evidently been "put back" to St. Stephen's Day.) This placed her for a day in the power of the men and boys of the island, who, in revenge for her treatment of their sex, hunted her mercilessly. When caught, the bird was placed on the end of a long pole, with its wings outstretched, and after being carried round the villages in procession, it was solemnly buried in the local churchyard, to the accompaniment of funeral dirges. But its feathers were preserved with pious care, for each of them was believed to protect its owner from shipwreck for a year. Indeed no Manx fisherman would venture to sea without such a safeguard. As the lads of the village paraded with the bird's corpse they chanted:

> "We hunted the wren for Robin the Bobbin,
> We hunted the wren for Jack of the Can,
> We hunted the wren for Robin the Bobbin,
> We hunted the wren for every one."[42]

This jingle is by no means a mere nonsense rhyme. As I have made it clear in another work, "Robin the Bobbin" is probably one and the same with the British god Beli, while "Jack of the Can" is "Kit of the Canstick," otherwise Will-o'-the-Wisp. It seems to me not improbable that these are allusions to some forgotten myth in which the wren and the other personages mentioned in the rhyme played the principal parts. Seemingly, we have to deal with three deities or spirits associated with light, for Beli has a solar connection, Will-o'-the-Wisp represents the fire of the marshes, and the wren was in one sense associated with the lightning and the oak.

Another Manx legend states that the wren was regarded by Manx fishermen as a spirit of the sea, which haunted the "herring track" and that a dead wren was placed aboard their vessels to protect them from storms.⁴⁸ A Lowland Scots rhyme called down curses on those who chased the bird:

"Malisons, malisons, mair than ten,
That harry the Lady o' Heaven's hen."

In Essex wrens were formerly chased by boys and killed and carried in procession with the words:

"The wren, the wren, the king of the birds,
St. Stephen's Day, was killed in the furze,
Although he be little his honour is great,
And so, good people, give us a treat."

This rhyme was also chanted in some parts of Ireland on the occasion of hunting the wren, and also in the Isle of Man.⁴⁴ The wren was certainly hunted in Kerry and Mayo. This also holds good of certain parts of France, where the youth who killed the wren was dubbed "King." Canon MacCulloch is of opinion that the wren may have had a totemic significance, that more anciently it was carried round the community to obtain its divine influence and then eaten and buried. The terms of an old Manx song make it clear that it was eaten on St. Stephen's Day.

The outstanding significance of the wren myth in its more modern sense and as recognized in the Isle of Man, seems to be that it was hunted to secure its feathers for use as protective talismans at sea. And let us remark that while the Manx myth makes the wren-spirit female and associates it with the sea and the herring-track, elsewhere it was regarded as male and as "King of the Birds," while nothing is said concerning its maritime connection. It should be indicated that the cuckoo, the squirrel and other creatures were also hunted in this and in other countries at certain seasons. It is notable, too, that these animals were hunted and slain only once annually, as totemic animals are by primitive peoples.

But it would also seem that the myth of the wren and the custom of its annual chase are much too widely distributed to permit us to account for them on totemic grounds alone. I am of opinion that in the Isle of Man the wren-spirit became confused nominally with Ran, the Norse goddess of the sea, whose name and legend must have been well known in an area so thickly settled by Norse folk as was Man. And this, I feel, accounts for the circumstance that in Man the wren was regarded as female and that a maritime connection with the bird was unknown elsewhere. Ran, says Grimm, drew drowned men to her in a net. To "fare to Ran" was to be drowned at sea. Ran, like the Irish merrow or mermaid and the sea-god Manannan or Manawyddan, who gave its name to the Isle of Man, was thought of as keeping the souls of drowned sailors "in pots turned upside down."⁴⁵ Here it is not inapt to note that the bone prison of Oeth and Anoeth, built by Manannan, the god of the Isle of Man, was "in the shape of a beehive," that is, it resembled a "pot turned upside down."⁴⁶" In the island, then, there appears to have been much confusion betwixt the Celtic myth of Manannan and the Teutonic legend of Ran. I may add that in Scotland the wren is known as "the wran," and I should not be surprised to learn that its name is, or was, so pronounced in the Isle of Man, though regarding this I can find no confirmation. Thus confusion arose between the names and legends of Ran and the wren. Note, too, that in the rhyme chanted by the Essex boys the wren is male, while in Waldron's legend it is female. This is one of the best examples within my knowledge that myth, especially in its "secondary" forms, is sometimes "a disease of language."

It is proper to say that our knowledge of the prison of Oeth and Anoeth is derived from a Welsh source only, but I think it is clear enough that the tale concerning it, or something closely resembling it, may well have been known in Man also in former times. Nor can I discern any difference between the Irish-Scots-Manx form of Manannan and his Welsh form Manawyddan, the last certainly being derived from Irish settlers on the Welsh coast.

But this mythic confusion concerning "wren" and "Ran" in the Isle of Man has obviously nothing to do with the wren legend as we find it elsewhere and must be separated from it absolutely, as a local growth. The Manx legend is eloquent of the myth of Ran, which must have been known in the island and thus was blunderingly employed to "explain" the hunting of the wren. In the first instance the wren can have had no association whatever with the Norse goddess Ran.

Among the Celts, the wren was a bird of augury and its chirpings were thought to be predictive of events to come. As has been said, the Irish Glossary of Cormac explains it as *drui-en*, a "druid bird." This nominally associated it with the oak tree, *derw* in its Old British plural form, and we know that this tree was regarded as a storage "tank" or reservoir of the lightning, the heavenly fire. The wren is thus the symbol or bearer of the celestial fire, precisely as is the robin, and that this fire was in some mysterious manner connected with those of the god Bel and of Will-o'-the-Wisp, seems not improbable, judging from the rhyme. It also seems clear that were the fishermen provided with the talisman of the lightning-bearing bird in the shape of one of its feathers, this, through the power of sympathetic magic, would safeguard them against lightning and storms at sea, although it may be that this part of the legend is due to confusion with the myth of Ran. The sacrifice and ritual eating of the bird was, I believe, gone through for a similar "reason"—that to partake of its flesh procured for one immunity from lightning. If you ate of the lightning-bearer you were fortified against the lightning itself, you had eaten "a hair of the dog" which might bite you, and, of course, you derived strength from the magical qualities of the celestial source whence the bird received its strange powers. Alternatively, the bird may have been devoured because of its association with the sacred oak tree, of which it seems to have been regarded as the genius, or indwelling spirit.

DRUIDIC FORMS OF DIVINATION

Although it seems possible that almost the entire system of Celtic occult belief had a Druidic origin, I have been careful in these pages to omit mention of any of its forms which are not definitely stated to have issued from a Druidic source. What were known as *coelbreni*, or "omen-sticks," are said to have been employed by the Druids for interpreting the future. As the sticks fell, so the diviner interpreted the fates.[47] Horrible indeed was the method by which the Druids divined future events after a human sacrifice. "The Druids," says Tacitus, "consult the gods in the palpitating entrails of men," while Strabo informs us that they stabbed a human victim in the back with a sword and then drew omens from the convulsive movements made by him in his death-struggles. Diodorus says that they augured from the posture in which the victim fell, from his contortions, and the direction in which the blood flowed from the body. From these, "they formed their predictions according to certain rules left them by their ancestors."[48]

Certain passages in Welsh literature might lead us to believe that the Welsh Druidic augurs were in the habit of divining from a species of frame called the *peithynen*, or "the Elucidator," sometimes alluded to as "the Druids' Wheel." Sir John Daniel (who illustrates this apparatus on page 136 of his book *The Philosophy of Ancient Britain*) says of it: "The Elucidator consisted of several staves called faith-sticks or lots, on which the judicial maxims were cut, and which, being put into a frame, were turned at pleasure, so that each staff, or bar, when formed with three flat sides, represented a triplet; when squared or made with four flat sides, a stanza (in verse). The frame itself was an oblong with right angles." In one of his poems Taliesin exclaims:

> "I am Taliesin,
> Chief of the Bards of the west,
> I am acquainted with every sprig
> In the cave of the Arch-diviner."[49]

And Llywarch Hen alludes to "the Elucidator" in one of his poems.[50] These ancient metres, however, obviously refer not to such an apparatus as Sir John Daniel describes, but to a system of divination from the sprigs of various trees, which formed a species of magical alphabet. There appear to have been three such alphabets in Ireland, and these have been described by O'Flaherty in his *Ogygia*, and by the present writer in his work *The Mysteries of Britain* (pp. 58–60). The Druids, it is said, also divined from the appearance of the roots of trees. Omens, too, were also drawn from the direction of the smoke and flames of sacred fires and from the condition or appearance of the clouds.[51] An Irish equivalent to the

Welsh "Elucidator" in its phase of a frame bearing carven maxims may perhaps be found in the practice of engraving ogham sentences on rods made of yew and divining therefrom. It was by such means that the Druid Dalan discovered the whereabouts of the beauteous Etain who had been borne off by the god Mider, her husband in a previous existence.

DIVINATION BY BULL-SACRIFICE

We must now consider those passages in ancient Irish and Scottish lore which tell of divination by means of the sacrifice of bulls through diviners or augurs who wrapped themselves in the hides of these animals. We have already seen that some such expedient was in use when a king was to be chosen by means necromantic. Keating alludes to the custom of the Irish Druids of making use of the hides of bulls offered in sacrifice for purposes of conjuration. They made wattles of the quicken-tree, or rowan, spreading the hides of the sacrificed bulls over them, with the fleshy side uppermost to attract the spirits who might provide them with the hidden information which they desired. This ceremony was known as "the wattles of knowledge."[52]

Now we possess a striking illustration of a survival of this Druidic rite in the Highlands and Islands of Scotland down to a late period in what is known as *taghairm*. The word signifies "an echo," that is of the voice of spirits consulted by a seer. The seer was wrapped in the hide of a newly slain bull and laid beside a waterfall, or at the foot of some precipice believed to be the haunt of spirits, or alternatively on the bank of a rivulet. In due time, the spirits visited him and communicated that which he sought to know, the fate of a family, the issue of a battle, or other information of importance. The seer was usually chosen by lot, and was violently rocked to and fro in the hide by four companions, who struck his hips forcibly on the ground. "What have you there?" asked one, to which another replied: "a log of birchwood," the intention being, perhaps, to delude the spirits that no human being was concealed in the bundle. The first speaker then cried: "Let our invisible friends appear from all quarters and relieve him by giving an answer to our questions." A swarm of diminutive spirits then rose from the sea and replied to the man's queries, as suddenly disappearing, after which the necromancers returned home.[53]

By their arts, the Druids of Ireland were enabled to discover the most suitable site for the erection of a royal palace. When Eachaidh, King of Connaught, desired to erect a mansion for himself, he consulted his Druids who, after due magical experiment, found that a site at Cruachan was the most fortunate spot on which to build it.[54]

DIVINATION BY DREAMS

As interpreters of dreams, the Druids were celebrated in the writings of antiquity. Eachaidh Mac Erc, a king of the Firbolgs, had an unusual dream, which he communicated to Cesarn, his chief Druid, who augured from it the approach of a powerful enemy, the Tuatha Dé Danann.[54] A list of charms and their significance is given in the tract preserved in the library of Trinity College, Dublin, of which I have already made mention, and this catalogue is claimed by O'Curry as of the nature of Druidic lore.[56] Much of the material in question has passed into modern folk-lore.

DRUIDIC PROPHECY

The Irish Druids appear to have excelled in the art of prophecy. An Irish Druid it was who prophesied to the Fomorian god Balor that he would meet his death at the hands of his grandson. Like numerous other divinities or monarchs in legend, when faced with such a contingency, he shut up his daughter Ethnea in an impregnable tower on the summit of an almost inaccessible rock on Tory Island. But the youth Mackineely, by the assistance of another Druid, defeated his intentions and gained access to the maiden, who gave birth to three sons, one of whom eventually slew Balor.[57]

Geoffrey Keating, whose time-honoured *History of Ireland* has furnished Celtic scholars with so much valuable material for the study of their theme, ransacked many volumes which in his day were still readily obtainable. In one of these, *The Etymology of Names*, which is mentioned in the "Book of Lecain," he found a tale which described how a Druidic prophet foretold to the Irish King Daire that he would have a son whose name should be Lugaidh, and that he should succeed to the throne. To give force to the prophecy, he advised that the monarch should call each of his five sons by the name of Lugaidh. The rightful heir would be he who should overtake and kill a fawn at the Tailltenn games. The Druid's prophecy was duly fulfilled.[58]

In the book known as *The Dialogue of the Two Sages*, a pagan Druidic bard is found prophesying concerning the future condition of Ireland under the Christian faith, in terms anything but hopeful. We have already seen how his Druids discussed with King Conn the origin and nature of the stone Lia Fail. Various prophecies are attributed to Fin MacCoul, who forecast future affairs in respect of the Druidic potency accorded him by his miraculous "thumb of knowledge." These appear to be related to the conquest of Ireland by the Anglo-Normans. The coming of St. Patrick to Erin is said to have been foretold in disastrous terms to the pagan monarch Loegaire by his two chief Druids, Lochra and Luchot Mael. O'Curry pleads for the authenticity and antiquity of this last foretelling.[59]

The word employed in describing such prophecies is *baile*, which in Gaelic implies "speech of excitement," or has some such significance suggesting frenzied utterance. The poem known as "The Fate of the Sons of Usnach" recounts how Cathbad the Druid foretold King Conchobar of Ulster that the maiden Deirdre would grow up to be the most beautiful woman in the world, but would be the unhappy cause of the death of many heroes.⁴⁰ We recall, too, that the Gaulish Druids prophesied the world-empire of the Celts in A.D. 70⁴¹ while more than one prophecy is attributed to Gaulish Druidesses, as I have already indicated.

A Druid prophesied to Cumhal Mac Art that were he to marry, he would meet death in the next battle he fought. But he married the King's daughter secretly. On the day following this event news came to hand that an engagement was toward. In the interval, a Druid had informed the King that his daughter's son would take the kingdom from him. Cumhal was duly slain in the battle, but his son, the celebrated Fin MacCovl, although his life was attempted by his grandfather, grew up to manhood and organized the Fenian band, although he never attained kingship.⁴²

In *The Life of St. Brigit* we read that a Druid foretold the greatness of that saint while yet she was unborn. Lughbran, another Druid, attached to the Court of King Crimthann, prophesied the birth of St. Ciaran of Clanmacnois and the wonders he would perform. A Druid prophesied to Modha Nuagat, King of Ireland, a seven years' famine to follow seven years of plenty, and advised him to store up corn and thus avert the calamity. The King accepted his advice with satisfactory results.⁴³

THE DRUIDIC ''EGG''

That symbolic and mystical object "the serpent's egg" has been the theme of numerous writers on Druidism. In this place I wish to deal with its legend in a strictly practical manner. The *locus classicus* concerning its tradition is, of course, to be found in *The Natural History* of Pliny. In the summer, he tells us, snakes gather and coil themselves into a ball, which is held together by their expectoration and a secretion from their bodies. The Druids say that serpents cast this into the air and that it must be caught in a cloak and not permitted to touch the ground. When thus obtained, he who secures it must leap upon a swift horse and make all speed from the scene, as the serpents will rapidly follow him until they are stopped by a stream. The best test of the authenticity of such a charm is that it will float against the current of a river, even should it be set in gold.

The Druids averred, Pliny continues, that such eggs can only be secured on a certain day of the moon. He adds that he had seen one of these eggs. It was round and about the size of a rather small apple. The shell was like a cartilage, and pock-marked. The Druids believed that it ensured success in law-suits and that its possession ensured the favour of princes. A man of the Vocontii, who had been honoured by a Roman knighthood, secreted one of these eggs on his person during a trial. But the stratagem served him not, and he was put to death by the Emperor Claudius, perhaps because he had superstitiously believed in the protection vouchsafed by the talisman.⁴⁴

This amulet was known to Celtic tradition as the *Glainnader* or *Glan-nan Druidhe*, "the Druid's glass." Some writers on the subject state that it is referred to by the Welsh bard Aneurin when he sings of:

"The quick-glancing ball,
The adder's bright precious produce,
The ejaculation of serpents."

Camden states that in some parts of Wales, Scotland and Cornwall people retained a superstitious belief in the origin and virtue of such "eggs." The island of Bardsey, remarks Meilyr, an old Welsh poet, was known as "the holy island of the Glain." "These *Gemmæ Anguine*," says Camden, "are small glass amulets commonly about as wide as our finger-rings, but much thicker, of a green colour, usually, though some of them are blue and others curiously waved with blue, red and white." The belief was handed down in folk-lore in Britain. Mr. Kendrick alludes to such snake-stones as have been found in Cornwall, Wales and Scotland, which in Wales and Ireland were known as "Druids' Glass." Many of these beads, he says, date from the first two or three centuries before the Christian era.[65]

But from Pliny's account of the Druidic "egg" it would appear to have been a fossil rather than a glass bead, an echinite or fossil sea-urchin or an ammonite, or fossil shell of an extinct mollusc, some of which are still known as "snake-stones" by peasants.[66] In the Highlands old spindle-whorls when found were called "adder stones" and were thought to give protection against the bite of a serpent.[67] In all likelihood an ancient tradition prevailed among the Celts that serpents were responsible for such "eggs," echinites or ammonites, and that they held magic potencies. And in later times these may have been imitated in glass. The folk-lore of Scotland is full of examples of magical stones and beads.[68]

DRUIDIC ASTROLOGY

Cæsar credits the Druids with a certain knowledge concerning astronomy when he states that: "they likewise discuss and impart to the youth many things respecting the stars and their motion."[69] "The knowledge of astronomy ascribed by Cæsar to the Druids," says Canon MacCulloch, "was probably of a simple kind, and much mixed with astrology, and though it furnished the data for computing a simple calendar, its use was largely magical. Irish diviners forecast the time to build a house by the stars, and the date at which Columba's education should begin, was similarly discovered."[70]

The legend of the Lia Fail recounts, as we have seen, how, when King Conn repaired one morning at sunrise to the battlements of Ri Raith, or the royal fortress of Tara, accompanied by his Druids, his intention was to watch the firmament, so that no hostile being from the air might suddenly descend upon Erin unknown to him. This precaution had assuredly an astrological significance. The ancients believed that hostile influences, usually spiritual, were in the habit of descending from the heavenly bodies. The Aztecs of Mexico envisaged these as great insects, spiders, scorpions, and so forth, and the belief appears to be associated in some way with that which held that elfin arrows were discharged from the aerial spaces. Strangely enough, this custom of King Conn was also carried out by Montezuma, the Emperor of Mexico, whose duty it was to rise several times during the night to inspect the heavens for signs of unfriendly presences.

According to Pliny, the Druids watched the course of the moon until this was auspicious for the cutting of the mistletoe.[71] We have seen, too, that the Druids were compelled to admit that they could not control the courses of the stars, so that it seems evident that they must have claimed such a power. "It is odd," remarks Mr. Allcroft, "that if Druidism was really so much concerned with astronomy, there should remain so little tradition of the fact . . . there is nothing to shew that druidical star-study amounted to more than that very simple and very useful applied astronomy which meets us on every page of Hesiod's *Works and Days* and Vergil's *Georgics*, and with which every Greek and Latin farmer seems to have been conversant. . . . Apparently the modern belief that Druidism included astronomy or astrology, or both, is a growth of the last two centuries or so."[72] I may add that my own researches fully corroborate Mr. Allcroft's findings. If (and I use the doubtful conjunction advisedly) the stone circles of prehistoric times have any association with astronomical science, it must have been a science of such a primitive kind as Mr. Allcroft refers to.

And in relation to the subject of the Druids and the computation of time, I may say that I do not believe the Coligny Calendar, discovered at Coligny towards the end of last century, and engraved on bronze plates, to be of Druidic origin. Indeed there is not a scrap of evidence of any sort to show that it has the slightest association with the Druidic caste.

MAGICAL FIRES OF THE DRUIDS

Druidic fires were sometimes set alight to halt the advance of an enemy. When King Cormac and his Druids had been worsted by Mog Ruith, the Druid of Munster, as narrated on a previous page, they took counsel among themselves and resolved to light a Druidic fire against the enemy. They sent their warriors into the forest to fell a number of quicken trees (the magical rowan, or mountain ash) and with the timber thus acquired large fires were lighted. It was resolved that if the smoke of these fires was wafted southward, Cormac and his men should follow the host of Munster, but if northward, the omens were in favour of a retreat.

Meanwhile Mog Ruith and the men of Munster were doing much the same thing. Mog Ruith then ordered each man of his host to give him a shaving from the shaft of his spear, and these he mixed with butter and rolled into a large ball, chanting a spell the while to the effect that the angry flame he was about to let loose might subdue that of his enemy. He then cast the magical ball into the fire, where it exploded with a thunderous report. He next blew a Druidical breath upward into the sky, where it became a great black cloud which rained down blood upon the plain of Cláiré and moved in the direction of Tara.

The rival fires now engaged in contest, chasing each other across the mountains and consuming all the trees in the countryside. Then did Mog Ruith call for his dark grey hornless bull hide and his white-speckled bird headpiece and his Druidic instruments, and thus accoutred, he flew upward into the air, turning the fires northward. In the firmament he was encountered by Cormac's Druid Ciothruadh, but Mog Ruith's power was the stronger, the fires descended into Cormac's camp and the Druid Ciothruadh crashed there along with them, so that the host of Cormac was put to utter rout. But Mog Ruith sent another devastating breath in the direction of his enemies, so that Cormac's three luckless enchanters were turned into the stones known as "the Flags of Raighné."[13]

A magical fire was produced by the Druid Lugaidh, who was known as Delbhaeth, or "the Fire-producer," for the purpose of lighting his five sons to their future inheritances. It divided into five streams, each of which led one of the youths on the path to fortune.[14]

Chapter XII

THEORIES CONCERNING THE ORIGINS OF DRUIDISM

Having reviewed the whole "document" of Druidism, and epitomized the entire range of information respecting it, we may now summarize the several theories which profess to explain its origin before drawing our final conclusions as to their value.

Mr. T. D. Kendrick is of opinion that the main facts associated with Druidism are to be found only in such records as have survived concerning its position in the Gaul of the first century B.C. The Druidism of Ireland, he thinks, is only to be explained incidentally by this governing factor. Celtic doctrine in the Marne area, he believes, must have been "built up on native faith," that is the religion of the tribes upon whom the Gauls imposed their rule, after the Gauls had occupied that area for some generations.

This mingled faith was then carried to Britain by those Gauls who had mixed with the native population of the Marne area, and in Britain it blended with the religion of the non-Celtic folk who then peopled our islands. But in the peaceful and appropriate conditions which marked the La Téne period in Gaul, the Celtic settlers there may have developed a priestly caste (the Druidic) at some time in the fourth or third century B.C. Druidism in Gaul, for Mr. Kendrick, is therefore Celtic religion after its fusion with "native" beliefs in the Marne area, while Druidism in Britain was a mélange of this Gaulish system with an aboriginal British cultus which itself had affinities with the native Marne faith with which Celtic belief had blended. The Druids as a hierarchy "were only subsequent Keltic servants of the Kelticised native faith in Gaul, a separate and accidental phenomenon of Gallic (not British) Druidism."[1]

Sir John Rhys saw fit to alter his views on the origins of Druidism more than once. In an early work he asserted that Druidism had been planted in Gaul by those Belgæ who had settled in Britain.[2] Later, he gave it as his opinion that no Belgic or Brythonic people ever practised Druidism.[3] Still later, he concluded that the Goidelic invaders of Britain borrowed their magic and Druidism from the folk of the *sidh* who afterwards became in the popular mind the fairies of folk-lore.[4] Again, he argued that Druidism had been developed by the Goidels of the Continent, or accepted by them from the aborigines.[5] In the last edition of his *Celtic Britain* he affirmed that Druidism had originated among the aborigines both of Gaul and Britain, who inherited it from common ancestors.[6] It was, therefore, so far as he was concerned, not a Celtic cultus at all, but would seem to have been most powerful "in those districts where a pre-Celtic population may naturally be conjectured to have survived in the greatest numbers, namely in the west of Gaul, in the west of Britain and in Ireland."[7]

Rice Holmes thought it "not unreasonable to believe" that the Celts had borrowed Druidism from some non-Aryan people. There was, he thought, "nothing to show that the Gauls whom the Romans first encountered had ever heard of it." He denied Rhys's statement that people of Brythonic race did not practise Druidism. Cæsar's account, he thought, made it clear that it was common to all the peoples who lived between the Seine and the Garonne, among many of whom "the Gallo-Brythonic element was predominant."[8] Holmes quoted as against his own view that Desjardins had pointed out that there was no evidence that Druidism existed in Cæsar's time in Aquitania or in the Roman Province and that it seemed clear from Cæsar's account that the Romans came in contact with the Druids for the first time when they had passed beyond the northern boundary of Roman territory. But Holmes rightly retorted that there was no evidence that Druidism did not exist in the Province, and that it probably flourished there before the inhabitants became Romanized.[9]

Frazer indicated resemblances between the Druidic religion and that of ancient Latium. The white steers sacrificed on the Alban Mount and in the Capitol at Rome, he says, "remind us of the white bulls which the Druids of Gaul sacrificed under the holy oak when they cut the mistletoe. . . . When we remember that the ancient Italian and Celtic peoples spoke languages which are nearly related to each other, we shall not be surprised at discovering traces of community in their religion, especially in what concerns the worship of the god of the oak and the thunder."[10]

M. Camille Jullian holds that Druidism was a Celtic institution of comparatively late appearance, which perhaps had its rise at some time in the third century B.C. He believes that Britain preserved more faithfully than the other Celtic lands the religious habits of the common motherland, retaining their most primitive forms and that this was the reason why the Gaulish Druids sent their novices to Britain for instruction. It may have been that an ancient native community existed in the island with foreign rites and teaching which supplied inspiration to the Druids.[11]

Mr. A. H. Allcroft, as we have seen, argues that Druidism was not a religion but "an organization (*disciplina*) which made of religion a means to political power." There is, he says, no trace of Druidism among the Celts of Spain, of Italy or of Galatia and it would seem to have been of late introduction in Gaul. In Cæsar's time it had small influence in Aquitania and the Narbonnaise. He is of opinion that it originated among the Belgæ, as Chartres, its centre, was under "Belgic hegemony." The Belgæ once conquered, Druidism disappeared as an influence. It probably flourished among the Belgæ of Britain, where it was extirpated when

Claudius effected the conquest of the island. The Goidelic and Iberian peoples did not readily submit to it.[11] In my view practically none of these assertions can be seriously entertained.

M. Salomon Reinach was of opinion that the Gaulish Celts accepted Druidism from some pre-Celtic people *en bloc*, as the later Romans adopted certain Oriental cults. He further asserted that when the Celts appeared in history Druidism was in its decline.[12]

D'Arbois de Jubainville maintained that the Druids were priests of the Goidels in Britain who imposed their faith upon their Gaulish conquerors, who then introduced Druidism to Gaul at some time about 200 B.C.[14] Sir G. L. Gomme was of the belief that the Druids were a pre-Celtic priesthood, as the faith they practised held much that was "non-Aryan," and was indeed the parent of witchcraft.[15]

Another supporter of the theory that Druidism was a "non-Aryan" faith was Julius Pokorny of Vienna, whose arguments are so interesting as to merit more than passing consideration. "Druidism," he thought, "has many features quite alien to the character of an Indo-European religion," and this is to be accounted for by the circumstance that the Druids were the priests of the pre-Celtic aborigines of the British Isles. "In historical times we find among the Irish kings traces of the former priestship which had originated in the furthest past ages from the divine adoration of mighty magicians"—otherwise the doctrine of the Divine King—"a belief which the Indo-European races had given up before they had left their common native home." But it is contrary to the evidence to assert either that the doctrine of the Divine King was solely an "Aryan" one, or that the Indo-European races had relinquished it at a period so early as Pokorny believes they did. So far from being "Aryan," it was entertained by the people of ancient Egypt, if indeed it did not originate in that country, as all the evidence goes to show. Pokorny, indeed, destroys his own argument when he states that "the Celts believed that there would be bad crops as a punishment for bad rulers," as this alone reveals that Indo-European folk had not deserted the doctrine.

In the British Isles, he continues, the Gauls had found an aboriginal race who had come over from the Continent in early times, and it was among them that Druidism had its rise. The Druids were magicians rather than priests of a well-defined religion, a notion which I have already shown to be ill-founded, if not insupportable. The worship of the oak, he argues, was certainly Indo-European. "If the Celts had had Druids who were already priests of the oak before the occupation of the British Islands, they certainly would have brought that worship with them to Ireland," yet we seldom hear of the oak in Irish literature, and "the Irish Druids are never mentioned in connection with the oak . . . The Druids must have been once the priests of a people who did not know the worship of the oak. But the oak-worship of the Celts is vouched for several times, therefore the Druids cannot have been originally a Celtic priesthood."¹⁰

But, as I said in a former chapter (VI), I think Pokorny greatly exaggerates when he asserts that the worship of the oak was unknown in Ireland and that its place there was taken by the yew tree. There are frequent references to sacred oaks in Irish literature. The circumstance that in the *Book of Leinster* we read that during a popular revolt every oak in Ireland bore only one acorn as a punishment for the manner in which the people had treated the King and the nobles, alone makes it plain that the oak was regarded as a sacred food-yielding tree, the central object of a cultus associated with that of the Divine King, as in Gaul. At the same time it must be admitted that the yew appears to have been more prominent in Irish Druidism and that it may have superseded the oak as a symbol. This, however, it seems to me, has no bearing on the question whether the Druids were originally a Celtic or a non-Celtic priesthood. That they were a Celtic priesthood in Gaul, where and when we first encounter them, we know. That they were also servants of the Celtic seasonal festivals in Ireland we are also aware. But the whole argument as to whether they were of "Aryan" or "non-Aryan," Celtic or Iberian origin is scarcely relative to the larger view of Druidic beginnings which I hope to be able to maintain in a later chapter.

Having summarized the outstanding theories relating to the origin of Druidism, let us now examine more particularly some of the arguments set forth in them. And first, as to the racial associations of Druidism. We find that Rhys, Kendrick, Reinach, Gomme and Pokorny, with varying degrees of insistence, adhere to the theory that Druidism originated among the "aboriginal" tribes of the Continent and Britain, that Frazer lays some stress upon its origin among the Latin-Celtic peoples, that Jullian finds that it was wholly a Celtic faith and that Allcroft considers it to have been exclusively a Belgic institution. Rice Holmes goes so far as to assert that there is "nothing to show that the Gauls when the Romans first encountered them, had ever heard of it." On the other hand, it may be said, with equal justice, that there is something to show that they had.

If the reference be to the period of the Gaulish invasion of Rome in 390 B.C., it should be remembered that the Romans observed the Gauls on that occasion only as an army and thus not in such circumstances as would be favourable to observing their religious characteristics. If it be to subsequent early contact, the Romans could scarcely have been unaware of the great Druidic settlement at Marseilles. Indeed *a Roman army went to the assistance of the Greek settlers in Marseilles against the Gauls as early as* 155 B.C., and by 120 B.C. the Romans had acquired the valley of the Lower Rhone by conquest. Druidism in Gaul had been in existence at least a generation or so before this, as Diogenes Lærtius's reference to it makes clear, quoting the writings of Sotion of Alexandria, who wrote about 200 B.C. It seems, therefore, idle and even absurd to suggest that Druidism was unknown to the Gauls when the Romans first encountered them in their own land.

More substantial is Holmes's belief, based on the account of Cæsar, that Druidism was common to all the peoples who lived between the Seine and the Garonne, and as we know that it was also established on the southern coast of Gaul, there is little question that it was the prevailing religion of the greater part of that country. But, as Desjardins remarks, the evidence for Druidism in Aquitania is lacking. The absence of all proof that it existed in the province is, as Holmes indicates, cancelled by the circumstance that that area had been thoroughly Romanized at an early date.

But there is good reason to believe that Druidism did not function throughout the Belgic portion of Gaul, despite the statements of Allcroft and others that it actually had its rise among the Belgæ. Had this people practised it, there can be little question that they would have continued to do so in Britain, where they made extensive settlements in the Southern areas in times immediately preceding the Christian era. But in a prolonged study of the history and general conditions of this Celto-Teutonic folk in Britain I have failed to discover even the slightest evidence that they ever embraced the Druidic cultus, or that they had even the least association with it whatsoever. The one reference which might seem to prove exceptional in this connection is that of Tacitus to the sacrifice or slaughter of the women of Londinium by the host of Boadicea in the grove of Andate or Andraste in the year 61. But as I have already said, the circumstances of dubiety which surround the cult of this goddess make it impossible to judge whether or not she had any associations with Druidism and this seems to me to remove the reference to her and her temple in Romano-Belgic London from the sphere of practical consideration so far as it relates to Druidic origins.

Canon MacCulloch, criticizing the theory of Rhys that the Druids were originally a non-Celtic priesthood, remarks that it fails for lack of historical evidence. "Everywhere they appear as the supreme and dominant priesthood of the Celts, and the priests of a conquered people could hardly have obtained such power over the conquerors." He regards such a situation as "incredible." He denies that Druidic practice was opposed to "Aryan" sentiment in its legal and priestly functions.[17] Macbain also maintained the "Aryan" character of Druidism. He compares it with the Brahman caste of India in its rigidly monopolizing and exclusive spirit.[18]

Such religious ideas as appear to have been known to the Druids were equally familiar to the peoples of other "Aryan" communities—Germans, Slavs, Greeks, Romans and Hindus. The writers of the Classical period indeed appear to have realized the underlying identity of the more outstanding figures of the several "Aryan" pantheons in a manner never approached by modern authorities on comparative religion. I certainly do not mean to imply that no leaven of "non-Aryan" faith or magic found its way into Druidic dogma and ritual. Such a negation would be absurd. Indeed so many religious and magical forms are common to both "Aryan" and "non-Aryan" peoples as to make it virtually impossible to distinguish between them at times. Actually the tests by which some traditionalists seek to do so are, in certain circumstances, glaringly incompetent for all practical purposes, and in face of this, I feel it is frequently impossible to draw any hard-and-fast boundaries.

Writing on the subject of the term "Aryan" in a recent work, Mr. Patrick Carleton has sharply criticized the laxity of its employment. "Probably," he says, "no scientific term has been so constantly misused by ignorant persons as has this one. Strictly speaking, the name Âryan ought only to be applied to those ancient European invaders of India and Persia and to their language. But that language is one of the great and important group called (from the fact that its branches extend from England and Germany to India) *Indo-European* or *Indo-Germanic*; and consequently 'Âryan' is sometimes stretched to cover the whole of the language-group and all the races who speak any branches of it. . . . The fact of the matter is that we are no more able to speak of an 'Indogermanic Race' than of a 'Semitic Race'." Nor is it possible, he avers, to identify and separately distinguish any Indo-Germanic race.[19] With his attitude I find myself in perfect agreement.

Whether Druidism were "Aryan" or otherwise, it is evident that it must have absorbed much of the so-called "Aryan" spirit. But that it also retained much of the character of a more primitive fetishism is clear from the traditions respecting it which we find in Ireland and Scotland. Indeed, we may safely accept it as authoritative that Druidism was, in its beginnings, like the religions of Greece and Rome, a primitive faith of the lower cultus which gradually assumed a more exalted status as it advanced in time, either because of its adoption by a Celtic people, or because of those evolutionary causes which quicken the growth of religious cults. This, however, is among the questions which must be answered in the next and final chapter.

Chapter XIII

CONCLUSIONS

"THE worship of the oak-tree, or of the oak-god, appears to have been shared by all the branches of the Aryan stock in Europe." With this solid fact behind us, as laid down by Frazer.[1] we can scarcely fail to arrive at a general, if not a particular conclusion concerning the origins of Druidism. Of this widespread worship of the oak the Druidic cultus is one illustration only, but it appears to have been, until the period of its cessation, not only the most faithful to the original type, but the most persistent in survival among those which made up the westerly group of the European oak-cults. While those of Greece and Rome became merged in a complex of other and later religious ideas, Druidism remained comparatively unimpaired. At the same time, the original design of the primitive oak-cult remained within the rite and content of the Roman pagan religion until the last, much as might an ancient dwelling upon which has been superimposed the structure of a more grandiose and more modern edifice.

The development of the oak-cult in Greece and Italy, regarding the earliest facts of which we possess trustworthy accounts, must have run parallel with that of the oak-cult among the Celts, so far as its several phases were concerned, and even to some extent in time. Indeed, we have already seen that in many respects its evolution took the same direction, therefore it is of the first importance for us in a comparative sense, as it serves to enlighten us not only respecting the rise and circumstances of Druidism, but regarding those phases of the Celtic cult concerning which we possess little or no evidence. The history of the oak-cult in Greece and Rome corresponds in so many instances with what we know of the Celtic oak-cult that it is reasonably safe to draw inferences concerning the latter in respect of what we do not know of it from known Greek and Roman circumstances.

We have seen that Classical writers reveal the existence of a primitive belief that early man relied upon the acorn as an article of food, from which we may safely assume that he worshipped the tree whence it was procured. At one of the earliest sanctuaries of this cult in Greece, that at Dodona, Zeus was worshipped in the oracular oak which grew there. The festival of the Little Daedala at Platæa, already described, reveals at least a part of the process by which the oak itself, or the spirit which was thought to ensoul it, gradually assumed godhead. Every few years an oak tree was selected by bird-auspices, cut down, and a rude image was made from its trunk. This was attired as a bride and was conveyed to the town of Platæa. The images thus made were collected and preserved until the period of the Great Daedala, which fell once in sixty years, when they were consumed by fire [2] The rite obviously refers to the marriage of the oak-god to the oak-goddess, and Frazer indicates that it is of the same class as the much later marriage of the King and Queen of the May, commonly celebrated in many parts of Europe. In my view, the intention of this rite was to quicken by a mimetic process the supposititious sexual instincts of the powers of vegetation. It is indeed clear from the Platæan instance that the oak, in that area at least, had come to be regarded as symbolic of the collective powers of vegetation, as indeed it was not only with the Druids, but as we have seen, among the folk of Old Prussia and the other Slavonic peoples. The Platæan ceremony symbolized the marriage of the lightning-god to the oak, while that of the Great Daedalus seems to have been a species of cumulative ceremony designed to excite abnormal or long-lasting powers of growth by a marriage of the fourteen idols to the god of fire and lightning at one and the same time. It was indeed such a "marriage" of the lightning spirit with the tree as we find referred to in the Irish "Dindshencas," where the lightning-bird weds with "Timber-Knots," the spirit of the oak tree.

In a later phase the oak-god Zeus was coupled with Dione, or Juno, at Dodona, and at Mount Cithæron he was periodically wedded to an oaken image of Hera. So, on the Alban Mount and on that of the Capitol at Rome, he was united to Juno, or her surrogate Moneta.³ As Frazer has shown, the Kings of Rome and Alba masqueraded as Jupiter in his form as a god of the oak, a proceeding which marked the monarch as the human representative of the oak-god. Romulus, the mythical founder of Rome, is said to have contrived machines which mimicked the roll of the thunder and the flash of the lightning, and in a sense this apparatus equates with the solar or lightning "wheel" of the Druid Mog Ruith, which he constructed with the aid of Simon Magus, and the "flying-machine" of the mythical British monarch Bladud.⁴

The ashes of the fires of the Vestal Virgins discovered at the Temple of Vesta in the Forum at Rome were those of oak-wood.⁵ There is indeed the most ample proof that the entire religion of ancient Rome originated in a cult of the oak. The same holds good of the worship of Egeria, or Diana at Nemi, the shrine of the golden bough. The very name of Egeria is derived from a root *æg*, meaning "oak."⁶

Moreover the sacrifice of white steers or bulls to Jupiter as god of the oak reveals an association between Latin and Druidic rite. Again, as I have said, the cult of the Arval Brethren at Rome indicates a close accord between Latin and Druidic rite and general sodalic procedure. These priests, twelve in number, were the servants of the old Roman goddess of cornfields, Acca Larentia, and held their worship in a grove five miles from Rome. The Emperors themselves were members of this cult, the festivals of which were celebrated at the beginning of May. Were their grove damaged by human action or by lightning, expiatory sacrifices were held to avert the evil consequences which might ensue. That they were closely associated with the Kingship and the ancestral worship of the *Lares* is known.

All this reveals the several phases or stages which the oak-cult in Greece and Rome underwent—the adoration of the oak as a food-giving tree, the personalization and later the deification of the tree or its genius, its union with the spirit of fire or lightning, the recognition that the "king," or priest of the oak, was the living representative of the spirit of the lightning or fire-god who fructified it and who mated with the spirit of the oak in marriage. The king or priest of the oak came to be regarded as responsible for the crop of acorns which the sacred tree and other members of its species yielded. This, in time, was extended to imply responsibility for all vegetable growth.

The association of the Divine King with the cult of the oak seems therefore to be revealed as a theory implicit in the earliest condition of that cult, as in other vegetation cults, though it seems probable that in later times it was inspired and amplified as regards its ideals and ritual by influences from Egypt at a remove, and possibly of a secondary and later character.

As we have seen, it was held by primitive peoples in Europe, as it still is in backward areas of the world, that the spirits of the dead inhabited trees. How far this belief is associated with, or conflicts with, the idea that the tree possesses a spirit or genius of its own is not precisely clear. "The souls of the dead," says Professor Krappe, "may go into trees, becoming indistinguishable from genuine vegetation spirits."⁷ Sir West Ridgeway laid it down that "the belief in . . . Tree, River and Mountain spirits, is merely secondary, springing out of the primary faith in the existence of human souls after the death of the body."⁸

That the spirits of the ancestors were regarded as presiding over the food-supply is known from their intimate association with the growth of cereal plants in the agricultural period, and it may be assumed that in food-gathering times they were also identified with the supply of provender. From ancestor to godling or god is but a step to the primitive mind, and rapidly enough the ancestral figure takes upon itself the supernatural and mythical characteristics of a genius or god, occult potencies crowd upon it and in time it assumes the complete panoply of a departmental deity.

I think that Canon MacCulloch reached the heart of the matter when he summarized his conclusions regarding the character of the Druidic cult. "Other Aryan folk besides the Celts," he wrote, "regarded the oak as the symbol of a high god, of the sun or the sky, but probably this was not its earliest significance." The prevalence of oak forests all over Europe and the circumstance that men once lived on acorns has, he says, been established by archæological evidence, for instance in Northern Italy. The folk of an oak region might well have adopted the oak as a representative of the spirit of vegetation—the embodiment of life and growth. "How, then, did the oak come to symbolize a god equated with Zeus?" Perhaps the earlier spirit of vegetation had become a deity with functions resembling those of Zeus. As Frazer has said, the oak-tree wood burned at the festivals was regarded as being taken from "the original storehouse or reservoir of the fire which was from time to time drawn out to feed the sun." "The oak," concludes MacCulloch, "thus became the symbol of a bright god also connected with growth. But to judge by folk-survivals, the older conception still remained potent, and tree or human victim affected for good all vegetable growth as well as man's life, while at the same time the fire strengthened the sun."•

After long consideration of the question of the origin of Druidism I cannot escape the conclusion that it had its beginnings in the Food-gathering age when extensive forests of oak covered the face of Europe from the Atlantic coast to the Urals. Its rise must, indeed, have been almost coeval with the appearance of the oak in Europe. As has already been said, the lake-dwelling folk of early Switzerland who settled in that area in what is known as the "Cortaillod" period of culture at a time which was probably some centuries prior to the year 2000 B.C., gathered and stored the acorn and constructed their lake-dwellings from oak timber, which they also used for firing. They were also farmers with a Neolithic equipment, who cultivated wheat and barley and gathered apples and plums. They may even have used stone ploughshares and they raised flocks of sheep and goats. They were fairly good carpenters, and cultivated flax which they wove into linen.

To the north of them dwelt other lake-dwellers, those of the Michelsberg Culture, and still others flourished in Upper Austria and elsewhere.¹⁰ It appears to me as not unlikely that it was among such Neolithic settlements that the worship of the oak assumed its more definite and concrete form. We cannot doubt, however, that the cult of the oak must also have been in vogue in other areas where the tree was the most salient object in the landscape, such as Denmark, Old Prussia and parts of Russia, Greece and Italy. Doubtless by the end of the Forest-culture of the Mesolithic or Middle Stone Age, or that period which fell between the Old and New Stone Ages, the cult of the oak had been developed so far as its salient features were concerned. But in what European area precisely it first came to fuller fruition must remain obscure for the present, and indeed it appears as unlikely that it will ever be identi-fied with any degree of definiteness, as such data as might assist the desired conclusion are entirely lacking.

Did Druidism reach Gaul with the Celts when they entered that area at some time in the seventh century B.C.? If it did, I am of opinion that it was merely as a later wave of a cult already established there. If a Celtic cult of the oak was then introduced by these immigrants, it must surely have encountered in Gaul a faith of a similar character, more lowly in its type, perhaps, which had already flourished there for ages. But the Celtic Druids may have brought to it somewhat more elevated standards. And such a conclusion may possibly account for the circumstance that in

Irish legend we read of a Druidic cultus in vogue among the "Fomorians" and other early Irish races whom the incoming Celts sought to displace.

One of the major difficulties to be faced in seeking to account for the long survival of so early a form of faith as was Druidism in Europe, is associated with the perplexing problem of the persistent continuance of a cult which must have had its origin in Mesolithic times. When the Food-gathering age came to an end why did the faith which it had engendered not also lapse? That it continued to flourish in Greece and Rome for centuries after the Food-gathering era—probably for over a thousand years—seems to be indicated, and that during this time its forms and rites had persisted and had become altered by an agricultural civilization hardly at all, excites surprise. Then, more or less abruptly, it appears to have been to a great extent superseded or at least partially outmoded by the rituals and forms of a more advanced faith in which great departmental deities and their worship prevailed, so that when the Romans at last encountered another form of it in Gaul in the time of Cæsar, they appear to have regarded it as a cultus more or less primitive, extraordinary and foreign to them, although they were able to equate some of its deities with their own.

The truth is, I believe, that in the Gaul of Cæsar's time the oak-cult was on the verge of some such supersession as it had met with in Greece and among the Latin peoples. The virtual collapse of the kingship in Gaul administered a shock to its principles and its authority. This was, indeed, the opinion of Rhys, but he further hints that a definite change was effected by the erection of the Gaulish Mercury, or culture-god, to the headship of the Gaulish pantheon.[11] Jupiter and Zeus, the ancient gods of the oak in Rome and Greece, were never displaced as heads of their respective pantheons, but the excess of novel attributes accorded to their "personalities" so altered these as almost to occlude their original status as "oak-fathers."

But the main reasons why Gaulish Druidism retained so much of its antique form and ritual as a definite cult of the oak must be associated with the fact that it constituted a powerful and conservative priesthood definitely unfriendly to change of any kind, in the aristocratic character of its sodality, the regulations and composition of which accorded its members the highest privileges, in the powers of superstition they wielded and in the ignorance in which they sought to keep the folk at large respecting their lore and knowledge. Such conditions did not exist in primeval Greece and Rome. Greece, as by a miracle, had suddenly acquired by the rise of its thriving city states a measure of free and democratic opinion such as the people of Gaul never enjoyed, whereas in Rome the idea of popular liberty and religious co-operation in the state ritual was the jealous care of its freemen. The Druidism of Gaul was indeed the last relic of the ancient oak-worship of Europe in a condition more or less fossilized, unless we except its probably derivative form as witnessed in the Ireland of the early Christian centuries. As for the reason why Druidism survived after the Food-getting age, we can find so many parallels to this in religious history of the survival of early cults that our question is readily answered. Again, the acceptance of the oak as a general symbol of vegetational increase, even in an agricultural age, and its priority and ancient sanction provide us with an equally cogent reply.

That the oak-cult ran much the same course among the Teutonic and Slavonic peoples it is by no means rash to assume. History affords us glimpses of it among the Teutonic peoples, although they certainly had no priesthood devoted to it, and we have seen that oak-cults flourished in more than one Slavonic area until a comparatively late period and that these evidently possessed a priesthood of their own. Other tree-cults associated with fruit- or nut-bearing trees also existed in Europe in primitive times, those of the apple and the hazel among them, but although we find traces of both in history and folk-lore, these are insufficient to permit of anything like definite statement concerning them, save the mere fact of their existence.

To summarize the conclusions here arrived at with such complementary remarks as may seem to be called for, we find that the ancient cult of the oak tree had a widely dispersed vogue in Europe from France to Russia, and as regards more southern areas, in Greece and Italy. That part of its history which is most fully known is associated with its floreat in Greece and Italy, and it provides us with a reasonably trustworthy account of the character and ritual of the cultus in its early form. Indeed, it casts light on those details of the Celtic oak-cult which are obscure.

The value of the acorn as an article of food to men and cattle was unquestionably the chief factor in the rise of an oak-cult in Europe. The acorn, indeed, came to be regarded as the gift or bounty of the spirit or supernatural power which resided in the oak, and at a later phase the branches and timber of that tree were also regarded as among its benefits. Because its wood was employed in the kindling of fires, it seems to have been presumed that the lightning-flash was produced by the friction caused by the rubbing together of gigantic oaken sticks in the firmament by supernatural agency, and it may be that these were conceived as coming from the branches of a great divine oak tree situated in the heavens, from which all meteorological phenomena proceeded. Perhaps the *mana*, or magical influence of this giant supernatural oak came to be thought of as a reservoir of vegetational growth, but concerning these latter possibilities we can only indulge in surmise.

In course of time, it is clear, everything about the oak tree came to be conceived as sacred—its trunk, its bark, its boughs and leaves, the mistletoe which was occasionally found upon it as a parasite, the birds which nested and sang in its branches. At some time a priest or "king" was selected as the human representative of its genius or spirit, and it was doubtless from this practice that the Druidic priesthood had its more definite development. A growing ritual, ever branching out into curious and minute particulars of ceremony, would demand an enlargement in the personnel of its ministry, a discipline would be established and that severe control which is dictated by the rigid fixation of rite and its inevitable and irrefragable constancy, would come into being. In the assumption of a "king" of the oak, who was probably sacrificed at stated intervals because of the diminution of his vigour, or for other reasons, we find the origin of that Divine Kingship so clearly associated with vegetation cults.

As to the time and place of the beginnings of the oak-cult, it seems to be coeval with the spread of the oak in Europe, and may have owed its later development to those lake-dwelling tribes who dwelt near areas heavily afforested with the oak tree, and who depended on and made such extensive use of its fruit and timber. There is, of course, the possibility that it arose not in one but in several areas similarly situated, but the evidence appears to point to the fact of its rise in one locality, and under such circumstances as prevailed in the Nile country in respect of the religious developments which arose there and which were due to the adoption of irrigation as an aid to the extensive cultivation of wheat and barley.

From the hypothetical region of its origin Druidism spread both eastward and westward, a more elaborate type of it entering Gaul with the conquering Celts, where it must almost certainly have encountered a more humble version of the oak-cult. Its precise relationship to the great pantheon of the Celtic races still remains among the obscurities. We have seen that Druidism recognized as its presiding divinities certain gods embraced in the Celtic pantheon, but what connections it had with the remaining members of that "Olympus" we are unaware. The self-same set of circumstances confronts us in the history of the pantheons of Greece and Rome, numerous members of which appear to have had no affinity with the ancient oak-cults of these countries whatsoever. But we do know that the assemblages of gods in question arose out of the amalgamation of numerous separate local cults of lowly beginnings, which had deified this or that power of growth or other factor thought to be beneficent to human necessity, and it may well be assumed that the same process took place in respect of the Celtic pantheon. The difference consisted in the greater potency of the oak-cult among the Celts.

When that broke down, consequent upon the fall of the kingship in Gaul, the Celtic pantheon still continued to be worshipped, even though that worship was adulterated by the introduction of Roman ideals, and this would seem to suggest that a wide difference of origin existed between Druidism, the cult of the oak, and the later developments of Celtic faith, and that Druidism had only prevailed and had functioned as the priesthood of the Celtic religion because of its superior organization, that it had, in short, as an established priesthood of most ancient institution, drawn into the scope of its religious function and control numerous other cults, while still deftly maintaining its own cultus as the nucleus of all.

REFERENCES

(This list serves also as a list of authorities quoted)

Chapter I

INTRODUCTORY

[1] See J. A. Wylie, *History of the Scottish Nation*, Vol. I, p. 95, note 1.
[2] J. G. Frazer, *The Magic Art*, Vol. II, pp. 362–3, and note 2.
[3] J. Rhys, *Hibbert Lectures*, pp. 221–2.
[4] Maximus Tyrius, *Dissertations*, Book VIII, chap. 8; and see Vergil, *Georgics*, III, 332.
[5] H. M. Chadwick, *Journal of the Anthropological Institute*, 1900, p. 34.
[6] A. Macbain, *Celtic Mythology*, p. 154.
[7] H. D'Arbois de Jubainville, *Les Druides*, pp. 11, 82–6.
[8] E. Anwyl, *Celtic Religion*, p. 44.
[9] T. D. Kendrick, *The Druids*, p. 16, note 1.
[10] J. A. MacCulloch, *The Religion of the Ancient Celts*, p. 293.
[11] J. E. Lloyd, *History of Wales*, Vol. I, page 42.
[12] A. H. Allcroft, *The Circle and the Cross*, p. 315.
[13] W. Ridgeway, *The Early Age of Greece*, Vol. I, p. 352.
[14] E. Anwyl, *op. cit.*, pp. 4–5.

Chapter II

DRUIDISM IN CELTIC AREAS

[1] Diogenes Lærtius, *Lives of the Philosophers*, Prooemium, Par. 1.
[2] H. D'Arbois de Jubainville, *Les Druides*, p. 12.
[3] Desjardin, *Géographie de la Gaule Romaine*, Vol. II, p. 515.
[4] H. D'Arbois de Jubainville, *Principaux auteurs de l'antiquité à consulter sur l'histoire des Celtes*, pp. 187–8.
[5] T. Rice Holmes, *Ancient Britain and the Invasion of Julius Cæsar*, p. 292, note 2.
[6] T. Rice Holmes, *Cæsar's Conquest of Gaul*, p. 525.
[7] Cæsar, *Commentaries*, Book VI, chap. XIII–XVIII.
[8] C. Jullian, *Cambridge Mediæval History*, Vol. II, p. 468.
[9] Cæsar, *op. cit.*, Book VII, chaps. IV, VIII, LXXXII; Rice Holmes, *op. cit.*, p. 130 ff.
[10] J. Rhys, *Hibbert Lectures*, pp. 231–2.
[11] Suetonius, *Claudius*, chap. 25.
[12] Pliny, *Natural History*, Book XXX, chap. 13.
[13] Pomponius Mela, *De Situ Orbis*, Book III, chaps. 2, 18 and 19.
[14] Fustel de Coulanges, *Comment le Druidisme à disparu*, *Revue Celtique*, Vol. IV, p. 44.
[15] Lucan, *Pharsalia*, Book I, 453.
[16] Tacitus, *Historiæ*, I, IV, chap. 54.
[17] Ausonius, *Commen, professorum*, IV, 7–10 and X, 22–30.
[18] A. E. Waite, *The Hidden Church of the Holy Grail*, p. 176 f.
[19] Julius Cæsar, *op. cit.*, Book VI, chap. XIII.
[20] Tacitus, *Annals*, Book XIV, chap. 30.

[21] Pliny, *op. cit.*, Book XXX, chap. 13.
[22] E. Hull, *Folklore of the British Isles*, p. 298.
[23] J. Fergusson, *Rude Stone Monuments*, pp. 5–6.
[24] T. D. Kendrick, *The Druids*, chap. V, *passim*.
[25] J. Rhys, *Lectures on Welsh Philology*, pp. 83–4.
[26] J. Rhys, *Celtic Britain*, p. 69.
[27] J. Rhys, *The Welsh People*, p. 83.
[28] H. D'Arbois de Jubainville, *Les Druides*, pp. 13, 22–3.
[29] T. D. Kendrick, *op. cit.*, p. 92.
[30] L. Spence, *Boadicea*, p. 72.
[31] Dio Cassius, *Roman History*.
[32] L. Spence, *op. cit.*, pp. 149–52.
[33] C. Squire, *Mythology of the British Isles*, p. 35.
[34] T. D. Kendrick, *op. cit.*, p. 100.
[35] J. E. Jackson, *Aubrey's Topographical Collection for Wilts*, p. 103.
[36] Nennius, *Historia Britonum*, chap. 40; J. H. Todd, *The Irish Version of Nennius*, p. 91.
[37] J. Rhys, *Hibbert Lectures*, pp. 224–5.
[38] J. Rhys, *Celtic Britain*, p. 70.
[39] J. A. MacCulloch, *The Religion of the Ancient Celts*, p. 300, note 6.
[40] W. J. Gruffydd, *Math Vab Mathonwy*, p. 266, note 88.
[41] A. Herbert, *The Neo-Druidic Heresy*, p. 5.
[42] A. Herbert, *op. cit.*, p. 131.
[43] T. D. Kendrick, *op. cit.*, pp. 27–8.
[44] C. Elton, *Origins of English History*, pp. 253–4.
[45] Roland, *Mona Antiqua*, p. 89.
[46] J. Toland, *The Druids*, p. 60.
[47] D. Wright, *Druidism*, p. 14.
[48] D. Wright, *op. cit.*, pp. 129–30.

Chapter III

DRUIDISM IN CELTIC AREAS (continued)

[1] W. F. Skene, *Chronicles of the Picts and Scots*, p. 31.
[2] W. F. Skene, *Celtic Scotland*, Vol. II, p. 114.
[3] Adamnan, *Life of St. Columba*, Book I, chap. 32.
[4] Adamnan, *op. cit.*, Book II, chap. 11.
[5] Adamnan, *op. cit.*, Book II, chap. 34.
[6] J. Hill Burton, *History of Scotland*, Vol. I, chap. IV.
[7] W. F. Skene, *op. cit.*, Vol. II, p. 119, note 72.
[8] G. Keating, *History of Ireland*, Vol. II, p. 32 (Dineen's edition).
[9] A. Mitchell, *The Past in the Present*, pp. 147 and 267 ff.
[10] T. Pennant, *A Tour in Scotland*, p. 330.
[11] A. B. Cook, *Folk-Lore*, Vol. XVII, p. 332.
[12] M. Martin, *Description of the Western Isles*, pp. 110–12.
[13] M. Martin, *op. cit.*, p. 166.
[14] E. Hull, *Folklore of the British Isles*, p. 300.
[15] E. Hull, *op. cit.*, p. 291.
[16] G. Keating, *op. cit.*, Vol. II, p. 65 (Dineen's edition).
[17] W. Beauford, *Collectanea Hibernica*, Vol. II, p. 208.
[18] G. Keating, *op. cit.*, Vol. I, pp. 203, 213, 217 (Dineen's edition).
[19] E. O'Curry, *Manners and Customs of the Ancient Irish*, Vol. II, p. 187.

[20] E. O'Curry, *op. cit.*, Vol. II, p. 108.

[21] J. Rhys, *Hibbert Lectures*, p. 222.

[22] T. D. Kendrick, *The Druids*, p. 132 f.

[23] A. Macbain, *Celtic Mythology and Religion*, p. 79.

[24] T. D. Kendrick, *op. cit.*, p. 199.

[25] E. O'Curry, *op. cit.*, Vol. II, p. 228.

[26] P. W. Joyce, *Old Celtic Romances*, pp. 106–9.

[27] C. Squire, *op. cit.*, p. 202.

[28] W. Y. Evans Wentz, *The Fairy Faith in Celtic Countries*, p. 444.

[29] T. Wright, *St. Patrick's Purgatory*, *passim*.

[30] G. Keating, *op. cit.*, Vol. II, p. 33 (O'Connor's edition).

[31] E. Hull, *op. cit.*, pp. 125–7.

[32] J. Bonwick, *Irish Druids and Old Irish Religions*, pp. 234–5.

[33] Strabo, Book XII, 5, 1.

[34] Arrian, *Cynegaticus*, p. 33 ff.

Chapter IV

THE DRUIDIC PRIESTHOOD

[1] Cæsar, *Commentaries*, Book VI, chap. 13.

[2] Pomponius Mela, *De Situ Orbis*, Book III, chap. 2.

[3] Cæsar, *op. cit.*, Book VI, chap. 14.

[4] J. Bonwick, *Irish Druids and Old Irish Religions*, pp. 14, 45.

[5] Diodorus Siculus, *Histories*, Book V, 31, 2.

[6] Strabo, *Geographica*, Book IV, 4, chap. 197, 4.

[7] Ammianus Marcellinus, chap. XV, 9.

[8] Lucan, *Pharsalia*, Book I, 449.

[9] Pliny, *Natural History*, Book XXX, chap. 13.

[10] J. A. MacCulloch, *The Religion of the Ancient Celts*, p. 300.

[11] D. Hyde, *Literary History of Ireland*, p. 88; P. W. Joyce, *Social History of Ancient Ireland*, Vol. I, p. 239.

[12] Ammianus Marcellinus, XV, 9.

[13] Diodorus Siculus, *op. cit.*, Book V, 31, 2–5.

[14] A. Macbain, *Celtic Mythology and Religion*, pp. 81–2; E. O'Curry, *MS. Materials of Ancient Irish History*, p. 248.

[15] E. O'Curry, *op. cit.*, p. 240.

[16] J. Bonwick, *op. cit.*, pp. 37–44.

[17] P. W. Joyce, *op. cit.*, Vol. I, pp. 424–34; E. O'Curry, *Manners and Customs of the Ancient Irish*, Vol. II, pp. 171, 179–228.

[18] E. Windisch and W. Stokes, *Irische Texte*, Vol. III, Part I, pp. 51–3; E. O'Curry, *op. cit.*, Vol. II, p. 171 ff.

[19] J. Bonwick, *op. cit.*, p. 39.

[20] Diogenes Lærtius, *Vitæ*, Proem I.

[21] C. Jullian, *Recherches sur la religion gauloise*, p. 102.

[22] T. D. Kendrick, *The Druids*, pp. 135–8; C. Jullian, *Cambridge Mediæval History*, Vol. II, p. 47.

[23] J. A. MacCulloch, *Religion of the Ancient Celts*, p. 298.

[24] A. Holder, *Altceltischer Sprachschatz*, Vol. I, 2046; F. Loth, *Revue Celtique*, Vol. XXVIII, p. 120.

[25] T. Rice Holmes, *Ancient Britain*, p. 293, note 2.

[26] T. Rice Holmes, *Cæsar's Conquest of Gaul*, p. 527, note 7.

[27] T. Rice Holmes, *op. cit.*, pp. 831–2.

[28] Origen, *Contra Celsus*, Book I, chap. 16.
[29] T. D. Kendrick, *op. cit*, pp. 79, 113–14, 199.
[30] J. Pokorny, *Celtic Review*, Vol. V., p. 1 ff.
[31] C. Jullian, *op. cit.*, Vol. II, pp. 68–9; *Histoire de la Gaule*, Vol. II, p. 87, note 3.
[32] J. A. MacCulloch, *op. cit.*, pp. 305, 311–12.
[33] E. Hull, *Folklore of the British Isles*, pp. 293–4.
[34] G. Keating, *The History of Ireland*, Vol. I, p. 302.
[35] O. Seyffert, *Dictionary of Classical Antiquities*, p. 74.
[36] A. Macbain, *op. cit.*, pp. 69–86.
[37] E. O'Curry, *op. cit.*, Vol. II, p. 228.
[38] J. Rhys, *Hibbert Lectures*, pp. 226–8.
[39] T. D. Kendrick, *op. cit.*, pp. 79–81.
[40] P. W. Joyce, *op. cit.*, T. J. Westropp, "Proc. R. Irish Acad." Vol. XXV, p. 313.
[41] Cæsar, *op. cit.*, Book VI, chap. XIII.
[42] A. Bertrand, *Religion des gaulois*, p. 280.
[43] G. Keating, *op. cit.*, II, pp. 273, 405 (Dineen's edition); E. Windisch, *Táin Bó Cualnge*, pp. 792–3 and note 2; *Irische Texte (Coir Anmann)*, Vol. III, p. 389.
[44] Strabo, Book IV.
[45] E. O'Curry, *op. cit.*, Vol. III, p. 145.
[46] Pliny, *op. cit.*, Book XVI, 249.
[47] J. G. Dalyell, *Darker Superstitions of Scotland*, p. 239.
[48] J. Dunn, *Táin Bó Cualnge*, p. 33.
[49] J. Rhys, *Celtic Britain*, pp. 73–4.
[50] Gildas, in Haddan and Stubbs, *Councils and Ecclesiastical Documents*, Vol. I, pp. 112–3.
[51] J. Rhys, *op. cit.*, p. 74.
[52] J. Rhys, *Hibbert Lectures*, p. 210 ff.
[53] Bede, *Ecclesiastical History*, chap. XXI.
[54] J. Rhys, *op. cit.*, 213.
[55] A. Herbert, *Britannia After the Romans*, Vol. II, pp. 69–70.
[56] J. A. MacCulloch, *op. cit.*, p. 304.

Chapter V

THE DRUIDIC PRIESTHOOD (*continued*)

[1] Cæsar, *Commentaries*, Book VI, chap. XIV.
[2] Pomponius Mela, *De Situ Orbis*, Book III, chap. 2, 18–19.
[3] E. Windisch and W. Stokes, *Irische Texte*, Vol. III; P. W. Joyce, *Social History of Ireland*, Vol. I, pp. 424–34.
[4] E. O'Curry, *Manners and Customs of the Ancient Irish*, Vol. II, pp. 201–2.
[5] J. Rhys, *Hibbert Lectures*, p. 223.
[6] C. Jullian, *The Cambridge Mediæval History*, Vol. II, p. 469.
[7] A. H. Allcroft, *The Circle and the Cross*, p. 312.
[8] Pomponius Mela, *op. cit.*, Book III, chap. 2, pp. 18–19.
[9] J. Bonwick, *Irish Druids*, p. 14.
[10] Giraldus Cambrensis, *The Topography of Wales* (Wright), p. 97.
[11] E. O. Gordon, *Prehistoric London*, p. 66; J. Toland, *History of the Druids*, p. 44, note 1.
[12] J. Dunn, *Táin Bó Cualnge*, pp. 31–2.
[13] Cæsar, *op. cit.*, Book VI, chap. XIII.
[14] C. Jullian, *op. cit.*, Vol II, pp. 468–9.
[15] G. Dottin, *l'Antiquite Celtique*, pp. 190–1.

[16] D'Arbois de Jubainville, *Revue Celtique*, Vol. VIII, pp. 519-25.
[17] D'Arbois de Jubainville, *Les Druides*, pp. 60–64.
[18] Strabo, *Geographica*, Book IV, 4, chap. 197, 4.
[19] Cæsar, *op. cit.*, Book VII, chap. XXXIII.
[20] T. Rice Holmes, *Cæsar's Conquest of Gaul*, p. 525, 3.
[21] Diodorus Siculus, *Histories*, Book V, 31, 2–5.
[22] Strabo, *op. cit.*, Book IV, 4, chap. 197, 4.
[23] E. O'Curry, *MS. Materials of Ancient Irish History*, p. 287.
[24] Pliny, Book XXIV, 11; Book XXV, 9.
[25] Windisch-Stokes, *op. cit.*, Vol. I, p. 215.
[26] P. Kennedy, *Legendary Fictions of the Irish Celts*, p. 269 ff.
[27] G. Keating, *History of Ireland* (Dineen's edition), Vol. I, p. 93; Vol. II, p. 173.
[28] T. D. Kendrick, *The Druids*, p. 140.
[29] J. Bonwick, *Irish Druids*, pp. 15–16.
[30] *Psalter of Cashel.*
[31] Lampridius, *Alex. Severus*, Book LIX, c. 5.
[32] Vopiscus, *Numerianus*, Book XIV.
[33] Vopiscus, *Aurelianus*, Book XLIII, chaps. 4 and 5.
[34] Strabo, *op. cit.*, Book IV, chaps. 4 and 6 ; Pomponius Mela, *op. cit.*, Book III, chap. VI; T. D. Kendrick, *op. cit.*, p. 138 ff Elton, *Origins of English History*, p. 25 ff.; G. Dottin, *op. cit.*, pp. 284–5; Rice Holmes, *Ancient Britain*, p. 217 ff.; J. Rhys, *Hibbert Lectures*, p. 196; S. Reinach, *Revue Celtique*, Vol. XVIII, pp. 1–8; C. Jullian, *Revue des etudes anciennes*, Vol. VI, p. 258.
[35] G. Frazer, *The Magic Art*, Vol. II, p. 241, note 1.
[36] J. F. Campbell, *Popular Tales of the West Highlands*, Vol. I, p. 24, XCIII.
[37] L. F. A. Maury, *Les Fées du Moyen-Age*, p. 28.
[38] Lady Charlotte Guest, *The Mabinogion*, pp. 323, 370.
[39] Cicero, *De Divinatione*, Book I, chap. XLI, par. 90.
[40] T. D. Kendrick, *op. cit.*, 80; S. Reinach, *Orpheus*, p. 179.
[41] J. Guenebauld, *Le Reveil de Chyndonax*, pp. 1–35.
[42] E. O'Curry, *op. cit.*, pp. 285–7.
[43] E. O'Curry, *Manners and Customs of the Ancient Irish*, Vol. II, p. 200; J. Rhys, *Hibbert Lectures*, pp. 137, 223.
[44] R. A. S. Macalister, *Tara*, p. 56.
[45] E. Hull, *Folklore of the British Isles*, p. 270.
[46] G. Keating, *General History of Ireland*, Vol. I, p. 128 (D. O'Connor's edition).
[47] W. Y. Evans Wentz, *The Fairy Faith in Celtic Countries*, pp. 81–2, note 2.
[48] E. O'Curry, *MS. Materials of Ancient Irish History*, p. 402 ff.
[49] E. O'Curry, *op. cit.*, pp. 271–2; G. Keating, *op. cit.*, Vol. I, p. 288.
[50] E. K. Chambers, *Arthur of Britain*, p. 95 ff.

Chapter VI

DRUIDIC THEOLOGY AND RITUAL

[1] T. D. Kendrick, *The Druids*, pp. 113–14.
[2] D'Arbois de Jubainville, *The Irish Mythological Cycle* (Best's trans.), p. 126.
[3] Pomponius Mela, *De Situ Orbis*, III, 2, 18 and 19.
[4] R. A. S. Macalister, *The Archæology of Ireland*, pp. 218–19.
[5] Strabo, *Geographica*, Book IV, 4, chap. 197, 4.
[6] Lucan, *Pharsalia*, I, 450–8.
[7] Ammianus Marcellinus, chap. XV, 9, 4.
[8] Maximus of Tyre, *Dissertations*, VIII, 8.

[9] C. Squire, *Mythology of the British Islands*, p. 260.

[10] J. Rhys, *Hibbert Lectures*, pp. 79–82; L. Spence, *The Minor Traditions of British Mythology*, pp. 156-8,

[11] E. O'Curry, *MS. Materials of Ancient Irish History*, pp. 224, 505.

[12] Diodorus Siculus, V, 31, 4.

[13] Diodorus Siculus, *op. cit.*, 31, 4.

[14] E. Anwyl, *Celtic Religion*, p. 47.

[15] J. G. Frazer, *The Magic Art*, Vol. II, pp. 12–50.

[16] J. G. Frazer, *op. cit.*, Vol. II, pp. 12, 16, 19.

[17] E. Hull, *Folklore of the British Isles*, pp. 127–30; J. Rhys, *op. cit.*, p. 358.

[18] G. Keating, *History of Ireland*, Vol. I., pp. 222–3 (Dineen's edition).

[19] J. Geikie, *Prehistoric Europe*, pp. 420 ff., 482 ff., 495; R. Munro, *Ancient Scottish Lake Dwellings*, p. 266.

[20] J. G. Frazer, *op. cit.*, Vol. II, p. 353, quoting W. Helbig, *Die Italiker in der Poebene*, pp. 12, 14, 16 ff. and 20.

[21] O. Seyffert, *Dictionary of Classical Antiquities*, p. 197; J. G. Frazer, *op. cit.*, Vol. II, pp. 358–9.

[22] Pausanias, IX, 3.

[23] J. G. Frazer, *op. cit.*, Vol. II, pp. 373–4.

[24] J. G. Frazer, *op. cit.*, Vol. II, pp. 361–2.

[25] J. G. Frazer, *op. cit.*, Vol. I, p. 42.

[26] J. Grimm, *Teutonic Mythology*, pp. 72, 172.

[27] L. Leger, *La Mythologie Slave*, p. 57 ff.

[28] J. G. Frazer, *op. cit.*, Vol. II., p. 366, note 2.

[29] J. Grimm, *op. cit.*, p. 176.

[30] J. Rhys, *Hibbert Lectures*, p. 221.

[31] J. A. MacCulloch, *The Religion of the Ancient Celts*, p. 198.

[32] Giraldus Cambrensis, *The Topography of Ireland*, chaps. XXXIV–VI.

[33] J. Pokorny, *The Origin of Druidism, Celtic Review*, Vol. V, No. 17, p. 19.

[34] E. Hull, *Folklore of the British Isles*, pp. 126–7.

[35] *County Folk-Lore, Leicestershire*, p. 26 ff.

[36] W. Hone, *Everyday Book*, Vol. II, p. 512 ff.

[37] A. Porteous, *Forest Folklore*, p. 190, quoting Loudon, *Trees and Shrubs of Britain*.

[38] B. C. A. Windle, *Tyson's Pygmies of the Ancients*, p. lxxxviii.

[39] L. Spence, *British Fairy Origins*, p. 29.

[40] J. Grimm, *op. cit.*, p. 461.

[41] J. Grimm, *op. cit.*, pp. 73–5.

[42] W. Y. E. Wentz, *The Fairy Faith in Celtic Countries*, p. 434–5, quoting Mahé, *Essai*, pp. 333–4.

[43] J. M. Mackinlay, *Folklore of Scottish Lochs and Springs*, p. 233.

[44] C. S. Burne, *Handbook of Folklore*, p. 35.

[45] J. G. Frazer, *op. cit.*, Vol. II, p. 371.

[46] J. G. Frazer, *op. cit.*, Vol. II, pp. 371–2.

[47] S. Baring-Gould, *Curious Myths of the Middle Ages*, p. 627.

[48] J. Aubrey, *Remains of Gentilisme and Judaisme*, p. 247.

[49] M. R. Cox, *Cinderella*, p. 478.

[50] W. Henderson, *Folk-Lore of the Northern Counties of England*, p. 17.

[51] C. Friend, *Flowers and Flower Lore*, pp. 305–6.

[52] Pliny, *Natural History*, XVI, 249.

[53] J. Cameron, *Gælic Names of Plants*, p. 45.

[54] J. A. MacCulloch, *op. cit.*, 163.

[55] J. G. Frazer, *The Golden Bough*, Vol. II, p. 189; O. Seyffert, *Dictionary of Classical Antiquities*, p. 338.

⁵⁶ D. Wright, *Druidism*, p. 167; Vergil, *Æneid*, IV, 513.

⁵⁷ W. Stukeley, *Medallic History of Carausius*, Vol. II, pp. 163–4.

⁵⁸ J. A. MacCulloch, *op. cit.*, p. 162.

⁵⁹ L. Spence, *The Magic Arts in Celtic Britain*, pp. 125–6.

⁶⁰ J. Aubrey, *op. cit.*, p. 89.

⁶¹ T. F. Dyer, *English Folk-Lore*, p. 11.

⁶² H. Friend, *Flowers and Flower Lore*, pp. 378–9.

⁶³ T. F. Dyer, *The Folklore of Plants*, p. 43.

⁶⁴ A. Porteous, *Forest Folklore*, pp. 230–1.

⁶⁵ Folk-Lore of Yorkshire, *County Folk-Lore*, Vol. II, pp. 279–80, note 1.

⁶⁶ W. Stukeley, *op. cit.*, Vol. II, pp. 163–4; J. Leland, *Itinerary*, Vol. IV, pp. 182–3.

⁶⁷ T. D. Kendrick, *The Druids*, pp. 124–5; J. Allies, *Antiquities and Folklore of Worcestershire*, p. 163.

⁶⁸ Cæsar, *Commentaries*, Book VI, chap. 17; Lucan, *Pharsalia*, III, 412.

⁶⁹ S. Reinach, *Revue Celtique*, Vol. XIII, p. 189 and pp. 193–9; A. Bertand, *Revue Archæologique*, Vol. XV, p. 345.

⁷⁰ C. Jullian, *Cambridge Mediæval History*, p. 464.

⁷¹ E. O'Curry, *Manners and Customs of the Ancient Irish*, Vol. II, p. 227.

⁷² W. Stokes, *Tripartite Life of St. Patrick*, Vol. I, p. 40.

⁷³ G. Keating, *General History of Ireland*, p. 305 (O'Connor's edition).

⁷⁴ J. Bonwick, *Irish Druids*, pp. 163–7.

⁷⁵ G. L. Gomme, *Ethnology in Folklore*, p. 140.

⁷⁶ G. Petrie, *The Ecclesiastical Architecture of Ireland*, Trans. Royal Irish Academy, Vol. XX, p. 69.

⁷⁷ E. O'Curry, *op. cit.*, Vol. II, p. 21.

⁷⁸ A. M. Hocart, *Kingship*, pp. 103–9.

⁷⁹ *Book of Armagh*, in W. Batham's *Antiquarian Researches*, Vol. II, p. xxix; Whitley Stokes, *op. cit.*, pp. 123, 323 and Intro., p. 159.

⁸⁰ G. L. Gomme, *op. cit.*, p. 87; W. Sikes, *British Goblins*, p. 355.

⁸¹ See L. Spence, *The Minor Traditions of British Mythology*, chap. II, for a full account of superstitions associated with British wells.

⁸² Lady Charlotte Guest, *The Mabinogion*, p. 6 ff.

⁸³ E. Hull, *Folklore of the British Isles*, pp. 194–5; J. A. MacCulloch, *op. cit.*, pp. 308–9.

⁸⁴ E. O'Curry, *op. cit.*, Vol. I, p. cccxxi ff.

Chapter VII

IDEAS CONCERNING THE AFTER-LIFE, FESTIVALS
AND SACRIFICE

¹ Diodorus Siculus, *Histories*, V, 28, 6.

² Strabo, *Geographica*, IV, 4, chap. 197, 4.

³ Pomponius Mela, *De Situ Orbis*, III, 2, 18 and 19.

⁴ Ammianus Marcellinus, XV, 9, 8.

⁵ Hippolytus, *Philosophumena*, I, 25.

⁶ Clement of Alexandria, *Stromata*, I, XV, 70, 1, and I, XV, 71, 3.

⁷ Valerius Maximus, II, 6, 10.

⁸ Herodotus, 4, C, 19.

⁹ Rice Holmes, *Ancient Britain*, pp. 295–6.

¹⁰ T. D. Kendrick, *The Druids*, p. 108.

¹¹ E. Anwyl, *Celtic Religion*, pp. 45–6.

[12] T. Rhys, *Hibbert Lectures*, p. 431.

[13] W. Y. Evans Wentz, *The Fairy Faith in Celtic Countries*, p. 368.

[14] D. Hyde, *A Literary History of Ireland*, p. 95.

[15] E. S. Hartland, *Primitive Paternity*, Vol. I, p. 19 ff.

[16] D'Arbois de Jubainville, *The Irish Mythological Cycle*, pp. 25–35.

[17] E. Windisch, *Irische Texte*, p. 136 ff.

[18] E. Meyer, "The Wooing of Emer," in *Arch. Review*, Vol. I, p. 70.

[19] H. D'Arbois de Jubainville, *op. cit.*, p. 191 ff.

[20] E. Hull, *The Cuchullin Saga*, p. 82.

[21] E. O'Curry, *Manners and Customs of the Ancient Irish*, p. 192 ff.

[22] A. Nutt, *The Mabinogion*, p. 307.

[23] D'Arbois de Jubainville, *op. cit.*, pp. 26, 196–7.

[24] L. Spence, *British Fairy Origins*, *passim*.

[25] L. Spence, *op. cit.*, p. 157 ff.

[26] J. A. MacCulloch, *The Religion of the Ancient Celts*, p. 258.

[27] J. G. Frazer, *The Golden Bough*, *passim*; J. A. MacCulloch, *op. cit.*, p. 256 ff.; E. Hull, *Folklore of the British Isles*, *passim*.

[28] J. Curtin, *Tales of the Fairies and Ghost World*, p. 72.

[29] G. Keating, *History of Ireland* (Dineen's edition), Vol. II, pp. 133, 247, 251.

[30] E. Hull, *Folklore of the British Isles*, p. 232.

[31] G. Keating, *op. cit.*, Vol. I (O'Connor's edition), p. 246.

[32] P. W. Joyce, *Irish Names of Places*, p. 216.

[33] L. Spence, *Myth and Ritual in Dance, Game and Rhyme*, p. 21.

[34] J. Rhys, *Hibbert Lectures*, pp. 409–11.

[35] For the feast of *Lugnassad*, see J. Rhys, *op. cit.*, p. 409 ff.; J. A. MacCulloch, *op. cit.*, p. 272 ff.; R. A. S. Macalister, *Tara*, p. 162 ff.

[36] J. G. Frazer, *The Magic Art*, Vol. II, p. 172; L. Spence, *British Fairy Origins*, pp. 33–35.

[37] E. O'Curry, *MS. Materials in Irish History*, pp. 618–22.

[38] R. A. S. Macalister, *op. cit.*, 154.

[39] T. D. Kendrick, *The Druids*, pp. 129–30.

[40] J. Ramsay, *Scotland and Scotsmen in the 18th Century*, Vol. II, p. 444.

[41] *Notes and Queries*, First series, VII, p. 353.

[42] T. D. Kendrick, *op. cit.*, p. 199.

[43] Cæsar, *Commentaries*, Book VI, chap. XVI.

[44] Strabo, *op. cit.*, IV, 4, chap. 197, 4.

[45] Strabo, *op. cit.*, IV, 4, chap. 198, 5.

[46] H. Gaidoz, *Esquisse de la Religion des Gaulois*, p. 21.

[47] Diodorus Siculus, *op. cit.*, V, 31, 2–5.

[48] Strabo, *op. cit.*, IV, 4, C, 198, 5.

[49] L. Spence, *The Gods of Mexico*, pp. 159–60, 217; E. Seler, Commentary on the *Aubin Tonalamatl*, p. 93.

[50] L. Spence, *Myth and Ritual in Dance, Game and Rhyme*, p. 37.

[51] S. Baring-Gould, *Curious Myths of the Middle Ages*, p. 113 ff.

[52] J. G. Frazer, *The Magic Art*, Vol. II, p. 11.

[53] Cassius Dio, *Roman History*, LXII, 7.

[54] P. Courteault, *Journal of Roman Studies*, Vol. XI.

[55] E. Hull, *op. cit.*, pp. 92–94.

[56] *Folklore Journal*, Vol. III, p. 281.

[57] A. Bertrand, *La Religion des Gaulois*, pp. 68–73, 252 and 368.

[58] J. A. MacCulloch, *op. cit.*, p. 163.

[59] J. Grimm, *Teutonic Mythology* (trans. Stallybrass) pp. 72–79.

[60] J. G. Frazer, *op. cit.*, II, pp. 366–7.

[61] A. Mitchell, *The Past in the Present*, p. 269.

[62] L. Spence, *The Minor Traditions of British Mythology*, p. 63.
[63] A. Mitchell, *op. cit.*, p. 275.
[64] J. Y. Simpson, *Proc. Soc. Antiq. Scot.*, Vol. IV, p. 33.
[65] J. Grimm, *op. cit.*, p. 608.
[66] J. Stuart, *Presbytery Book of Strathbogie*, p. 104 f.
[67] Gordon Cumming, *In the Hebrides*, p. 194.
[68] R. M. Ferguson, *Rambles in the Far North*, p. 71 f.
[69] J. Evans, *North Wales, The Beauties of England and Wales*, Vol. XVII, Pt. I, p. 36.
[70] W. Hone, *Everyday Book*, Vol. I, p. 431; R. Hunt, *Popular Romances of the West of England*, pp. 212–14.
[71] H. Griffith, *The Rigveda*, Vol. II, p. 299 ff.
[72] K. Macdonald, *Social and Religious Life in the Highlands*, p. 31.
[73] *Transactions of the Gælic Society of Inverness*, Vol. XXV, 1, p. 129.
[74] G. Henderson, *Survivals in Belief Among the Celts*, p. 265 ff.
[75] J. Kemble, *The Saxons in England*, Vol. I, pp. 525–28.
[76] L. Spence, *Magic Arts in Celtic Britain*, pp. 96–7.
[77] M. A. Murray, *The God of the Witches*, p. 31.

Chapter VIII

PLACES OF WORSHIP

[1] J. Toland, *A Critical History of the Celtic Religion and Learning*, p. 60.
[2] T. D. Kendrick, *The Druids*, pp. 4–12.
[3] *Ancient Laws of Ireland*, Vol. I, p. 164.
[4] T. D. Kendrick, *op. cit.*, p. 147.
[5] E. Hull, *Folklore of the British Isles*, p. 124.
[6] C. Jullian, *Cambridge Mediæval History*, Vol. II, pp. 460–1, 466.
[7] G. Henderson, *Survivals in Belief Among the Celts*, p. 186 ff.
[8] P. W. Joyce, *Irish Names of Places*, pp. 499–500.
[9] P. W. Joyce, *op. cit.*, p. 499.
[10] A. E. Bray, *Traditions of Devonshire*, Vol. I, p. 90 ff.
[11] T. D. Kendrick, *op. cit.*, p. 151.
[12] Lucan, *Pharsalia*, III, p. 399 ff.
[13] T. D. Kendrick, *op. cit.*, pp. 153–4.
[14] F. Stevens, *Stonehenge: To-day and Yesterday*, pp. 22–3.
[15] Geoffrey of Monmouth, *Histories of the Kings of Britain*, Book VIII, 10, 11.
[16] J. Rhys, *Hibbert Lectures*, pp. 194–5.
[17] L. Spence, *British Fairy Origins*, p. 180 ff.
[18] J. G. Frazer, *The Magic Art*, pp. 162–165.
[19] T. D. Kendrick, *op. cit.*, p. 188.
[20] S. Reinach, *Comptes-rendu de l'Academie des Inscriptions et Belles-lettres*, 1892, 4° serie, XX pp. 6–7.
[21] A. H. Allcroft, *The Circle and the Cross*, Vol. I, chap. XI, p. 259 ff.
[22] J. Fergusson, *Rude Stone Monuments*, p. 27.
[23] R. A. S. Macalister, *The Archæology of Ireland*, pp. 103–109.
[24] E. Hull, *op. cit.*, p. 299–300.
[25] L. Siret, *L'Anthropologie*, p. 268 ff.; W. J. Perry, *The Children of the Sun*, pp. 499–500; *The Growth of Civilization*, pp. 63–75.
[26] D. T. Kendrick, *op. cit.*, pp. 156–93.
[27] J. A. MacCulloch, *The Religion of the Ancient Celts*, pp. 281–2.
[28] A. Macbain, *Celtic Mythology and Religion*, p. 181 ff.

[29] Polybius, *History*, II, 32, 6.
[30] Livy, XXIII, 24.
[31] C. Jullian, *op. cit.*, p. 466.
[32] Diodorus Siculus, *Histories*, V, 27.
[33] Gildas, *The History*, II, 4.
[34] A. H. Allcroft, *op. cit.*, Vol. I, p. 299.
[35] M. Felibien, *Recueil historique*.
[36] Pomponius Mela, *De Situ Orbis*, III, 2, 18 and 19.
[37] V. G. Childe, *The Dawn of European Civilization*, p. 2.

Chapter IX

DRUIDISM AND THE DIVINE KINGSHIP

[1] A. M. Hocart, *Kingship*, pp. 1–5.
[2] W. J. Perry, *The Children of the Sun*, p. 130 ff.
[3] J. G. Frazer, *The Magic Art*, Vol. I, pp. 366–7.
[4] J. Rhys, *Hibbert Lectures*, p. 231.
[5] Nettleship and Sandys, *Dictionary of Classical Antiquities*, p. 541.
[6] T. D. Kendrick, *The Druids*, pp. 197–8.
[7] E. Hull, *The Cuchullin Saga*, p. 271–3.
[8] E. Hull, *The Folklore of the British Isles*, pp. 272–3.
[9] Dion Chrysostom, *Orations*, xlix.
[10] W. G. Wood-Martin, *Pagan Ireland*, p. 352.
[11] G. Keating, *The General History of Ireland*, Vol. I, p. 231 (O'Connor's edition).
[12] G. Keating, *op. cit.*, Vol. I, p. 243.
[13] E. Hull, *op. cit.*, pp. 92, 292.
[14] E. Hull, *op. cit.*, pp. 276–8.
[15] J. G. Frazer, *op. cit.*, Vol. II, p. 361.
[16] J. A. MacCulloch, *Religion of the Ancient Celts*, p. 202; D'Arbois de Jubainville, *Les Celtes*, p. 51.
[17] J. G. Frazer, *op. cit.*, Vol. II, pp. 120–9.
[18] J. G. Frazer, *op. cit.*, Vol. II, p. 379.
[19] E. Davies, *The Mythology and Rites of the British Druids*, p. 484.
[20] R. A. S. Macalister, *Tara*, p. 127 ff.
[21] E. Hull, *op. cit.*, pp. 274–5.
[22] R. A. S. Macalister, *op. cit.*, p. 131 ff.
[23] E. O'Curry, *MS. Materials of Ancient Irish History*, p. 620.
[24] R. A. S. Macalister, *op. cit.*, p. 127 ff.
[25] L. Spence, *The Magic Arts in Celtic Britain*, p. 99 ff.
[26] A. Nutt, *Studies on the Legend of the Holy Grail*, p. 8.

Chapter X

INFLUENCE OF OTHER CULTS ON DRUIDISM

[1] R. Borrow, *Asiatic Researches*, p. 489.
[2] W. J. Phythian-Adams, *Mithraism*, p. 37.
[3] J. Rhys, *Hibbert Lectures*, p. 224.
[4] E. Hull, *Folklore of the British Isles*, pp. 295–6.
[5] Whitley Stokes, *Lismore Lives*, pp. 215–16.
[6] E. MacCulloch, *Guernsey Folklore*, pp. 145–6.

[7] F. E. Warren, *Cambridge Mediæval History*, Vol. II, p. 504.
[8] J. Jamieson, *An Historical Account of the Ancient Culdees*, p. 29.
[9] W. Skene, *Celtic Scotland*, Vol. II, pp. 276–7.
[10] H. Elder, *Celt, Druid and Culdee*, p. 136.

Chapter XI

DRUIDISM AND THE MAGICAL ARTS

[1] Pliny, *Natural History*, XXX, 13.
[2] Origen, *Contra Celsum*, Book I.
[3] J. Rhys, *Celtic Britain*, pp. 70–1.
[4] W. Stokes and D'Arbois de Jubainville, *MS. Harleian*, 5280; C. Squire, *Mythology of the British Islands*, p. 72.
[5] O. Connellan, *Transactions of the Ossianic Society*, Vol. V.
[6] A. Macbain, *Celtic Mythology*, p. 80.
[7] Adamnan, *Life of St. Columba*, chap. XXXIV.
[8] E. O'Curry, *The MS. Materials of Ancient Irish History*, p. 272.
[9] *Revue Celtique*, Vol. XII, p. 81.
[10] J. Bonwick, *Irish Druids*, pp. 51–2.
[11] W. Y. E. Wentz, *The Fairy Faith in Celtic Countries*, p. 344.
[12] A. MacBain, *Celtic Mythology*, p. 81.
[13] D'Arbois de Jubainville, *The Irish Mythological Cycle* (English trans. I. Best), p. 138.
[14] W. Y. E. Wentz, *op. cit.*, p. 52.
[15] J. A. MacCulloch, *The Religion of the Ancient Celts*, p. 322.
[16] L. Spence, *The Magic Arts in Celtic Britain*, pp. 59–61.
[17] Whitley Stokes, *Lives of the Saints*, p. xxviii.
[18] E. O'Curry, *Manners and Customs of the Ancient Irish*, Vol. II, p. 198.
[19] J. A. MacCulloch, *op. cit.*, p. 325.
[20] E. O'Curry, *op. cit.*, Vol. II, pp. 204–5.
[21] E. O'Curry, *op. cit.*, Vol. II, pp. 216–17.
[22] C. Squire, *op. cit.*, pp. 83, 87, 174.
[23] E. Hull, *Folklore of the British Isles*, pp. 173–4.
[24] E. O'Curry, *op. cit.*, p. 209–12; E. Hull, *op. cit.*, p. 176.
[25] Windisch-Stokes, *Irische Texte*, Vol. I, p. 213; D'Arbois de Jubainville, *Cour de Litterature Celtique*, Vol. V, p. 186; E. O'Curry, *op. cit.*, Vol. II, p. 208; E. Hull, 176–7.
[26] E. Hull, *op. cit.*, p. 177 and note 1.
[27] E. O'Curry, *op. cit.*, Vol. II, pp. 199–200.
[28] Agobard, *Contra insulsi vulgi Opinionem de Grandine et Tonitruis*. See *Patrologia Latina* (ed. Migne), civ, 147 ff.
[29] Gervase of Tilbury, *Otia Imperialia*, I, 13.
[30] See Appendix to O'Curry's *MS. Materials of Ancient Irish History*, No. CXXXVI, p. 625, and the same work, pp. 401–2.
[31] Geoffrey of Monmouth, *History of the Kings of Britain*, Book II, chap. X.
[32] See A. H. Sayce, in *Y Cymmrodorian*, Vol. X, pp. 207–21; L. Spence, *Legendary London*, pp. 179–82.
[33] E. Hull, *op. cit.*, pp. 184–6.
[34] C. Jullian, *Cambridge Mediæval History*, Vol. II, p. 462.
[35] Diodorus Siculus, *Historical Library*, Book V, chap. XXI.
[36] E. O'Curry, *op. cit.*, Vol. II, p. 224; R. I. Best, *Eriu*, Vol. VIII, pp. 114–26; K. Meyer, *Mélusine*, Vol. V., p. 85, Vol. X, p. 113; E. Hull, *op. cit.*, pp. 77–8.

[37] S. Reinach, *Catalogue Sommaire du Musée des Antiquites Nationale*, p. 31; Strabo, IV, 46.

[38] J. Toland, *A Critical History of the Celtic Religion*, p. 174 f.; Pompeius Troganus, in Justin, Lib. 24, cap. 4.

[39] Trevelyan, *Folk-Lore and Folk-Stories of Wales*, pp. 81–2.

[40] Giraldus Cambrensis, *Itinerarium Cambriæ*, Book I, chap. II.

[41] G. Henderson, *Survivals of Belief Among the Celts*, p. 96.

[42] G. Waldron, *Description of the Isle of Man*.

[43] C. Hardwick, *Traditions, Superstitions and Folk-Lore*, pp. 237–8.

[44] W. Yarrel, *British Birds*, Vol. II, p. 178; W. Harrison, *Mona Miscellany*, p. 156.

[45] J. Grimm, *Teutonic Mythology* (Eng. trans. Stallybrass), Vol. I, pp. 311–12; Vol. II, p. 311.

[46] J. Rhys, *Hibbert Lectures*, p. 667.

[47] E. Davies, *Celtic Researches*, p. 300.

[48] Tacitus, *Annals*, XIV, 30; Strabo, *Geographica*, IV, 4, 4; Diodorus Siculus, *Histories*, V, 32.

[49] E. Davies, *op. cit.*, p. 248.

[50] E. Davies, *op. cit.*, pp. 249–53.

[51] E. O'Curry, *op. cit.*, Vol. II, pp. 224–5.

[52] G. Keating, *History of Ireland*, Vol. II, p. 349.

[53] M. Martin, *Description of the Western Isles*, pp. 110–12.

[54] G. Keating, *op. cit.*, Vol. I, p. 211 (O'Connor's edition).

[55] E. O'Curry, *op. cit.*, Vol. II, p. 188.

[56] E. O'Curry, *op. cit.*, Vol. II, pp. 223–4.

[57] D'Arbois de Jubainville, *op. cit.*, p. 118 ff.

[58] G. Keating, *op. cit.*, Vol. I, p. 190–1 (O'Connor's edition).

[59] E. O'Curry, *MS. Materials of Irish History*, pp. 383-398.

[60] E. Hull, *Cuchullin Saga*; G. Keating, *op. cit.*, Vol. I, p. 212.

[61] Tacitus, IV, 54.

[62] J. Curtin, *Myths and Folk-lore of Ireland*, p. 204.

[63] D. Wright, *Druidism*, pp. 103–5.

[64] Pliny, *Natural History*, XXIX, 52.

[65] T. D. Kendrick, *The Druids*, pp. 125–6.

[66] T. D. Kendrick, *op. cit.*, pp. 127–8.

[67] J. G. Campbell, *Witchcraft and Second Sight in the Highlands and Islands of Scotland*, p. 84.

[68] J. G. Dalyell, *The Darker Superstitions of Scotland*, pp. 140–2, 400, 411; J. M. Macpherson, *Primitive Beliefs in the North-East of Scotland*, pp. 259–62; J. M. Mackinlay, *Folklore of Scottish Lochs and Springs*, pp. 243, 257, 336.

[69] Cæsar, *Commentaries*, Book VI, chap. XIV.

[70] J. A. MacCulloch, *op. cit.*, p. 248.

[71] Pliny, *op. cit.*, XVI, 249.

[72] A. H. Allcroft, *The Circle and the Cross*, Vol. I, pp. 263–4.

[73] E. O'Curry, *Manners and Customs of the Ancient Irish*, Vol. II, pp. 213–16.

[74] E. O'Curry, *op. cit.*, Vol. II, pp. 220–1.

Chapter XII

THEORIES CONCERNING THE ORIGINS OF DRUIDISM

[1] T. D. Kendrick, *The Druids*, chap. V, *passim*.

[2] J. Rhys, *Lectures on Welsh Philology*, pp. 83–4.

[3] J. Rhys, *Celtic Britain*, p. 69.

[4] J. Rhys, *Celtic Folk-lore, Welsh and Manx*, Vol. II, pp. 623, 685.

[5] J. Rhys, *The Welsh People*, p. 83.

[6] J. Rhys, *Celtic Britain*, p. 69.

[7] J. Rhys, *Hibbert Lectures*, p. 229.

[8] T. Rice Holmes, *Ancient Britain*, pp. 289–92.

[9] T. Rice Holmes, *Cæsar's Conquest of Gaul*, p. 525.

[10] J. G. Frazer, *The Magic Art*, Vol. II, pp. 188–9.

[11] C. Jullian, *Histoire de la Gaule*, Vol. II, pp. 88–9; *Cambridge Mediæval History*, Vol. II, p. 471.

[12] A. H. Allcroft, *The Circle and the Cross*, Vol. I, p. 308 ff.

[13] S. Reinach, *Revue Celtique*, Vol. XIII, p. 189.

[14] H. D'Arbois de Jubainville, *Les Druides*, p. 12 ff.

[15] G. L. Gomme, *Ethnology in Folk-lore*, pp. 58, 62.

[16] J. Pokorny, *The Origin of Druidism, Celtic Review*, Vol. V, p. 1 ff.

[17] J. A. MacCulloch, *The Religion of the Ancient Celts*, p. 293 ff.

[18] A. Macbain, *Celtic Mythology and Religion*, p. 84.

[19] P. Carleton, *Buried Cities*, pp. 137–8.

Chapter XIII

CONCLUSIONS

[1] J. G. Frazer, *The Magic Art*, Vol. II, p. 358.

[2] J. G. Frazer, *op. cit.*, Vol. II, p. 140 ff.

[3] *Livy*, XLII, 7, 1; *Dio Cassius*, XXXIX, 20, 1.

[4] J. G. Frazer, *op. cit.*, Vol. II, p. 180.

[5] G. Boni, *Notizie degli Scavi*, May 1900, pp. 161, 172 (Quoted by Frazer, *op. cit.*, Vol. II, p. 186, note 1).

[6] A. B. Cook, "Zeus, Jupiter and the Oak," *Classical Review*, Vol. XVIII, p.366.

[7] A. H. Krappe, *The Science of Folk-Lore*, p. 90.

[8] W. Ridgeway, *Dramas and Dramatic Dances*, p. 251.

[9] J. A. MacCulloch, *The Religion of the Ancient Celts*, pp. 199–200.

[10] V. G. Childe, *The Dawn of European Civilization*, pp. 272–82.

[11] J. Rhys, *Hibbert Lectures*, pp. 231–2.

INDEX

INDEX

A

Acorn as an article of human diet, 13, 72; stores of in prehistoric Europe, 73; classical references to its food-value, 74; as a Puritan emblem in England, 78, 177

After-life, Druidic ideas respecting the, 91 ff.

Airbe druad, the magical hedge of the Druids, 149

Alphabets, supposedly Druidic, 159

Amangons, king, legend of, 137–8

Andate, or Andraste, the goddess, 28; location of her cult, 107–8, 170

Andriou, A Druid of Guernsey, legend of, 142

Anglesey, Druidism in, 25

Annwn, "The Spoils of Annwn," a mystical poem, 55

Aquitanians did not practise the Druidic faith, 19–20

Arval Brethren of Rome, a priesthood resembling the Druids, 50, 173

Astrology, Druidic, 163–4

Augury, auspices, of the Druids, 154–5

B

Bards, Druidic, 46; their course of instruction, 46–7; practice of incantations among, 47; their influence and sacrosanct character, 47

Beallteinn (Beltane, May 1st), a Celtic festival, 99–101; Druidic associations of, 100–2; human sacrifice at, 104

Belgæ, did not practice the Druidic faith, 19–20, 170

Blocc, Bluicne and Moel, three Druids of Tara, 65

Boadicea (Boudicca), her possible association with the goddess Andate or Andraste, 107–8

Britain, Druidism supposed to have had its origin in, 20; traditions of Druidism in, 28 ff.; Druidic place-names in, 29 f.; no data for existence of Druidism in Southern, 30 f., 34

Bull, pagan priests wearing its hide, 110–12

"Bull oaks" in England, 77

C

Cæsar on the Druids, 20–2; value of his account, 21; ratified by other classical writers, 21

Calendar, the Celtic, 99

Cathbad, an Irish Druid, 64

Cattle, white, herds of in Britain, 112–16; their possible preservation for sacrifice, 115–16

Cattle, sacrifices of, in later times, 109–10

Cernunnos, a Gaulish deity; as a Druidic god, 69–70

Chartres, as a meeting-place of the Druids, 20, 22, 102, 128

Christianity, its associations with Druidism, 141; struggle between the cults, 142

Chyndonax, a Mithraic priest in Gaul, described as a Druid, 64

Coelbreni, or omen-sticks, 159

Colleges, Druidic, 42, 57 f.

Creation, Druidic idea of, 86–7

Cromm Cruaich, a primitive Irish deity, 108

Culdees, an early Christian sect, associated by some authorities with the Druidic faith, 143–4

D

Daedala, the, a festival of the oak-cult of Zeus, 172 f.

Darvellgadarn, idol of, a probable survival of Druidism, 84–5

Diogenes Lærtius on the Druids, 19

Diviciacus, an Æduan Druid, 24, 51–2, 64

Divination, Druidic forms of, 159 ff.; by the *Coelbreni* or omen-sticks, 159; by the "Elucidator," 159; by human sacrifice, 159; by bull-sacrifice, 160; by dreams, 160–1

Divination by sacrifice, 105–6

Divine Kingship (and king), doctrine of the, 12, 37, 130 ff.; in Ireland, 39; and reincarnation, 98; main theory concerning the, 130–1; expansion of the idea of the, 131–2; cult of among the Celtic peoples, 132–3; its connection with Druidism, 133; in Ireland, 133–4; hostages given for Irish kings, 134; king responsible for the failure of the crops, 134; must be free from bodily blemish, 134; association of with sacred trees, 134–5; ritual marriage of the, 135; slaughter of the, 136; British legend relating to the, 137; summary of the connection of the, with Druidism, 138